Edward Said
The Charisma of Criticism

This insightful critical biography shows us an Edward Said we did not know. H. Aram Veeser brings forth not the Said of tabloid culture, or Said the remote philosopher, but the actual man, embedded in the politics of the Middle East but soaked in the values of the West and struggling to advance the best European ideas. Veeser shows the organic ties connecting his life, politics, and criticism.

Drawing on what he learned over 35 years as Said's student and skeptical admirer, Veeser uses never-before-published interviews, debate transcripts, and photographs to discover a Said who had few inhibitions and loathed conventional routine. He stood for originality, loved unique ideas, wore marvelous clothes, and fought with molten fury. For twenty years he embraced and rejected, at the same time, not only the West, but also literary theory and the PLO. At last, his disgust with business-as-usual politics and criticism marooned him on the sidelines of both.

The candid tale of Said's rise from elite academic precincts to the world stage transforms not only our understanding of Said—the man and the myth—but also our perception of how intellectuals can make their way in the world.

H. Aram Veeser is Associate Professor at The City College of New York. He is co-author of *Painting Between the Lines* (2001), and editor of *The New Historicism* (1989), *The New Historicism Reader* (1994), *Confessions of the Critics* (1996), and *The Stanley Fish Reader* (1999). Besides his work as a writer and critic, Veeser pursues outside interests that range from drawing and painting to motorcycling and competitive rowing.

Edward Said
The Charisma of Criticism

H. Aram Veeser

LONDON AND NEW YORK

First published 2010
by Routledge

2 Park Square, Milton Park, Abingdon, Oxfordshire OX14 4RN
52 Vanderbilt Avenue, New York, NY 10017

Routledge is an imprint of the Taylor & Francis Group, an informa business

First issued in hardback 2019

Copyright © 2010 Taylor & Francis

Typeset in Sabon by Wearset Ltd, Boldon, Tyne and Wear

All rights reserved. No part of this book may be reprinted or reproduced or utilized in any form or by any electronic, mechanical, or other means, now known or hereafter invented, including photocopying and recording, or in any information storage or retrieval system, without permission in writing from the publishers.

Notice:
Product or corporate names may be trademarks or registered trademarks, and are used only for identification and explanation without intent to infringe.

Library of Congress Cataloging-in-Publication Data
Veeser, H. Aram (Harold Aram), 1950–
Edward Said : the charisma of criticism / Harold Aram Veeser.
p. cm.
Includes bibliographical references and index.
1. Said, Edward W. 2. Critics–United States–Biography. 3. Intellectuals–United States–Biography. 4. Scholars–United States–Biography.
5. Palestinian Americans–Biography. I. Title.
CB18.S25V44 2009
801'.95092–dc22   2009032554

ISBN13: 978-0-415-90264-9 (hbk)
ISBN13: 978-0-203-84619-3 (ebk)

For Cyrus

Contents

Abbreviations ix

Foreword x

A Note on the Title of this Book xii

1. The Charisma of Edward Said 1
   Discursion 1 ("That Bastard, Said") 20

2. Beginning Again 23
   Discursion 2 ("Your Name Is Aram") 36

3. Emergence 40
   Discursion 3 ("Before He Was An Arab") 57

4. Academostardom 61
   Discursion 4 ("Smart Jewish Boys") 81

5. Secular Criticism 83
   Discursion 5 (The Way He Taught Then) 103

6. Rhetoric and Image 106
   Discursion 6 (Ambition) 113

7. On Stage 116
   Discursion 7 ("Up to the Standard") 136

8. Later Visions 139
   Discursion 8 (Abu-Machiavelli) 156

9. Marquee Intellectual 158
   Discursion 9 ("I'm Very Upset") 172

10. Political Roughhouse 175
   Discursion 10 ("Partial Credit") 191

11. Dropping the PLO 194
   Discursion 11 ("Wonderful Cheeses") 202

12. Said in History 204

Notes 221

Bibliography of Works Cited 246

Index 255

Abbreviations

B	*Beginnings* (1975)
CI	*Culture and Imperialism* (1993)
JC	*Joseph Conrad and the Fiction of Autobiography* (1966)
Late	*On Late Style: Music and Literature Against the Grain* (2006)
ME	*Musical Elaborations* (1991)
O	*Orientalism* (1978)
OofP	*Out of Place: A Memoir* (1999)
PolD	*The Politics of Dispossession* (1995)
QP	*The Question of Palestine* (1979)
RI	*Representations of the Intellectual* (1994)
RoE	*Reflections on Exile and Other Essays* (2000)
Sky	*After the Last Sky* (1986)
WTC	*The World, the Text, and the Critic* (1983)

Foreword

A book as wide-ranging as this one depends on the generosity of many friends and colleagues. First, I would like to acknowledge the immense work of those who read and commented on the entire manuscript: Bruce Robbins, Vincent Pecora, Gerald Graff, David Kunzle, and an earlier, anonymous reviewer for Routledge. Jeffrey Williams contributed what I believe must be the most thorough and penetrating reader's report ever written, and I am also grateful to Hertha Schulze for pressing me to realize the book's final, outrageous form. All these readers made the manuscript unimaginably better than it could have been without their help. I would like to thank Matthew Byrnie and Stan Spring at Routledge for their unflagging support of this project, Allie Waite and Wearset for creating a beautiful and expressive format, and Carl Gillingham for copyediting.

As I was developing this project, I was particularly thankful for colleagues who provided venues for presenting it in earlier incarnations: Amitava Kumar, Michael Sprinker, Bernard McGuirk, and James E.B. Breslin. Their suggestions and comments helped shape my ideas in important ways.

Equally important have been the many conversations I forced on friends and colleagues, including Timothy Brennan, Arnold Browne, Barbara Burke, Carla Cappetti, Angharad Coates, Scanlynn Daniel, John Dewind, Jim Dingeman, Gaynor Ellis, Zeyad Essa, Jean Howard, Jane Marcus, Carmel McMahon, Matthew Mead, Stephen Moore, John Mowitt, Eva María Woods Peiró, James Shapiro, Else Vieira, Hasanthika Sirisena,

Gayatri Spivak, Fiona Wilson, Gregory H. Williams, Hanne Winarsky, Joshua Wilner, and Peter T. Zoller.

For the photographs I wish to thank The Wylie Agency; the *Columbia Daily Spectator* and its photographer Richard Howard (richardhowardphotography.com); the Columbia University Archive and the Columbiana Library; Alinari/Art Resource (New York); Getty Images; photographer Jean Mohr; photographer Robert McNeely (*The Clinton Years: the Photographs of Robert McNeely* [New York: Callaway, 2000]); *The Reagan Library and Museum*; Associated Press Images and photographer Ruth Fremson; photo researcher Paul Cronin; and *The Albany Times-Union*. I am grateful to Public Services Archivist Jocelyn K. Wilk for turning up the photograph on the cover of this book.

Several generous fellowships and grants enabled me to complete my work. I would like to thank the Tanner Humanities Center of the University of Utah, the Office of Research Assistance of The Wichita State University, the National Endowment for the Humanities, the Research Foundation of the City University of New York, the Professional Staff Congress representing the faculty of The City University of New York, and the Harvard Center for Literary and Cultural Studies (now the Harvard Center for Literary Studies).

A few sections of this book were published in earlier forms by SUNY Press, *Politics and Literature*, and *the minnesota review*. I thank these publishers for permission to reprint these articles in their altered form.

A Note on the Title of this Book

Originating in the Greek word kharisma, "gift" or "divine favor," from kharizesthai, "to favor," from kharis, "favor," charisma refers to a rare trait found in certain human personalities. Usually it includes extreme charm and a magnetic quality, sophisticated communication skills, an uncanny (or even supernatural) ability to lead, charm, persuade, inspire, and influence people, as well as the capacity to draw the attention and admiration (or even hatred if the application of such charisma is perceived to be negative) of others. Related terms are grace, exuberance, equanimity, mystique, positive energy, *joie de vivre*, extreme charm, personal magnetism, personal appeal, "electricity," chemistry, and allure. Unusual calm, confidence, assertiveness, dominance, authenticity, and focus often factor in, as do superb abilities of persuasion and oratory.

1
THE CHARISMA OF EDWARD SAID

He loves a country and he leaves.
[Is the impossible far off?]
He loves leaving to things unknown.
By traveling freely across cultures
those in search of the human essence
may find a space for all to sit ...
Here a margin advances. Or a centre
retreats. Where East is not strictly east,
and West is not strictly west,
where identity is open onto plurality,
not a fort or a trench ...
  "Mahmoud Darwish bids farewell"

Edward Said was often photographed. He had a knack for organizing the image, typically appearing as a richly upholstered six-footer, his bold stripes and patterns from a Savile Row tailor, hair like black whipped cream. Hearts throbbed for him. But the best-known image is very different. In it, he is throwing a stone at an Israeli guardhouse. Instantly published around the world, this photo instigated calls for Said's dismissal from Columbia University with a corresponding passionate rush to his defense. No other photo captures so economically Said's ability to make your head snap back and wonder, *Can he really get away with that?*

Said's career blended erudition, pride, audacity, eloquence, magic, power, and a good location. A prominent, self-declared Western humanist, presenting himself as a raging Jeremiah or a

2 • The Charisma of Edward Said

Romantic outsider—the Manfred of Lord Byron, stalking the Higher Alps and spitting poison at Europe; or a Jonathan Swift, gnashing imprecations at Western civilization. To put it like that announces the self-division that cleaves Said's whole enterprise. He was Western to the bone. His chosen doubles were Western heroes, riven and tormented figures such as Lawrence of Arabia, whose self-description as "a standing civil war" fascinated Said because it named his own condition. His interest in bisected eccentrics, the Genets, Vicos, and Conrads, lay in his quest to avoid the

Figure 1.1 Said throwing stone (source: Getty Images).

fateful stalemating of the contradictory gifts he saw in Lawrence, a civil war fought to a standstill. Said's intractable contradictions produced a kind of restless energy—and no end of academic tut-tutting from his more cautious colleagues—but nothing held him back. He was, of course, an intellectual rake, a fundamentally unpredictable character whose ultimate professional and cultural centrality never extinguished his charming eccentricity.

Friends admired Said's charisma and enemies feared it. Charisma means different things to different people. Max Weber's description, which is fundamental to ensuing definitions and debate, was grounded in religion. In Weber's famous paradigm, the supreme charismatic figure, Jesus, blazes briefly only to have his brightness dimmed as the Christian church reduces his one-of-a-kind example into offices, sinecures, rituals, repetition, rote formulas, and gray bureaucracy. Charisma turns into routine.[1]

Middle-class students who entered graduate school during the U.S. war on Vietnam prized Weber's definition of charisma because it threatened and rebuked established institutions. The first generation of Said's students tended to chant, "Tune in, turn on, drop out." About the university specifically, their directive was, "Shut it down!" By contrast, John Guillory feels "the Weberian motif of the 'routinization of charisma,'" has little application to academic people. It has been tacitly assumed to apply equally well, he writes, to religion and academic literary criticism, but literary critics' charismatic authority "was never exclusive of, nor incompatible with, [their] institutional authority."[2] For Guillory, an unmodified use of Weber's version of charisma obscures its real workings at the university. Our thinking about superstar literary critics "will not advance very far if its divergence from the Weberian 'ideal type' is not acknowledged at the outset" (Guillory 1993: 244–245). Yale Professor of Comparative Literature Paul de Man serves as Guillory's example of post-Weberian charisma, but arguably Said could work even better.[3]

Guillory shows how badly the Weberian paradigm fits academia. Not only are literary critics sadly incomparable to Jesus Christ, they also develop exclusively within the institutions that train, house, reward, package, and market them.

Unlike religious charismatics, critics are inseparable from their institutional wrappings. Harold Bloom would not be Harold Bloom were he working at Burger King. His identity resides in his institutionality: he is Yale Professor of English Harold Bloom. And that is true, *mutatis mutandis*, across the board. Derrida would not be Derrida were he not J. Derrida, *agrégé* of the *École Normal Supérieure* in Paris. Quality presses (such as Harvard or Gallimard) make their own contribution to a growing reputation, as do *TLS* or the *London Review of Books*, by providing prominent reviews that in turn produce invitations to speak at "R-1 [Doctoral research]" universities. Only a broad, expensive, coordinated effort can give a lowly English professor the pearly luster of charisma. It happens only to a few. And those few are produced: they do not produce themselves.

Two events occurred around 1981, just as Said achieved the first peak of his notoriety. One was the rise of literary theory superstars who attracted the attention of the general literate public. The other was a debate over literary professionalism. Guillory offers a plausible explanation for the first. Theory stars were, he writes, "the free agents of pure charisma. It is not difficult to see that the deployment of this category was driven by the interests of competitive university administrations, for whom the content of theory, subversive or otherwise, was largely irrelevant." He concludes, "What mattered was that the charisma of the master theorists could be converted into bureaucratic prestige" (1993: 254–255).

Guillory's materialist account of this competitive market for theorists depends heavily on Pierre Bourdieu, the late French sociologist who updated Marxist materialism by adding his own important studies of "symbolic capital." A panoply of workers and institutions labor to confer symbolic value on certain persons and objects. Consider the famous example of Marcel Duchamp's work, "The Fountain." To acquire value beyond its retail price as a common piece of manufactured plumbing, the dealers, the gallery, reviewers with their training and experience, art journals, academic quarterlies, biennales, conferences, underground publications, auction houses, and art investors must collude in "consecrating" it as a work of art.⁴ An equally diverse array of interlocking institutions invest in the literary critic, and receive the benefits of the star that they have consecrated. Bourdieu insists that

> the charismatic ideology of creation ... prevents us asking who has created this "creator" and the magic power of transubstantiation with which the "creator" is endowed ... thereby avoiding any enquiry beyond the artist and the artist's own activity into the conditions of this demiurgic capability.⁵

In Said's case, by 1981, the thirty-two-year-old tennis-playing clotheshorse of 1967 was well on his way to demiurgic status. Bourdieu's materialist version of charisma suggests just how that happened.

Bourdieu offers an amusing account of the typical *professorial* gestures and tricks: "verbal acrobatics, hermetic allusion, disconcerting references or peremptory obscurity, as well as the technical tricks ... such as the concealment of sources, the insertion of studied jokes or the avoidance of compromising formulations."⁶ He might well have added to the list the professorial practice of grandly denouncing his own profession. American critic and fervent pro-professionalism gladiator Stanley Fish was always particularly incensed by this ritual of self-flagellation. The institutionally created critic-professor is actively encouraged to display independence, even to the point of attacking the institution itself. Doing so enhances the university's own socially consecrated role as the sanctioned place for freedom of speech.

Said's own exhortations for professorial courage must be seen in this light. The final chapter of his manifesto on the intellectual vocation, entitled "Speaking Truth To Power," identifies himself as one of a tiny band "whose stentorian voices and indelicate imprecations are hurled at humankind from on high" (*RI* 7). He is "someone able to speak the truth to power, a crusty, eloquent, fantastically courageous and angry individual for whom no worldly power is too big and imposing to be criticized and pointedly taken to task" (*RI* 8). He is "someone whose place it is publicly to raise embarrassing questions, to confront orthodoxy and dogma (rather than to produce them), to be someone who cannot easily be co-opted by governments or corporations" (RI 11). Much more of the same follows, in this book and elsewhere, but that last phrase deserves careful attention. Bourdieu's measured account of charisma as a valued corporate commodity renders Said's idea that intellectuals can avoid compromise with governments and corporations romanticized, if not self-contradictory.

A look at Said's own record proves Bourdieu right. Whenever Said broke with norms of decorum, his employer, Columbia University, sprang to his defense. After he threw his famous stone at Israel, and calls were heard for his disciplining and dismissal, the University Provost Jonathan Cole issued a public defense of Said's right to "speak" and gave no inch of ground to his critics. Said supporters hailed Columbia for this act of rare courage. By this means, the university further established its pristine integrity as a utopia of individual freedom, where even the upper administration could speak its mind without constraint. Some insiders even saw Cole's letter as a throwback to feudal standards of personal loyalty: after all, Cole was Said's squash partner.

But the hard-hearted might conclude that neither love nor Romanticism nor an anti-corporate impulse made Columbia defend Said. Other Said-inspired upheavals, such as the revelation that he had exaggerated some details of his past, were also instantly slapped down by Columbia. After devoting so much institutional energy and authority to establishing so charismatic a professor, the university was determined to protect its investment. Said was fond of saying, with a conspiratorial twinkle in his eye, "They let me get away with this because I dress so well." The truth is that "getting away with this" was precisely what Columbia paid him handsomely to do.

The university was not alone. In keeping with Bourdieu's assertions, other institutions also defended the consecrated bearer of charisma. The liberal press (which is another industry devoted to charisma-production) also repeatedly sprang to

Said's defense. A way to understand the attack upon and defense of Said is to compare the treatment given to Jackson Pollock circa 1955. The vulgar fulminated that their five-year-olds dripped paint better than Pollock, while experts recognized his genius and praised it. Supporting Pollock became a mark of social, intellectual, and cultural superiority. In Said's case, political superiority was involved as well. Each institution and corporation had its policy. For example, in the midst of an uproar over his purported habit of falsifying his past, the *London Review of Books* commissioned a well-known pro-Palestinian muckraker to write a piece about the controversy. When he turned in the 5,000 studiously researched words, the editors killed his article because he admitted that Said had exaggerated.[7]

Accepting Bourdieu's reading deflates Said's proclamations of the courage demanded to speak truth to power. "If the institution tolerates and so strongly encourages disrespect for the accessories and even the institutional rules," writes Bourdieu, it does so in "the service of the institution and through it the institution's social function" (Bourdieu and Passeron 1977: 124–125). Unsurprisingly, that function is the conservative one of reproducing the social system as it is. For Said, real intellectuals (read: himself and his followers) stand alone while throngs hurl insults and labor ceaselessly to bring these heroes low. But his football-coach-like commands to show steely courage when telling off the institution belong to the scripted routines of professorial conduct. Far from subverting the social and political norms, these fervent proclamations—always delivered in a seasoned preparatory-school bark—strengthen the power that they hope or purport to oppose.

The stone-throwing episode marked the end of Said's political arc and the planetarity of his charisma. Completely apolitical until 1967, he entered the public fray as a writer trying to correct misperceptions of the Arab peoples that had come to his attention during the "six-day war." He excelled in this as-yet-unnamed cultural criticism, and his successes brought him to the center of PLO power. By 1974 he knew Yasir Arafat and the PLO elite. In 1979 he was meeting quietly with U.S. Secretary of State Cyrus Vance and almost worked out a deal for an independent Palestinian state. Throughout the 1980s he hobnobbed with MacNeil and Lehrer, Ted Koppel, Phil Donohue, and other media *machers*. He debated ambassadors and heads of state. By 1990, he had taken on the aura of a political prophet.

In addition to Said's anointment by Ivy League institutions, he was an expert practitioner of the irrational aspect of charisma. Linked by Weber to "the berserk with manic seizures of frenzy," the foundational theory of religious charisma tied it to prophets, outsiders, and pirates. Organization men or women were excluded from possessing it.[8] Bourdieu points to this irrational core, comparing charismatic professors to magicians who induce their audiences to suspend disbelief.[9] Said's ability to get very angry on short notice enhanced this aspect of his charisma and made him a most compelling television talk-show presence. His righteous anger grabbed the television viewer by the lapels and made Said's style a perfect fit for the sound-bite era.

But Said finally became frustrated and bored with the media. By the end of the twentieth century, he had tired of the "local" American scene and gone outside Europe itself. He withdrew from celebrity glitz, and, apart from low-key televised conversations with Charlie Rose, focused on the Middle East, Asia, and the Southern cone. His purest political statement was the photo, in which, sans his trademark finery, he had gone down to the dusty streets of the *intifadah* and taken his station beside the anonymous *shabab* and revolutionary children who had nothing left to lose. It is a penitential, revisionary, and profoundly moving self-portrayal.

When I met Said on the Columbia campus in 1968, he was still an Englishman. He embodied a style of high conservatism prey to fits of wild improvisation. His continual revolutions and intellectual self-transformations made him a charismatic teacher and his graduate seminars were pure inventions of the theoretical imagination. One was called "Egotism" and another was entitled simply "Repetition." He invented a lexicon that no writer can do without today: Orientalism, worldliness, culture and imperialism, "intellectuals," Palestine itself. None of these concepts would have their current urgency if Said had not lent them the force of his intellect as well as the glow of his celebrity.

Said's intellectual and political lives curved along comparably rounded arcs. Starting as a literary theorizer who gave that epithet part of its forbidding air of impossible difficulty, he soon abandoned the theory craze and found an audience wider than the academy. Calling his method "worldliness," he published a trio of books, *Orientalism*, *Covering Islam*, and *The Question of Palestine*. This trilogy cracked the airless vessel of French-inspired literary theorizing and barged into the exclusive clubrooms of Middle East scholarship. It let in the raucous, populist, vulgar, and comic atmosphere of real people—the public men and society women, the mountebanks, tyrants, and thugs who make the world go round. Orientalism had its glamour, after all: scholars and statesmen, artists and adventurers, poets and prelates all had their featured moments in Said's study. By conjuring with these varied figures, the eccentrics and writers like Richard Burton and Chateaubriand, the political rhinos like Balfour and Cromer, by meeting them all on their own terms, Said took on much of their reflected glamour, variety, and exoticism. Reversing Bourdieu's model, he does not passively wait to receive charisma from institutions of Orientalism; he steals it with his swashbuckling pen. Bourdieu might respond that the literary institution remains the author of this demolition job, since the institution itself weaned him on Aristophanes, Lucian, Pope, and Swift, and taught him the ferocious art of flaying dunces. Nonetheless, he chose his own models, always favoring a literature that was "parasitic on what it responds to" (*WTC* 78). *Orientalism* is at once a searing attack, an elegy, a work of literary criticism (for none of the examples is there by accident), and an inspired essay of cultural criticism.

Perhaps we tend to see Said as more isolated than he was. He was never without gifted peers, and there were some monumental talents among his American and French contemporaries, particularly Michel Foucault and Jacques Derrida. Said conveniently identified this pair with the two strands of theory that shaped him and precipitated his anxiety of influence.[10] When two charismatics meet, however, there can be only one issue: combat. "In principle only one side can be in the right" (Weber 1968: 51). By 1983 Said's celebrated renunciation of literary theory was inevitable. He ceased to pay homage to the thirty-year French theoretical Renaissance, but he never ceased to admire it, remaining soaked in its values and struggling to extend them. Foucault may have helped to start the train of thought that led to Said's interest in local knowledge, much as Derrida and his American counterpart, Paul de Man, led to his brilliant re-conception of literature as a form of rhetoric. But Said was not a proto-postmodernist. He stands up for the individual human will—even when no justification can be found. "Foucault believes that in general the individual text or author counts for very little," he wrote. "Empirically in the case of Orientalism (and perhaps nowhere else) I find this not to be so" (O 23). Why there and nowhere else? He offers no argument and no rationale. It is his one article of faith.

Said's deepest meditations study the survival of genius within deadening routine, the oppositional force of the individual among institutions or schools of thought. As a like-minded rebel, he had to admire Foucault's sovereign contempt for professional rules. Reluctant to credit his direct competitor for critical charisma, however, he looked around for a substitute progenitor. Somewhere he discovered as his ally the antique philologian, Gian'battista Vico.[11] This eighteenth-century Neapolitan schoolmaster was an unabashed idealist who fashioned a powerful response against the dominant materialist thought of his time. He could stand in for deconstruction because he too asserted the primacy of rhetoric over logic. Vico wrote that the first primitive people ("stupid, insensate, and horrible beasts") thought and spoke in poetry. They felt rather than thought; they imagined rather than abstracted. All they had, mentally, was a poetic ability to make metaphors.[12] They were irrational, but their irrationality made them more productive, powerful, and

From Said's Memorial to Foucault

Foucault emerged out of a strange revolutionary concatenation of Parisian aesthetic and political currents, which for about thirty years produced such a concentration of brilliant work as we are not likely to see again for generations. His major positive contribution was that he researched and revealed "technologies" of knowledge and self that beset society, made it governable, controllable, normal, even as these technologies developed their own uncontrollable drives, without limit or true rationale. His great critical contribution was to dissolve the anthropological models of identity and subjecthood underlying research in the humanistic and social sciences. Instead of seeing everything in culture and society as ultimately emanating either from a sort of unchanging Cartesian ego, or a heroic solitary artist, Foucault proposed the much juster notion that all work, like social life itself, is collective. The principal task therefore is to circumvent or break down the ideological biases that prevent us from saying that what enables a doctor to practice medicine or a historian to write history is not mainly a set of individual gifts, but an ability to follow rules that are taken for granted as an unconscious a priori by all professionals. More than anyone before him Foucault specified rules for those rules.[13]

creative. In refusing to consider culture and society as involuntary effects of the environment, and by inflating poetry to the status of the single, substantial shaping force of civilization, Vico's ideas understandably appealed to an English professor, as they appealed to another Vico devotee, James Joyce. It was Vico's flamboyance and unrepentant humanism that recommended him to the equally flamboyant characters of Joyce and Said. But even more so it was his cavalier disdain for ordinary rules. Vico was himself charismatic—though distant enough in time so that, unlike Foucault, he needn't be fought to the death. Though both were subverters of Enlightenment faith in Reason, Vico was the more surprising. An Enlightenment figure himself, he hinted that the Enlightenment was pregnant with the anti-Rationalist seed of its own undoing,

Vico was a strangely modern voice, urging "something outside mere logical sense." He was unrestrained by the Apollonian orderliness of the printed page, and he had nothing of the faded monkishness that Said understandably loathed. Indeed he was hardly rational at all. Along with his positive appreciation of poetry, he offered an unusually negative valuation of syllogism, sorites, and logic. For him, the fall of civilization resulted from the rise of the status of reasoned thought. Each cycle of rise and fall reflects ever-increasing abstraction. The history of human society consists largely in what Weber calls the routinization of charisma: the growth of prose out of poetry, reason out of fan-

> **Said's Initial View of Vico**
>
> No reader needs to be reminded of how peculiarly organized [Gian'battista Vico's] book [*The New Science*] is, nor of how eccentric in the alternation of opacity with blinding force, or directness with interminable and digressive detail, is its style. For that I think we must blame not only Vico's lonely, eccentric originality, but also his insight that there is always something outside mere logical sense to be engaged and dealt with when human reality is discussed. This is the body, whose untidy, immediate, sprawling largeness becoming intelligent and fit for social history is Vico's real subject. Vico inevitably seems not to be in full control of what he says, not to be fully aware of what he is all about.... Vico's unhappy style also communicates a loss of immediacy, as if the prolixity of descriptive language trying to recapture the bodily directness of "poetic" thought were a demonstration of mind trying unsuccessfully and inelegantly to recover glad animal movement.[14]

tasy, democracy out of autocracy. This evolution culminates in the ironic awareness that all the original poetic perceptions, and the institutions based upon them, are false. Wheeling from primitive anarchy to civilization and back to barbarism can by no means be called cumulative advancement. "Progress" is hardly the word for such a sequence, for the arrival of abstract reasoning heralds the imminent end of human society. Ironic consciousness leads to social disintegration. Predictably, when society collapses, a new age of bestial irrationality begins, but this era is even worse than the first, for now humans have thought themselves into the condition of "beasts made more inhuman by the barbarism of reflection than the first men had been made by the barbarism of sense" (Vico 1970: para. 1106). Nowhere had any Enlightenment figure so roundly endorsed irrationalism.

Vico spoke powerfully to Said, who endorsed self-contradiction and dismissed the claims of consistency. "Charismatic authority is specifically irrational in the sense of being foreign to all rules" (Weber 1968: 52). Said found Vico's antinomian views a bracing affront to the posturing of American scholars and *raissoneurs* who proclaimed the indisputable, scientific rationality of doctrines such as racism, Orientalism, and Eurocentrism, or for that matter to the professionalized literary scholars who identify with the American Medical Association in their assurance that each year they offer ever-better diagnoses and improved services.[15] Keeping faith with poetry, with its flashes of perception in defiance of all rational categories, was the true idealism.

The second influential strand of contemporary theory, that of deconstruction, entered Said's repertoire largely in the displaced form of Vico. Both deconstruction and Vico demolished Enlightenment Reason's arrogant self-assurance. Said's style itself was a self-contradiction; he used his own version of Vico's poetic speech to wrest an active function away from the pure passivity of abstract thought. Both his prose style and his thought persistently demonstrate his devotion to poetic speech, his distrust of abstractions, and his dismissal of Panglossian faiths of all kinds—especially the kind called radical communism. "My reading of Adorno," Said wrote at the end of his life,

> with his reflection about music at its center, sees him as injecting Marxism with a vaccine so powerful as to dissolve its agitational force almost completely. Not only do the notions of advance and culmination in Marxism crumble under [Adorno's] rigorous negative scorn, but so too does anything that suggests movement at all.
>
> (*Late* 14)

Nonetheless, Said moved away from high theory on a bridge made up of theory's own insights. What he called "disciplines of detail" was the "local knowledge" under whose banner marched interpretative anthropology, sociology, the New Social Movements, and New Historicism. What he called "speaking truth to power" encompassed the "rhetorical" arts of persuasion and delivery.[16] This was a different version of rhetoric than in deconstruction or in the sub-disciplines of rhetoric and composition. Today rhetoric is usually understood as expression (*elocutio*), meaning figurative language. This was the aspect seized upon and revived by deconstruction and other theories (e.g., Hayden White's *Metahistory*) that sought to revitalize literary studies with a (very strange) return to rhetoric. Rhetorical Invention was also encroaching on the traditional literary syllabus, with Freshman Composition being taught not as literature courses but as "rhet/comp" courses.[17] But, while there were many deconstructors and composition-rhetoric people, only Said championed the art of delivery. He alone proposed that a critic by definition had to fight for a political movement.

His later work followed a theoretical journey to the promised land of Local Knowledge mapped out by his intellectual generation.[18] "Think Globally, Act Locally" condenses this idea to back-bumper proportions. Having revolted against the subject (call it consciousness or the author) by using anti-humanist firepower (the statistical table, the philological laboratory, the stagecraft of culture), Said turned on his anti-humanist French allies, cut loose their structuralist and postmodern weaponry, and dove into an American-anthropologically inflected strategy of local action. Once he landed in local knowledge, he never turned back. *The Question of Palestine* offers 238 pages of local knowledge, only five of which are devoted to anything even vaguely theoretical. From then on, descriptions of the Palestinian situation grew into a series of studies of a single, local problem in media and culture (*Covering Islam* [1981], *After the Last Sky* [1986], *Blaming the Victims: Spurious Scholarship and the Palestinian Question* [1988], *The Politics of Dispossession* [1995], *The End of the Peace Process: Oslo and After* [2000], *From Oslo to Iraq and the Road Map* [2004], plus hundreds of biweekly columns for *Al-Majalla*, and then *Al-Ahram* and *Al-Hayat*, periodicals published in Europe and Egypt for a largely Arab readership). The books came faster and faster because they were empirical studies or responses to current events.

Said's later polemical essays, to say nothing of his public speeches, required colorful reactions, and the research they called for was collateral to his journalistic activism. The impulsiveness and subjectivity that appeared evocative but untrustworthy in literary studies gave him tremendous presence on mass media, in auditoriums, and in the press. His strength lay in those two long-neglected planks of the rhetorical curriculum: memory and delivery. His charisma grew, and his audience grew with it.

Passionate reactions to events in Said's local journalism had the effect of emphasizing his personality. This partly erased his earlier alliance to thinkers like Derrida and Foucault—who had de-centered, fragmented, and dispersed the sources of human achievement—and, like them, he became an intellectual celebrity. In other words, the process of breaking away from the humanist thinkers of Enlightenment and Victorian culture and confirming the death of the author led back to the very image of a white mythology that he had once worked so hard to kill off. His own identity was bound up with charisma-drenched Romantics such as George Gordon, Lord Byron, a much earlier public heartthrob who also yoked a literary career to a revolutionary politics, subordinated logic to poetry, and celebrated the East at Europe's expense.

In important respects, Said remained true to his first impulses. His last unfinished books flaunted the self-contradictions with which he always seemed so comfortable. In *Humanism and Democratic Criticism*, his particular brand of crusading liberal politics offered prescriptions, remedies, and solid promises that all would turn out well, if only people would follow his advice. That reassuring optimism was checked sharply in *On Late Style*, with its pessimistic message that, truth be told, all systems of traditional and rational authority stamp out human individuality. These two books flatly contradict each other. They meet in just the sort of conflagration that incinerates all modestly rational identities. He said all that he felt had to be said, and if the messages seemed inconsistent, so much the worse for consistency. That said, *Late Style*, with its off-beat title and its convalescent heroes, was by far the more Saidian and successful book.

Considered in light of *Late Style*'s meditation on failure, alienation, and death, his last "political" initiative—an orchestra composed of young Arab and Israeli musicians—appears as both an atonement and a withdrawal. It seemed to reverse his long-held conviction that a creative person had to be rooted in a political movement. The orchestra stood outside of any political movement. Instead, it reestablished an aesthetic realm divorced and protected from the sphere of ethics and politics. But this was the very separation that Said had always fought against. Perhaps he felt that the orchestra could serve as an aesthetic projection of a political goal.[19] At the same time, the West–Eastern Divan Workshop and Orchestra crystallized his own style of rhetorical performance. With no logical argumentation at all, it simply showed that Jews and Arabs could literally harmonize their differences. It was eloquence of a non-logical, even somatic kind.

The unlaid ghost of Jonathan Swift looms over this story. Swift recognized that an idea and a conquest usually arrive together. Allied to a nascent political force, the Irish community, which he played a part in creating, he walked the line between criticism and communal solidarity. He had no interest in philosophical consistency; he was compelled by shame and disgust. He was accused of poisoning the wells of high cultural enjoyment, and his self-contradictions were noted. Said sympathized with all these tendencies. He might well have been thinking of himself when he said of Swift, pay less attention to the ideas and more "to the deployment and disposition of his energies, his local performances" (*WTC* 82).

Said's career, his thought, his style, are all understood best through the lens he provides in his essays on Swift. There he writes:

> We do him a greater service if we accept the discontinuities he experienced in the way he experienced them: as either actual or imminent losses of tradition, heritage, position, history, losses located at the center of his disjointed verbal production.
>
> (*WTC* 65)

Added to the disjointedness expressive of "actual or imminent losses," "most of [Swift's] writing was precisely occasional: it was stimulated by a specific occasion and planned in some way to change it" (*WTC* 56). In that praise for occasional writing, one could read a very early prediction of Said's much later vast production of occasional and polemical writings about Palestine. The accent on writing in order to change specific occasions also holds steady right to the end. Call it Charismatic Activism, which begins only when the established social order is set aside: "the artist who is fully in command of his medium nevertheless abandons communication with the established social order of which he is a part and achieves a contradictory, alienated relationship with it."[20]

Said's roots were entangled with an older, native tradition. While he was finishing graduate school at Harvard and applying for his first professorship at Columbia, Lionel Trilling still presided over the Columbia College English Department. Jacques Barzun, Henry Steele Commager, and Meyer Schapiro strode like Colossi on College Walk. They had an aura and expected to receive due deference within the hothouse confines of South

Field, Hamilton Hall, and the insular neoclassical campus perched like a tiny Athens atop the hill above Harlem. Said was much younger than these examples of eminence grises, but he was unmistakably Ruling Class.

Both Trilling and Said were ethnic men in what was still, in pockets, a White Anglo-Saxon Protestant redoubt. Like Trilling, Said believed that writing communicated more through its form than by its explicit statements—although unlike Trilling, he held that "no synthesis is conceivable" and that the privileged forms are "anachronism and anomaly" (*Late* xiii). Both men were cultural critics. They gave their respective historical moments a "ruling personage," which is, as Taine explained, "the model that contemporaries invest with their admiration and sympathy."[21] It was appropriate that Said won the first annual Lionel Trilling Award for his book, *Beginnings: Intention and Method* (1975).

When Trilling was still a Columbia College undergraduate, he had written a pair of short stories about two young men on the make. In each story, a young university man needs to repress the crude but eccentric and brilliant—and very Jewish—side of himself.[22] Although Trilling possessed a charisma of his own, the painful insecurities and self-consciousness displayed by the characters in these early stories are the antithesis of grace, exuberance, equanimity, mystique, positive energy, joie de vivre, charm, personal chemistry, allure, potency, in short everything Said embodied.

In Trilling's story, the would-be-assimilated narrator denies his own Jewish roots by snubbing the alarmingly déclassé Hettner. In writing a short story about this fraught self-betrayal, Trilling was gnawing at a central ethical dilemma in then-contemporary Jewish intellectuals' young lives. He tried to keep his secret-sharer Hettners at arm's length.[23] Geraldine Murphy, Trilling's best critic, calls him the "shrinking violet." He always wore a pressed suit and looked unbearably worried, as if he were physically gulping back down the earthy, uncultivated Hettner concealed within himself. At most, this indecorous (for Gentiles) Jewish core was permitted a brief cameo appearance

> **"Impediments" by Lionel Trilling**
>
> If you sit next to a man in class and if, in a bashfully forward sort of way, he insists upon whispering during the lecture a series of ironic comments on the professor's capabilities, and if, when the notebooks have snapped shut and the cigarettes are being lighted, he suggests accompanying you to your next class, you can only be polite enough to smile at the comments, offer him a cigarette and hold up your end of the conversation as you cross the campus. Hettner forced me to these perfunctory courtesies. I did not like the fellow, a scrubby little Jew with shrewd eyes and full, perfect lips that he twisted out of their crisply cut shape ...
>
> He sat silent as he sampled the vitalized tea. He was wearing a blue serge suit, very shiny and worn, and a grimy tie. The suit was the only one he had, I knew, for he was poor, yet I very much resented it. Blue serge suits are all well enough, very handsome things, in fact, but when they are threadbare and lustrous they are detestable. A man may be as shabby as he pleases in a rough cloth, tweed or cheviot, and still look gay and interesting, but untidy blue serge gives him the look of a shop assistant.[24]

in Trilling's juvenile work of fiction, which was published in *Menorah Journal* for a presumably Jewish audience. It was a most discreet self-meditation.

Said had none of Trilling's uptightness and timidity. He had come of age amid worldwide decolonization and liberation movements. Perfectly assimilated and socially superior, more European, more bourgeois, more cultivated than his peers, he was instantly more "at home" in the Ivies than Trilling ever could have been. No one believed he was an Arab, above all a Palestinian, for he looked supremely at ease in every suit he wore, down to his gym suit. His privileges, his money, his British boarding-school voice, his looks, his athleticism, his easy sexuality: the symbolic capital was inexhaustible. He could afford to be nice to anybody he liked, even, on occasion, to lumpish, lower-middle-class, not-very-interesting characters from upstate New York.

The successes of Jewish assimilation inhibited Trilling in ways that Said could ignore. If Said showed little anxiety on any occasion, he had less reason to: he had few competitors.[25] Where were the Palestinian Prousts, Adornos, Abby Warburgs, Bernard Berensons, Peggy Guggenheims, Gertrude Steins, and Philip Roths? His first experiment with ethnic narrative, entitled "Cairo Recalled" and written for the Condé Nast glossy *House & Garden*, is a field day of social privilege.[26] Soirees, manicured playing fields, armies of white-clad servants, lawn tennis, regal courtyards, cotillions, and concerts, and parties, and wonderful clothes: "their poignancy for me is that I am certain they will never recur."[27] An opulent Jewish drawing room was banal, cliché; a Palestinian world of *luxe et volupté* had jaw-dropping novelty.

Unembarrassed by anything, Said openly declared that he was a work in progress, going public to pursue his disputes with the PLO, making sure his political battles played out before as big an audience as he could find, turning his life into a fight card that announced the successive and concurrent bouts. He had to go looking for fights because, in most respects, he was totally at home. His account of Bicker at Princeton gives a small but telling example. Three of the exclusive eating clubs vied to get him as a member, while his less desirable roommate looked on, increasingly distraught. Said finally consented to join the club that threw in the roommate as part of the deal. His open-armed acceptance by WASP America sorted rather ill with his self-concept as a Romantic outsider. And at some point around 1972–3, a conscious act of abdication took place. He decided to become an Arab.

"That Bastard, Said"

I heard of Said before I even got to Columbia. I went to New York in late March, when my upstate gulag was locked in dirty

Figure 1.2 Edward Said (source: University Archives, Columbia University in the City of New York).

snow. Sparrows and pigeons were scavenging around the trashcans when I reached Morningside Heights, and my host and sometime evil companion, Cousin Barbara, introduced me to her roommate, Mary Wise. Mary was a leggy Minnesotan who had attended the then-entirely WASP preparatory school for girls, Dana Hall. On this bonny day, she was talking about her thesis advisor, Edward Said.

Having done her M.A. under Said, she now wanted to enter the doctoral program in English and Comparative Literature at Columbia, and he had just refused to write her a letter of recommendation. Barbara and I shifted uncomfortably. Conspiratorial glances accompanied every mention of Said. What did that mean? I knew it had something to do with romance or even sex. Mary's rope of dark blonde hair was working loose out of its French twist. We were outside, in the garden of International House that stood just across Claremont Avenue, opposite Barbara's Deco-glass apartment building foyer. As Mary went through what she had said and what Said replied, she began to rub her slingbacks together. One of them eventually dropped off and made a hollow noise on the flagstone sidewalk.

"God!" Barbara exclaimed. "He sounds like such a bastard. He is *such* a bastard!"

I pieced together a rough impression of this bastard. He was young, brilliant, an Arab, sexy, unpredictable, arrogant, unyielding, unfeeling—in fact, a total *bastard*. After a while, the breeze off the Hudson picked up, and we decided to go. Mary leaned on me getting back into her shoe. And for my part, I had made up my mind. I would go to Columbia and major in English.

2
BEGINNING AGAIN

A social and historical critique which does not consider the conflictual structure of its own discursive operations will only reproduce the constraints it is seeking to displace.
                                                    Samuel Weber

The infamous thing has made itself: made itself without thought, without conscience, without foresight, without eyes, without heart. It is a tragic accident,—and it has happened. You can't interfere with it. The last drop of bitterness is in the suspicion that you can't even smash it.
                                                    Joseph Conrad[1]

The popular image of Said as an activist/ideologue locked into his own doctrine is the opposite of the Said I encountered at Columbia, a restless character who could not embrace any position or idea without simultaneously pushing it away. Foes painted him as an evil ideologue-automaton who was the implacable agent of much bigger forces. Friends rewrote him to make him consistent, logical, and imitable. But friends and foes alike tried to routinize and institutionalize his charisma. In consequence Said's colorful world has gone gray, and younger critics getting him second-hand conclude that "Said wasn't even boring."[2]

"Secular criticism" was Said's phrase for what he did, and few critics have the faintest idea what he meant by that. Timothy Brennan proposed one popular version—a genetic Said. Brennan argues that Said's oeuvre constitutes a fully planned and tightly consistent working out of a few basic themes.

He sees evidence that Said possessed a blueprint that he systematically went about filling over several decades, without wavering or backfilling. I would call Brennan's the single-minded Said, though he adds the further unbelievable observation that Said's interview with *Diacritics* contained all the later themes "fully formed." He seems to suggest something like intelligent design:

> [*Beginnings*] in fact records that broad-ranging but also limited list of motifs that occupy Said for the better part of his career, and that first are mentioned as a whole in an interview for *Diacritics* in the Fall of 1976.... All of the interests associated with a much later period of his writing are there, fully formed.... The interview is like a compendium of which the rest of his career is a patient and deliberate elaboration.[3]

A number of things are wrong with this view. System, totality, sticking to a limited plan, patience—these are not phrases Said brings to mind, not even to his own mind. "I hate systems," he more than once declared. The Hegelian idea of a planned or intuited totality could hardly apply to a man who almost never used the word dialectic and who mocked holism in favor of "local performances" and "disposition of energies." Hearing him respond to hecklers would demonstrate that patience was not one of his virtues.[4] Brennan's adjectives more accurately describe Brennan himself. Second-to-none in his intensive knowledge of Said's work, Brennan has persistently drawn a portrait of Said as an activist who never changed his mind, following a long tradition of critics using Said as a trampoline. By reading him so completely against the grain, Brennan ends up portraying an imaginary figure, one who is far more consistent, orchestrated, planned, and fulfilled than the rather more interesting character of the actual Edward Said.

Writing appreciatively of Jonathan Swift's "Tory anarchy," Said lauded the Irish churchman for his sportiness, his refusal to reconcile his contradictions, and his distaste for contemporary systematizers like Locke and Hume.[5] When smart commentators pointed out that his ideas were inconsistent, Said never apologized. "I like ... doubt and uncertainty," he stated in one interview. "I hate systems and I hate determinism and it seems to me the whole idea is to fight them." In another he added, "I simply gave up and figured that one is moved in ways that are quite mysterious ... who wants to be consistent?"[6]

In his memoir, he celebrates himself as self-contradictory:

> I occasionally experience myself as a cluster of flowing currents. I prefer this to the idea of a solid self, the identity to which so many attach so much significance. These currents, like the themes of one's life, flow along during the waking hours, and at their best, they require no reconciling, no harmonizing.
>
> (*OofP* 295)

The situation of not being fully formed and not having a "solid self" indicates the depth of Said's antipathy to anything like Brennan's "deliberate," tight-lipped, Leninist revolutionary who unswervingly enacts a twenty-five-year plan, all of it "fully formed" on Day One, completely consistent and frighteningly hostile to anything outside itself. Although Brennan wants to enhance Said's political impact, he ends up reducing it, for dogmatism was inimical to Said's greatest effects.

Besides the totally consistent Said, the critics also propose a double-plotted Said. With this model the critic attempts to deal with Said's patent self-contradictions by honoring them with words like "paradox" and "hybridity." A fine example of this method is the first Routledge volume about Said, Bill Ashcroft and Pal Ahluwalia's *Edward Said: The Paradox of Identity*.[7] In it, Said takes on the virtues of a poem as the old New Critics understood poems: a whole, unified structure held together by its apparent tensions, paradoxes, and ironies. Their choice of words tells the story: having thrown up their hands at finding no apparent consistent thread, they revert to an outmoded vision of the critic as a container of contradictions, high-strung, hypertense, and all wound up. They turn Said into Lionel Trilling.

Joseph Conrad, the subject of Said's first book, traced the perils of both passivity and vigorous action. He traced them, more significantly, through a series of would-be, failed charismatic heroes. This conundrum seemed exactly right to Said. In *Joseph Conrad and the Fiction of Autobiography*, he shows Conrad actively seeking a way out of the overwrought, angst-ridden role bequeathed to him by the previous generations of American critics. Conrad posed a comparatively inglorious choice: human experience is either anonymous chaos or stupid Egotism. Said must have felt himself confronting the very same two alternatives. "This, of course," he begins, "is the Schopenhauerian dilemma, and we shall consider later how close Conrad is to the German arch-pessimist" (JC 13). From the fatally vain hero of *Nostromo* to the foolhardy but commanding captain of "The Secret Sharer," from the destructively charismatic James Wait in *The Nigger of the Narcissus* to the most famous Conradian charismatic of all, Mr. Kurtz, Conrad was obsessed with the use and failure of charisma.

Said was fascinated that Conrad successfully promulgated a false image of himself as a commanding, deeply peaceful old sea salt and master storyteller, while in fact he was a tormented and insecure outsider. In Conrad's books, would-be Romantics such as Lord Jim, Nostromo, and Mr. Kurtz invariably fail. The Romantic blaze of self-immolating glory they seek eludes them, and they simply peter out. Babbling some nonsense like "Incorruptible!" or "The horror!" they end spiritless, disembodied, and sunk in their own moral defeat. The collapse of the charismatic project appears again and again, in figures from James Wait, to the prophetic Mr. Kurtz, to the beguiling Nostromo—in every book, a would-be charismatic figure occupies the mysterious center.

Conrad's violent images of his atelier as a kind of infernal workhouse stuck with Said. In both writing and politics, connectedness meant confinement to Said, although he also recognized confinement as a fundamental condition of creative life. If Conrad compared the writer's life to being a "convict ... chained to his knowledge" (JC 25), his grandeur also stemmed from the immobility a writer imposes on himself.[8] The sweaty image of rescuing experience from chaos remained the central image of Conrad's working philosophy: "Either one loses one's sense of identity and thereby seems to vanish into the chaotic, undifferentiated, and anonymous flux of passing time, or one asserts oneself so strongly as to become a hard and monstrous egoist" (*JC* 13). Said agreed with Conrad that these rescues ultimately fail. He liked Conrad's emphasis on the nobility and elitism of Sisyphus:

> One must drag the ball and chain of one's selfhood to the end. It is the price one must pay for the devilish and divine privilege of thought; so that in this life it is only the elect who are convicts—a glorious band which comprehends and groans but which treads the earth amidst a multitude of phantoms with maniacal gestures, with idiotic grimaces. Which would you be: idiot or convict?
> (Conrad's letter to Marguerite Poradowska; quoted in *JC* 25)

Conrad seems to suggest that charisma forms like a diamond, only under extraordinary pressure.

Critics and readers have overlooked this crisis-element in Conrad, yet it is precisely that sense of extremes that recommended him to Said. Critics tend to get snagged on the slightly unfamiliar phenomenological terms Said deployed. One London reviewer obsessed by plain style complained of Said's obscure and "turgid" theorizing. "The fuggy, hypnotic style," he wrote, is "a result of [Said's] conviction (restated [in *Beginnings*]) that criticism is at least as original and creative as art."[9] Of this outrageous idea, the reviewer comments:

> The assumption is ludicrously gratuitious [*sic*] because transparently self-regarding, and the stylistic results can be gruesome. A reviewer has noted that Said's first work [*Joseph Conrad*] was "a turgidly phenomenological study of Conrad." In this book I can discern only trace elements of the phenomenology. But the turgidity has not proved quite so easy to shake off.

By today's standards the *apparatus criticus* of *Joseph Conrad* is bluntly straightforward, the kind of thing eighteenth-century plain-stylists like Hugh Blair and Horne Tooke would have applauded. Such is fashion. The editors of *The Edward Said Reader* explain its then fearsome technique in accessible terms:

> Published in 1966, *Joseph Conrad and the Fiction of Autobiography* was Said's first book, a revision of his dissertation, which he wrote at Harvard University under the direction of Monroe Engel and Harry Levin. It was, as Said wrote, "a phenomenological exploration of Conrad's consciousness." The book drew on the literary criticism of what was known as the Geneva School, a group of literary critics centered on Georges Poulet, Jean Rousset, and Jean Starobinski. Espousing a view of literature and criticism based on the philosophies of Husserl and Merleau-Ponty, the Geneva critics held that literary works were embodiments of authorial consciousness. As J. Hillis Miller wrote, the Geneva critics saw literary criticism as the "consciousness of consciousness."[10]

But the editors forget the main point: that the book was meant to challenge and dissent from both historical criticism and formalist New Criticism, the dominant factions in North American English Departments. Despite Said's interest in form, which his fellow critic Terry Eagleton is perfectly correct to ascribe to Said, he resisted the formalistic New Critics when they forbade discussions of authors' biographies or intentions, readers' responses, or historical parallels.[11] These critics even gave historicism scary names such as "the intentional fallacy" and "the affective fallacy." Said's first book was a homage to these "fallacies." He committed the affective fallacy over and over by showing how Conrad played to his intended audience, leading them to conclusions and painting for them a rosy, false picture of himself as a masterly retired sea captain who steered his literary career with a commander's sureness and self-satisfaction. Conrad was apparently buttressing his own charisma.

Said's overwhelming question about the way charismatic individuals are formed put him completely out of sync with the dominant academic current. From the New Critical point of view, Said's whole study was hopelessly anthropomorphic. He argued that only an act of human will can "rescue" a meaning from the swamp of undifferentiation. As always in Said, the problem is to resolve the Kantian dilemma: how can the subject and object somehow be reconciled? Conrad's answer was by sheer brute will and force, "a kind of mental convulsion lasting two, three or more days—up to a fortnight—which leaves me perfectly limp" (LL, II.25 in *JC* 50). Said emphasized the difficulties and the struggle of writing in an unkind, unrelenting, and oppressive world. "The actual experience of writing was usually so hateful, the expense of creating art so great, the results so uncertain," that Conrad seemed almost unhinged by the process (*JC* 51). Reviewers of Said's book seemed disappointed when they failed to get the neat analysis or pathologization of Conrad they had expected. Instead, Said gave fascinated accounts of Conrad's horrors without taking a clinical view of them. In one letter, Conrad described human society as great knitting machines that "knit you in and knit you out." As a fantasy of painful penetration and mutilation, this rivals Kafka at his most brutal.

Said's long campaign to defend human will actually resurrected pessimism against his own will when he performed what Gayatri Spivak slyly calls "repetition in rupture."[12] Obsessed with avoiding passivity and mobilizing will power, he vastly inflated the threat of terminal passivity, inanition, and sloth. He agreed with Schopenhauer on this point. Both felt "shame at the will to live at all costs" (*JC* 98). His drive to attain conventional honors, pleasures, successes, and comforts was isochronal with his embarrassment at having any of these things.

For Said, the category of passivity outweighs any other topic. He discussed passivity more than geography, political force, performance and narration, determinism, historical inevitability, amateur versus professional literary criticism, lack and repression, hegemony, late style, transformation, or the discipline of details. Although it is true that he also warned against unbridled egotism and imposition of the will on the world, in his nearest approach to consistency, he defied passivity in all of his writing

> **Said on Conrad**
>
> Conrad's achievement is that he ordered the chaos of his existence into a highly patterned art.... Because he, like so many of his characters, lived life at the extreme, he was more acutely conscious of community.... Driven back on his individuality, he accepted its burdens and its uncompromisingly pessimistic vision of reality.
>
> (JC 196)
>
> There was for him no available movement of defiance, as there had been for his father, in which to play a part. He had to create the movement, his role in the movement, and the gesture of defiance all on his own. Such, as he understood it, was the cruel joke played on him by history when it offered him only a stunted, incomplete legacy of national identity, dissipated in an obscure and chaotic world.
>
> (JC 38)
>
> Conrad had characterized existence as a huge knitting machine that "has evolved itself out of a chaos of scraps of iron." The description itself is a weird mixture of grotesque humor and piteous self-commentary. Its particular urgency is conveyed by the lengths of fantasy to which Conrad went in order to make a point, the kind of murky background he drew on for a moment, then dismissed, and the horrifying repetitiveness he saw in the entire sequence.
>
> (JC 33–34)

and most of his performances. Passivity threatened to kill charisma.

"Ducking a fight," running away, "chickening out," meek, pliant, soft, submissive, on a string, spiritless, tame, lacking mettle, gumption, push, or initiative, mama's boy: no phrases emasculate quite so well as these. The terrible threat of a disabling passivity hangs like a sword over charismatic heroes.[13]

Florilegium: Passivity

Beginnings

The writer is not at liberty to make statements.

(258)

A poetic or literary career does not reflect the man's life, it absorbs it, overwhelms it, gets on top of it.

(262)

Orientalism

faced with the obvious decrepitude and political impotence of the classical Orient ...

(79)

The passive, seminal, feminine, even silent and supine East.

(138)

a mere Oriental, who, for creative purposes, is a thing dead and dying—a mental mummy.

(193)

The World, the Text, and the Critic

A writer-author suggests the glamor of doing, of bohemia, of originality close to the real matter of life (always we find this closeness of reality and originality); a critic scholar-author suggests the image of drudgery, passivity, impotence, second-order material, and faded monkishness.

(128)

[Lukács] shows the increasing retreat of the subject into passive, privatized contemplation ... more and more divorced from fragmented realities, Lukács then depicts modern bourgeois thought as being at an impasse, transfixed and paralyzed into permanent passivity.

(231)

continued

the contemporary critic still uselessly transfixed by pure form and often gullibly enraptured by an uncircumstanced structural poetics.

(271)

After the Last Sky

The tension between teachers and students remains, but better the tension than the peace of passivity, or the unresisting assent to authority.

(44)

Culture and Imperialism

Above all, we accept censorship as we do nearly everything else that has been forced on us in this miserable, damp, and gloomy period of mediocrity and defeat, because we say that we are powerless, the world is against us, Zionism and imperialism have won.

(72)

What distinguishes the truly struggling intellectual is ... the conception of his or her work as activity, not as *passive contemplation*.

(210)

It is as if we have been anaesthetized as a people, unable to move, unable to act. They take the land, and we watch, or, more probably, we don't even watch.

(291)

The Politics of Dispossession

Palestinians in Lebanon, most of whom are stateless, poor, permanently stalled.

(xliv)

A Palestinian UNRWA official ... I noticed how anxious he was to avoid the word *passivity*.

(7) [italics in the original]

> *Out of Place*
>
> I seemed to myself to be nearly devoid of any character at all, timid, uncertain, without will.
>
> (3)
>
> Why did I allow myself to be so powerless, so "weak"—the word was beginning to acquire considerable resonance in my life—as to let him assault me with impunity?
>
> (42)
>
> *The End of the Peace Process*
>
> The overriding impression I got was of energetic, agile, and perceptive young men simply wasting their time and lives immured in the dingy flat, waiting for some change in the situation, hoping for a deus ex machina to get them living again.
>
> (86)

In light of the preponderant theme of passivity in Said's work, neither "wise passivity" in the Romantic tradition of William Wordsworth nor the Greek "middle voice" (neither passive nor active) in Greek grammar, nor the therapies for passivity in popular self-help books seemed terribly germane. Only when I realized that passivity was equal to trauma did it begin to fit in with Said's project for secular criticism. Calling trauma "passivity" was a way to demand action from victims. It was a way to combat acquiescence, a goad and a challenge. In *Orientalism*, we overhear a colonial administrator affirming that the Arabs are "all, nationally speaking, more or less in *statu pupillari*." These "passive, fatalistic subject races" were generally thought to have lolled about and guaranteed for the East "its backwardness, its silent indifference, its feminine penetrability, its supine malleability" (O 206). Said responds by calling for action.

But sheer heroic action wasn't enough either. "There were two Conrads," Said wrote, one "a passive agent, the other an unreliable master" (*JC* 67). Whereas Conrad moans that he is "painfully aware of being crippled, of being idle, of being useless," he equally distrusts men of action, writing "there is impulsive action on the one hand and ineffectual reflection on the other" (*JC* 89). Neither alternative is satisfactory (*JC* 4). In fact, "the trouble with unrestrained and militant egoism is that it becomes an imperialism of ideas, which easily converts itself into an imperialism of nations" (*JC* 140). Said's *bête noire*, Orientalism, was, he said, a "technique for turning vast geographical domains into treatable, and manageable, entities.... Europe and Asia were *our* Europe and *our* Asia—our *will* and representation, as Schopenhauer had said" (*O* 115, italics in the original).

Romantic political ideas offered a charismatics that was political but not tyrannical. Said became an early American fan of Georg Lukács, but solely as an imaginative writer, and a fanciful one at that, anomalously without Lukács' Marxism.[14] Elsewhere he wrote that Lukács' "proletariat" in no respect resembles any actual working people. He insists that they are purely "the theoretical antithesis to capitalism," and "can by no means be identified with a ragged collection of grimy-faced Hungarian laborers."[15] Lukács remained the Romantic Idealist in the German tradition who, before his conversion to Marxism, had written so feelingly of Goethe and Schiller.[16]

Said's view of history was equally Romantic and Idealist. His avatar in this respect, his twin separated by a 150-year gap, was the founder of the Romantic School of historiography, Jules Michelet (1798–1877). Like Said, Michelet revered Vico; his first published work (1827) was a translation of Vico's *The New Science*. In his *History of France* (1856), Michelet also expressed a Saidian impatience with secondary, scholarly literature. He set aside the fancy, scholarly explanations that had accrued with the centuries and returned to the unsophisticated and imagistic thoughts of the earliest human speakers. Like Vico, he believed that the human mind had two layers: an individual, conscious mind, which pursued selfish, short-sighted, and self-destructive ends; and a collective human mind, that extracted long-term good from these selfish acts. "Michelet *emplotted* his histories as dramas of disclosure, of the liberation of a spiritual power fighting to free itself from forces of darkness."[17] This idea of luminous emergence informs much in Said's life, work, and politics, the way for example that he contrived, in the course of a fifty-minute lecture, to emerge from a balled-up, hunched over, larval introvert into an expansive Monarch butterfly soaring from one corner to the other.

What emerged was Said's entry into politics. In his imagination, the Palestinian liberation movement became a romantic and inspired quest to shake off the injustice of dispossession. Palestinians were being made to pay exorbitant compensation for the crimes of European anti-Semitism—crimes they had not committed and scarcely knew. In that sense, Said flirted with, and perhaps exploited, the lure of extreme radical romanticism, whose unholy excitements took the form of third-world liberation movements. In "the late '60s and early '70s," Said recalled, "a tremendous enthusiasm and romantic glamour attached to the rise of a new movement out of the ashes."[18] Liberationist romanticism weighed against the abiding, stereotypically Orientalist sin of fatalism and passivity that Said unequivocally rejected. "I don't want to be interpreted as saying Palestinians are innocent, or that as a people they have been passively tolerant of their fate. Such words as innocent have no place in discussions of this sort" (*PolD* 171). His statement takes the form of a confession ("we did wrong"), yet it carries the content of an assertion ("at least we were active, not passive"). This contradiction is redolent of Said's repetitious dramas of emergence, of his strategies of embrace-plus-expulsion or betrayal/abandonment.

In 1966 Said was tussling with a "tormented stasis" that seems to have had him stuck on four levels: personal, aesthetic, critical, and political. He had escaped Cairo, where his family belonged to the *khawaga* bourgeoisie. Palestinian and Syrian foreigners, the Saids had never been entirely accepted in Egypt and became still more impotent after the Nasserite rebellion of 1953, which resulted in the torching and ruin of his father's prosperous business. The family was stymied, immobilized, many of them on the run from a now-conquered Palestine. Inexplicably, his father used Edward's name on some business documents that imperiled his further travel to Egypt.[19] Edward entered a long half-life as an isolated youngster and young adult marooned in America. He wrote about his first year at Mount Hermon boarding school in Massachusetts: "The utter loneliness at Mount Hermon seemed heightened three weeks after I returned to school in early January. We were entombed" (*OofP* 240). A general sense of solitude seems to have persisted through his years at Princeton and even later, in graduate school at Harvard, although at least one of his sisters came to the United States as well. His stylish English clothes and his languages set him apart. His literary and critical interests, historicist and phenomenological, grated against the reigning bias of New Criticism and empirical historicism. Politically, the Arabs were being ignored and, in 1967, suffered a military defeat by Israel—a humiliation reiterated joyously in the American press and by Said's colleagues and students at Columbia, the most Jewish college in the Ivy League. His unhappy marriage to Maire Kurick-Said ended within the year.[20] He was truly stuck. In retrospect, it seems almost inevitable that he chose to write a book in homage to the inwardly tortured Conrad. The book created a monument to a self he was about to bury—the would-be charismatic hero who succumbs to devastating flaws.

"Your Name Is Aram"

My introduction to Edward Said took place in his office in Hamilton Hall on the Columbia campus in September 1968. I had just arrived from Guilderland, New York, my large public suburban high school that squatted beneath the old Helderberg Mountains, one of many in the tri-city area of Albany, Schenectady, and Troy. My parents never took me on the requisite before-first-semester-of-college shopping trip, and I hadn't known to ask. So I arrived garbed in my high-school uniform: tan stretch jeans, a cut-off yellow football sweatshirt, and low-top white Converse sneakers. The wry New Yorkers in the Registrar's office had turned me away, telling me I needed my advisor's signature. Leaving Kent Hall I could see South Field, where hedges had been trampled during the riots the spring before and unruly students had gouged deep dirt paths across the tatty lawns. While adult-looking graduate students wearing pressed shirts or kipas went briskly about their business, my bell-bottomed peers milled around the sundial, looking for action.

I found Said's office in the dim old oak hall. Just as I approached, his door opened. He came out, fast. I registered the black cashmere blazer he wore over a wide-striped tailored shirt. Of course, coming from the provinces, I didn't know his coat was cashmere or that his shirt had been commissioned from an English haberdasher. All I knew was that he looked like nothing else this seventeen-year-old boy had seen in his life: pressed and polished, full of eye and hand contact, a busy man of the world who was nonetheless courtly and attentive to me, only a lost student asking for his signature. I wondered where he was going, that he should be in such a rush.

"Professor Said?"

"I'm on my way out." He paused, caught himself, smiled. "Make it quick."

"Hi. My name is Harold Veeser and ..." I hesitated. "You're my advisor."

"Oh, yes. How do you do, then ... (pause) ... Harold. So, then, you must have some little card for me to sign. Ah, yes, there it is, just give it over here." We moved back into his office. It smelled citrusy, and I noticed a vase of cut flowers. "Oh, look, [now he was delighted] your middle name is Aram. Why don't you use it? So you must be ..."

"Armenian," I said, happy we had established this because I knew he was an Arab.

"Well, then, I suppose you speak some Armenian?"

At this juncture Said put his arm around my shoulders. I was stunned. "Well, no, a couple of words."

"That was a piece of negligence, Aram. Why didn't you learn it?"

"Well, my father, he's German. There wasn't a lot of Armenian spoken."

He narrowed his glance and gave me an impatient half smile. "My dear boy, a way can always be found. If you want it." He tilted back his head and handed me the card. "You haven't progressed very far with this, have you?" His voice had a lilt now. Was it mockery? "Your courses, you see, need to be written in here." He pointed a long, elegant finger to a line on the card.

I took a deep breath. "I wanted to ask you about courses," I stammered. I was feeling a bit confused. Was he being friendly? Or was he insulting me? "I'm an English major." Immediately I felt stupid. Of course I was. He was my advisor.

"That's the idea. But you see"—he pointed to a fat lump of yellow gold on his wrist—"It can't be today. I'm late for an appointment. This is just not the time. Why don't you come round later this week?" He opened his drawer and pulled something out.

"Professor, I have to register now ..." I insisted. He's living up to his reputation, I thought, putting me down, making me ashamed of not knowing Armenian, rushing me out of here. I had to get my boast in there. "I tested out of freshman English, so I don't know what English course to take."

"Harold, I would love to discuss all this with you, and I will when you come in for a longer chat." Now he was up. He took me by the arm. He liked me. "I want to talk to you about the Armenians, too." Then I noticed his chummy grasp was steering me closer to the door. As we reached it, he smiled broadly. "You sign up for Professor Michael Rosenthal's course," he said, holding open the door. "The Bloomsbury Circle. He's fantastic, a brilliant intellect. Look, I'll sign the form." From his inside pocket, he plucked a gold pen the size and thickness of a frankfurter to autograph my program. I glimpsed a matte amethyst stone in his chunky gold cuff link. "And it was really an immense pleasure to meet you, Harold." He gripped me by the shoulder. "You must come in and see me. Good-bye."

I found myself standing in the hall, having just experienced for the first time Said's gift for extraordinary intimacy and steely, dismissive rejection—simultaneously. This pattern of embrace-plus-expulsion distinguished so many of his involvements—with literary theory, with the PLO, in fact, with everything except his personal relationships and his dedication to Palestine, which never wavered. The meltingly warm embrace overlaid a cold and steady gaze, like two transparencies on an overhead projector.

3
EMERGENCE

The miracle of [society's] constitution lies in the fact that in each of its revolutions, it finds in the very corruption of the preceding state the elements of the new form which is able to redeem it.
   Jules Michelet, "Principes de la philosophie de l'histoire"[1]

Performance is only part of a larger activity: of shaping a self out of the materials in which it is immersed, like the figure of Michelangelo's captive.
                               Richard Poirier, *The Performing Self*

By late 1967 Said had decided to step off the beaten track. He was resolved to break out of all his prisons: marriage, political silence, the persona of the tweedy English professor. Only one item remained unchanged: he still could not occupy a position for five seconds before he began to evacuate it. He received tenure and a sabbatical leave, resolved to end his unhappy marriage, and, what turned out to be most important, agreed to write his first political essay. He began a second book and this time plunged headfirst into the exciting critical developments coming out of Europe and especially France.

   Compared to the lucubrations on tormented stasis and murderous knitting machines in *Joseph Conrad*—that dark love tryst with failure—*Beginnings: Intention and Method* is a bright and optimistic comedy. In writing it, Said was able for a few brief years to occupy completely the generous framework of comic narrative. According to Northrop Frye's definition, which loomed over the critical field while Said was in graduate school, in comedy what normally happens is that a young man wants a young woman, that his desire is resisted by some opposition, usually paternal, and that near the end of the play some twist in the plot enables the hero to have his will.²

French literary theory played both parts: the exciting siren and the blocking humor. The siren promised to lift him right out of the suddenly decrepit, dowdy ranks of his colleagues, often pompous, Anglophilic men who quoted only themselves. Generational splits bisect most academic departments, and in 1967 this tense stand-off of old versus young was sharpened by the bottle-throwing, angry, and obstreperous student body. While siding with the new theorists, *Beginnings* also saw that their ideas threatened to bring down the curtain on any possible independent social action. Powerful currents of determinism and political quietism ran right through all the thinkers he now discussed: Freud, Nietzsche, Conrad, Canguilhem, Barthes, Derrida, Foucault, and a passel of other Modernist and contemporary structuralist thinkers.³ Although he shows enthusiasm for the as-yet relatively unknown (and therefore intriguing) theories of European structuralism and deconstruction, he finally rejects them all because they seem to undermine the potency of the conscious human will. To advance his ongoing fight for the efficacy of will and against passivity, he develops a theory of "molestation," which applies to novels as they evolve toward the Modernist period. He argues that proto-Modernist novelists increasingly feature the battle between will and determinism, and show that willed human fictions are inevitably eroded by reality. Thematically, this theory of "molestation" confirms Schopenhauer, for it demonstrates that a purely willed reality is subject to attack by more fundamental realities. The titles of influential novels such as *Lost Illusions* and *Great Expectations* announce this theme in advance, and the European novel is rife with characters such as Julien Sorel and Frederic Moreau, whose ambitions and projects inevitably fail—cautionary examples for the ambitious Said. Lost illusions overtake the novelists as well as their protagonists. *Nostromo*, with its succession of invalidated or qualified narrations and failed narrators, including Captain Mitchell, Decoud, Dr. Monygham, and Emilia Gould, amply canvasses the many ways to fail to tell a story. For five chapters, Said explores disenchantment—a theme that has always signaled the end of charismatic originality and the onset of settled, disillusioned rational authority. He probes and develops his theory that narrations can no longer succeed, that the narrative impulse itself has been rendered sterile. The final, sixth chapter of *Beginnings*, "Conclusion: Vico in His Work and in This," follows this chronicle of literary self-subversion. It is the sole chapter named for a single writer, and about that writer Said has only good things to say. In his eyes, Vico merits unreserved approval. Said and Vico merge as one. This happy union with an out-of-place Enlightenment oddball, tacked on to a book about post-structuralist French theory, gives *Beginnings* the form of a traditional comedy: the blocking humors finally removed, the marriage can be consummated. Disenchantment is itself disenchanted, and the book, having

---

Said's Praise of Vico

Vico's tendency was to turn away from schematic methods that could be lifted out of his text; instead, he advocated wideness of scope, broad comparisons, the love of detail linked to large universal principles—all intended to load down schemata beyond usefulness. The power of Vico's rhetoric always takes one away from method, rationalistically [sic] considered, to knowedge [sic] as pathos, invention, imagination—with their pitfalls unobscured.... Everywhere in Vico's work there is to be found the sometimes paradoxical play between, on the one hand, learning, tradition, history, method, pedagogy—in short, applied and pure reason in all their dynastic forms—and on the other hand, originality, personality, the marvelous, detailed, and often heroic style in all its dispersed forms.

(B 368–369)

survived its encounter with theory, swings open onto a new set of possibilities.

Said appears stunned by the sight of his own bisected image mirrored in Vico. The "paradoxical play" between "learning, tradition, history, method, pedagogy, pure and applied reason in all their dynastic forms" and "originality, personality, the marvelous, detailed, heroic dispersed forms" is every bit as Manichean as those masque/antimasque productions of the English royal absolutist court. Said's claims are outlandish: Vico, a terrible and incompetent narrator, anarchic and sloppy, seems implausible as the solution to narrative breakdown. He displays the kind of instability and final impenetrability that characterize Said himself. "For the modern reader," Said admits, "*The New Science* is not a tidy book, and its often postponed arrival at any sort of conclusion makes it perhaps a bad example of expository prose" (B 354). This admission is even more fitting for his own prose, and were Vico alive, he would be within his rights to splutter out a "Tu quoque!" But, by definition, charisma always banishes logic and defies rational calculation. Said has never written a decent conclusion: he's all about erosion, evacuation, and abandoning positions, not closure or driving points home. In a Said paragraph, things don't come together. They come apart.

Said as well as Vico specialized in releasing intellectual energies without the predictable rhetorical machinery of climax and closure. Vico exemplified prose that succeeded without ever arriving at any kind of conclusion. His great life's work "was not a tidy book." In some way, therefore, he authorized Said's own stylistic vagaries. Vico's thought "parallels my key arguments throughout the preceding five chapters" (B 357). These parallels include Vico's tendency to emphasize "the lateral and the dispersed rather than the linear and the sequential," his selection of "a special, idiosyncratic problem" to write about, his "topics for critical analysis that do not fall neatly into the categories" of normal investigation, and overall his interest in "the instability, and the richness, of a text as practice and as idea" (B 357). With these four features—dispersed argument,

> **Examples of Vico's Style**
>
> Irony certainly could not have begun until the period of reflection, because it is fashioned of falsehood by dint of a reflection which wears the mask of truth. Here emerges a great principle of human institutions, confirming the origin of poetry disclosed in this work; that since the first men of the gentile world had the simplicity of children, who are truthful by nature, the first fables could not feign anything false; they must therefore have been, as they have been defined above, true narrations.[4]
>
> That which is metaphysics insofar as it contemplates things in all the forms of their being, is logic insofar as it considers things in all the forms by which they may be signified. Accordingly, as poetry has been considered by us above as a poetic metaphysics in which the theological poets imagined bodies to be for the most part divine substances, so now that same poetry is considered as poetic logic, by which it signifies them.[5]
>
> Here begins also a philosophy of authority, a second principal aspect of this Science, taking the word "authority" in its original meaning of property. The word is always used in this sense in the Law of the Twelve Tables, and the term *auctores* was accordingly applied to those from whom we derive title to property. *Auctor* certainly comes from *autos* (= *proprius* or *suus ipsius*); and many scholars write *autor* and *autoritas*, leaving out the aspirate.[6]

idiosyncratic topics, uncategorizability, and instability—neither neat nor schematic nor linear nor straightforward—you never really know exactly where you are—in the middle of his argument, near the end, or still in the prologue. You have a sense of fecundity and instability, as if the topic might take off in a number of branching directions, all of them potentially intriguing, novel, and useful. Yet this sense of imminent abandonment or departure can be unsettling. Not everyone will happily surrender to the unpredictable cascades of charismatic genius. Obviously it is not a style for the faint-hearted or for anyone who insists on orderly exposition. Said's style has been lamented as widely as it has been celebrated. Nonetheless, this unsettled and tremulous style made him an academostar second to none.[7] Wrapping *Beginnings* with a chapter on Vico proved a bounteous as well as a defiant way to conclude.

The best analysis of Said's style was one of the earliest, and what we could now name as Vichian elements are deftly identified. The author resorts to the language of natural disasters, with spurts, slippage, and floating debris:

> Let us try now to characterize in a general way the performance of Said's writing. It appears, in the first place, to be done very fast, or at least in spurts that correspond roughly to the division of paragraphs. The impression of speed is enhanced by what to an academic reader must seem a scandalous disregard of the usual norms of editorial attention. The argumentative line within the paragraph tends to illustrate the textual movement the French call *dérapage*, a slight slipping from sentence to sentence whose effect is produced under the rhetorical aegis of ellipsis. The argument tends to move laterally, rather than pointedly, reaching out as it proceeds for allusions, bits of quotation, pieces of authority, fragments of stray remembrances.[8]

In this intuitive, sympathetic assessment, three of the elements that Said found in Vico reappear: the lateral and the dispersed rather than the linear and the sequential, the instability, the fecundity. Not coincidentally, the style is the man: *dérapage* equally well describes Said's "slippage" in other situations: his slippage out of the PLO, out of High Literary Theory, out of English literature into postcolonial thought, out of intimacy into objectivity. The general impression is that of a rock climber moving up a cliff face, grabbing allusions, bits of quotation, pieces of authority, fragments of stray remembrances, new lines of argument, ascending laterally or in a zig-zag, anything but a direct vertical route.

One of the great mid-century puzzles afflicting literary criticism was how difficult-to-read theory could have come to dominate a field previously consecrated to belletristic limpidity. In Said's case, careless prose aggravated the intellectual difficulty of theory. Stylistically, slippage or *dérapage* is conventionally thought of as a weakness, and Klein is bemused as he writes up violation after violation. My colleague at Marymount College, Sister Emanuela, used to call this sort of divagacious prose "the Wandering Willy." Indeed, Klein implies that Said reduces the reader to the kind of passive suffering that Said himself despises, what Klein calls "the impotence one feels in the presence of student prose whose inadequacies are apparent but whose exact pathology is hard to diagnose" (1978: 83). He chooses this example from Said's *Beginnings*:

> Subject (*sujet*) in its more exact context means the thinking subject or the speaking subject, the subjectivity that defines human identity, the cognito [*sic*] that enables the Cartesian world of objects. The influence of the thinking subject in Western thought has, of course, been profound. Not only has the subject guaranteed ideas of priority and originality, but also ideas, methods, and schemes of continuity and achievement, endowing them libidinally with a primal urgency underlying all patterns of succession, history and progress.
>
> (B 293)

Taking this passage apart, Klein's red pen is just a blur.

> Suppose you had to grade these sentences! Or had to invent some irony to put in the margin next to the profundity of a sentence like the second one! You might then begin to measure the failure Said's writing represents, at the risk of underestimating its extraordinary power.
>
> (1978: 84)

Dérapage is not entirely debilitating:

> Said's thought never creates the illusion that you can predict where it is going; and when it arrives at the end of its thrust,

you rarely have the feeling that a telling blow has been struck. The force of the writing is impulsive; the ellipses are signs of the spurted gaps that interrupt the forward progress of the line and slide the argument in its movement of *dérapage*, at the same time derailing it and *providing its energy*.

(1978: 86, italics added)

Slithering about can be good art: witness the tango expert or clay-court tennis champion. What Said called Vico's "often postponed arrival at any sort of conclusion," Klein calls a pronounced feature of Said's own conclusion-shy prose.[9] Klein seems unsure just how this "energy" is produced, but he applauds the strange rhythms so unlike the crisp and decisive prose that executives are expected to write. You could say this is prose designed precisely to outrage bureaucratic standards.

This same quality of *je ne sais quoi* draws further comment from another early analyst of Said:

> a recurrent figure in Said's writing ... [is] that of Mind in difficult or troubled confrontation with the world. It is not the Cartesian mind, however, since it is not treated as something apart from the world, looking into it; rather it is a Vichian mind, a consciousness at first merely potential, literally buried in the human body, from which it must fight to emerge, to make itself.[10]

How intriguing that the human body should make an early appearance here in Gorman's remarks.[11] But then Gorman, remembering that he inhabits the cerebral world of academe, hears the screaming alarms set off by this gauche intrusion of the body and proceeds to describe its "fight to emerge" as a wholly theoretical affair. A third critic, Richard Poirier, understands Said's fight viscerally and literally, as it should be parsed. Poirier brings both features together in the most productive image of all. One of Michelangelo's four unfinished statues known as "The Captives," now housed at the Academia in Florence, adorns the cover of the work Said invariably cited, Poirier's best and most widely known book, *The Performing Self*.[12]

Figure 3.1 Captive by Michelangelo (source: Alinari/Art Resource, New York).

Emergence • 49

In this book, Poirier advances a unique appreciation of captivity, of being mired in a situation and fighting one's way out of it. His moving account of the image on the book jacket cover has great importance. There, Said would have seen the reproduction of a body straining to emerge from the crude block of stone; its right leg, of tree-trunk solidity, pushing up like a weightlifter squatting five plates; the left arm cocked, biceps engorged, elbow jutting forward. The hand and forearm push at what would be the back of the head.

> Except that there is no head. Where it would be is instead a heavy block of stone. So that it is as if the arm and hand, with awesomely sustained and patient exertion, were trying to push off the imposing weight which imprisons the head. The communicated effect is not of aspiration but of some more elemental will toward attainment of human shape and human recognition.
>
> (Poirier 1971: xv)

Can this sweaty scene really be allied to cool charisma? It can, from Said's point of view. What Said took from this image was the exertion, the emergence of human form, and above all the endlessness and internality of effort. The crucial insight is that "the imagined head cannot be conceived except as part of the material that will not willingly yield itself to the head's existence" (Poirier vii). A Laocoon-esque entanglement rules out any possibility of rupture, separation, or even liberation. All this means that pride in one's "beginnings," one's past and heritage, is a crucial element of hacking out one's individuality. It demands

> Negotiation, struck compromise with the stubborn material of existence, be it language or stone. The fact that the statue was left in its unfinished state provides a surpassingly eloquent image of the strenuousness, even, sometimes, the violence, required by this effort.
>
> (Poirier 1971: viii)

When the artist depicts the straining aspirant locked within the stone, he really is musing about his own struggle:

> The workings of Michelangelo with the stone are thus of a piece, quite literally so, with the seeming exertions of the captive within it: both of them would summon the power required for the composing of a self otherwise lost to the material from which it might be formed.
>
> (Poirier 1971: viii)

With that, Poirier suggests how the brutal efforts proper to a slave bear some resemblance to the Apollonian freedom proper to the great sculptor. We know from Said's meditations on Vico how fascinated he was by Vico's descriptions of humanity—only prospectively human and trapped in the bodies of giants—laboriously extracting itself from the passions and instincts that rule over the mind. In Said's case these were the habits of Cairo, the structure of patriarchy that governed his nuclear and extended families, and the colonial mentality of subservience. Something of the same labor emerges in "The Captive," but, far from a blue-lipped, painful experience, in Poirier's view, the captive's exertions amount to a "self-discovering, self-watching, finally self-pleasuring response to the pressures and difficulties" of making, sculpting, writing, or self-fashioning:

> When a writer is most strongly engaged by what he is doing, as if struggling for his identity within the materials at hand, he can show us, in the mere turning of a sentence this way or that, how to keep from being smothered by the inherited structuring of things, how to keep within and yet in command of the accumulations of culture that have become a part of what he is. Much of cultural inheritance is waste; it always has been. But only those who are both vulnerable and brave are in a position to know what is waste and what is not.
>
> (Poirier 1971: xvi)

A monumental task done with careless ease: the quality that Baldessar Castiglione called *sprezzatura* looms large, 500 years on, in what we today call charisma. Poirier conceives of a brave if vulnerable subject who keeps some volition and autonomy although trapped within, who manages to fight for room to breathe, and who achieves an identity apart from that of the malevolent machine that encases him. For the Palestinian–Egyptian intellectual, the smothering body includes Balfour's 1919 promise to Zionism, the "bolus" of fantasy that comprises the libelous tradition of Orientalism, and the Israeli conquest of Palestine—the *nakba*. But it also includes the oppressive weight of Arabness itself, the hypocritically pro-Palestinian Arab regimes, the whole ungainly and malevolent geopolitical landmass with its corrupt tyrants and its ostrich-like insularity.[13]

In politics as in literature, Said wrote about captivity. From his initial foray into this political realm, he was determined to extract a human image of the Arab from a farrago of misrepresentations. In "The Arab Portrayed," his first political essay, he set out to extract a human form of Arab people. Yet he knew that the Arab past could not simply be ignored or leapt over.

As a native Palestinian and founder of a secular party in Syria, Ibrahim Abu-Lughod, the older Palestinian-American who commissioned Said's first political essay, presented himself as Said's bridge to secular Arab political thought. But he also sought to routinize and bureaucratize what Said preferred to keep independent. He was the one who persuaded Said that they must have an organizational base. That base was, indeed, base. Said found its membership stupid, but Abu-Lughod checked him: "If you want a higher level of abstraction, you go somewhere else."[14] They proceeded to build a safe, nurturing zone where the traumas of the past could be re-experienced and articulated by a group of victims. Their effort was reminiscent of marginal immigrant authors, non-mainstream Americans who worked out their identity issues within the protected pages of ethnic literary journals.[15] Abu-Lughod insisted on organized collectivity. His evident pleasure in setting up a board of directors, trustees, officers, banquets, conventions, meetings, referenda, and journals runs at a sharp angle from Said's loner sensibility.

Two models of authority clash in Abu-Lughod's story: the bureaucratic-rational organization that he himself wants, and the charismatic authority of a "star like Edward" who "doesn't

Interview with Ibrahim Abu-Lughod, December 29, 1991, at his Home on Sheridan Avenue, Evanston, Illinois

A-L: I drew [Edward] to it, you see. I drew him into it.... It was a brilliant invention, as it were. It could happen only in America. That we got the professors, we got the lawyers, the doctors, and the engineers, i.e., a certain cut in society. We were pragmatic about it. In America you have to have an organization in order to have somebody listen to you unless you become a star like Edward. Now Edward doesn't need an organization. But Edward didn't exist in those days. So we needed the organization. We needed literature that we could produce. And we did. We did really brilliant social-institutional work. Prior to 1967, we had no such thing! We needed the mass, the critical mass. Needed the collective work. And that institution became the one that did it. We relied on the lawyers and engineers to give us the back-up support, to pay the dues and all of that. And they accepted our sort of leadership, in terms of our collection of intellectual material, political material. The book, for example, about the '73 war: Well, that was part of our production. We did it as a collective, literally. We have over a thousand members, around fifteen hundred members, from all over America. So we became known to each other. So, once a year, we met as a group. Our conventions number sometimes a thousand people. It was an incredible, what I used to call a clambake. You are snatched by the graduate students who are writing this dissertation and they want to talk to Edward, they want to talk to me, they want to talk to that one—because their advisors don't know a God-damned thing about the Middle East! [laughter] So Edward got to know all—what he called, "the same fools again." Sure, they are the same fools. But they are the professors, you know [more laughter]—you can't complain about them. That's what we got! [Edward] certainly came to these meetings. He gave papers. All the earlier writings that he did, we commissioned in relation to these meetings. The things we invented! We were addressing ourselves to serious issues. He did it ... partly, he saw the response. And that's when he split with the Orientalists. Some of the Orientalists used to come to these meetings, and they would complain to me how unfair he is, compared to me. And then they would grab him sometimes to educate him "You don't know the Orientalist tradition—I mean you are external to this." Then he would laugh at them. But that's when he did it. And the Arabs began to focus on him and to give him the support that he not only probably deserved but that I think he ... he valued. They don't read him. They don't read his *Beginnings*. They don't read his *Conrad*. That's not their bag. But they listen to what he says. And what he says is good. They recognize quality.

HAV: Out of the organization [the Arab-American Association of University Graduates] the book [*The Arab Israeli Confrontation*] was published. Were there also articles in the *Journal of Palestine Studies*, things like that?

A-L: We issued the *Arab Studies Quarterly*. We founded that—Edward and I founded it. I can show you the original letter that I wrote. It took five years, six years to produce it, from the time of its conception. It became a reality in 1979. He and I were the first editors. That was our brainchild! Both that magazine and the Institute of Arab Studies. The Institute partly came as the result of interaction between the two of us.

continued

> I remember distinctly when the idea developed. He went to give a lecture in Abu Dhabi [United Arab Emirates].... He came back. He said, "You know"—we used to see each other a lot then. We still do, but I think we did more, because I traveled a lot then. I went to New York all the time. He now travels, you can't catch him—he said, "You know, there's nothing like ... there's no think tank. We don't have a think tank in the Arab world, to advise these people." He wrote a proposal. Then he and I went to the financiers, trying to impress them with the idea that we need a think tank. And it wasn't even a Palestinian think tank, it was an Arab think tank. But we thought that of all places it must be here in America where you have some freedom—I mean we're aware of the constraints in the Arab world, and we went to a law firm in New York, mediated by this financier, and they actually drafted the bylaws for us.

need an organization" and who ridicules the members as "fools." Poirier's "Captive" is apropos as an image for Said's involvement with the Arab-American Association of University Graduates. Around 1975, he seemed fully committed to Vico and to the AAUG. Could he finally have settled down? No, he couldn't. And yet the restive Said who was unsatisfied in his first marriage, his life as a literature professor, his role as an importer of French literary theory, or his role as an immigrant seeking assimilation also recognized that his charisma derived from his willingness to struggle with each of these involvements, to work himself forcefully through them, to place his own qualities of ease, defiance, and effort above any claims made by rationality, bureaucracy, or impersonal routine.

The fragmentation of the self as an unfinished figure chimed exactly with Said's patient, astringent toil within his enveloping, empowering blocs: the AAUG, the professorial chair, the Pales-

Interview with Ibrahim Abu-Lughod [continued]

A-L: Edward likes to be "in." But he has very little patience to be "in." If he is not "in," he is really upset. But once "in," he has terrible patience. Eventually, when we created—and I don't know if you have gotten into this history—the Institute of Arab Studies for which he is a co-founder and the only chairman of the board, and then it got dissolved, essentially. I have never seen him happier. More than the first—we were about, maybe, twelve or fourteen people, when we had our dinner and our first meeting, as it were. He was *so happy* at that meeting. Must have been end of 1979 or 1980. He was *so happy* because he *found his people*. It was an ethnic thing.... But I said, "He's not going to sustain it." [laughter] "Because he can't!" You know, "You're a bunch of fools." [more laughter] And he was. He wanted to be *in*, because he had been so much out of it in America.

HAV: Wasn't all this a big distraction from his serious bid to become the greatest North American literary critic?

A-L: You see, he was part of Egypt, part of the Palestinian community in Egypt, so when he came to America, he was essentially severed from everything collective. Then the AAUG brought him in, then he was elected vice-president of the Association, and then he was given recognition by the Association. So he felt better that he is incorporated into this great ethnic network, as it were. But it's too broad, and it's too vague.... But we used it for mobilization to enable the intellectuals among us, who were active in politics, to have some base of support.... But the Institute was his group.

continued

> It was more elite. And he was as happy as a lark that he was finally accepted by the cream of this community, that elects him to their boss. And he had not been boss yet. Although he says that he never wanted to be chairman of the [English] department, or a good citizen of the department, because he is a dissident. Well, maybe. But you want some measure of acceptance. And I think he knew his worth. There is no question about it: he doesn't suffer from doubt about himself. He knew that he is accepted as an intellectual, as a leading figure. But he also wanted to be accepted within the Arab community as a preeminent Arab. It had nothing to do with his literature. But he wanted to be accepted. And at the Institute, he was accepted. He became the boss. He was the chairman. He could sit in the chair and pontificate to us, and blast us, you know: "You are not doing this, you are not doing that." And then talking, any way he wanted to. And we took it from him. But he couldn't sustain it for a long time either. [laughter]

tinian spokesmanship. He understood that these organizations blessed him with cultural capital and symbolic value. But expressive power was so concentrated within himself there was no need to break completely away. As for the bureaucracies, he lent unexpected dazzle to their norms and routines. What university or pro-Arab group would refuse to honor someone who possessed such reserves of feeling or so unrestrained a passion for public speech?

From the point of view of building the AAUG, a charismatic member may actually threaten the organization. Abu-Lughod recounts how the members were ready "almost to lynch" Said when he played the role of Master of Ceremonies: his undisciplined style enraged them. Up to this point, Said's incipient charisma appeared in a largely negative light: although his work attracted a great deal of attention within literature studies, his critics had noticed a certain turgidity of exposition, a tendency toward self-contradiction, an undisciplined slippage or *dérapage*, a poverty of argumentation, and a failure to reach decisive conclusions.

The turning point came when he turned all those debilities into strengths and began staging his own struggles. Instead of feeling chastened and trying to write more clearly, consistently, logically, and conclusively, he found ways to accept and even dramatize his own weaknesses. In Romantics such as Conrad, he discovered the rich value of self-tormented stasis, in the neoclassical Vico, a preference for the lateral and the dispersed rather than the linear and the sequential, the value of seeking a special, idiosyncratic problem to write about, the use of topics for critical analysis that do not fall neatly into the categories of normal investigation, and above all the love of instability. He developed a style of his own that preserves all his natural tendencies. It retains the chaos of his original instinct and makes of that chaos his own emerging "form." Dynasty versus dispersion, history versus personality, method versus the marvelous, tradition versus originality: Said respected both sides of the Vichean divide. But while there were many to advocate rational method and corporate professional conduct, the other side had only one advocate: Edward Said. He alone gave equal time to the Vichean values he had identified in *Beginnings*: "knowledge as pathos, invention, imagination—with their pitfalls unobscured." Only he "loaded down schemata beyond usefulness" and stood up for "originality, personality, the marvelous, detailed, and often heroic style" (*B* 368–369).

"Before He Was An Arab"

Milton Berle made a joke about Doris Day: "I knew her before she was a virgin." I knew Said before he was an academostar. "The Said we knew," my classmate Sean Wilentz said recently, "was not the Said the world knows. We knew him when he was a Princeton Man." Wilentz, now a Princeton professor of

58 • Emergence

Figure 3.2 Student demonstration at Columbia University, Fall 1968 (source: Richard Howard, www.richardhowardphotography. com).

history (and a reigning expert on the American working-class), was recalling Said's poshness and self-assurance. But his use of the indefinite article also tells a tale. For Said was one of many, just another extremely privileged kind of man.

When I met Said, he was unmistakably Ruling Class. His intellect, his reportedly exotic origins, and his academic fame were all very well. But what really caught my attention were his social ease and polish, his vast helpings of money and manners, his rich clothes, his easy arrogance, and his boarding-school purr. He really *was* Princeton.

At this epoch, it was customary for radical students to "liberate" college classes. The professor of a liberated class was expected to stand aside and accept the verdict of History. I don't think anyone tried this on Said, who once used his umbrella to brush aside two friends of mine, who were kissing on the Hamilton Hall stairwell. I recall one occasion when he addressed the Columbia chapter of Students for a Democratic Society, who were very big on liberating classrooms and even whole buildings. Students, visiting radicals, Harlem residents, and street people had pressed into Hewitt Lounge in the student center. Imagine a group who had the political moderation of Robespierre and the sartorial verve of the Hell's Angels, and you'll have a pretty fair grasp of the scene.

An audible stir up in the front let me know Said had arrived. What followed was a series of tiny collisions and Gestalt readjustments. As he entered Hewitt Lounge, the person speaking, Josie Biddle Duke, drew to a rapid close:

> All right, people, please, quiet. Dig it. We're strong, we're solid, we're going to shut it down. We need to link arms with all parts of the radical community. We welcome support from all sectors of the university. Tonight we are getting some of that support, we are getting some solidarity, man, and it's coming tonight from a faculty member, a professor in the English Department. I'm going to stop there because you, you know, the professor has arrived. This is Professor Edward Said. Professor Said of Columbia University. Professor Said is going to make a statement. Professor Said!

He declined to mount the Victorian coffee table that had been serving as the speakers' dais. He was tall enough to be seen and the crowd sort of stepped back and gave him some room. He was visible this way and could move around a bit, too. His preamble was subdued, his shoulders hunched, his eyes lowered, his voice quiet. He promised to make four points, the final one about the Palestinians. As he made them, his animation grew. His hand came into play. He straightened up. His diction became richer, even a bit fanciful. His fourth and final point resonated through the large room: "And have you in SDS ever said so much as a word on the Palestinians' behalf?" He searched the assembly, daring someone to answer. "No, you haven't!" The dandy-like and introspective professor had morphed into a swingeing Palestinian Billy Sunday. Now he piled fact upon fact, a fifth, sixth, seventh point heaped on his promised four. "And my final point is this"—here, a quick smile answered our laughter—"is that you call for 'many Vietnams.'

Well, Palestine today IS another Vietnam!" It was a tour de force.

I witnessed such transformations many times. Suddenly, the buttoned-down precision of his prologue would take off like a Jimi Hendrix solo—not the weed-like proliferation of a Dickens novel nor the schizoid meanderings of a Beckett monologue nor the predictable going-one-better of a John Leguizamo, but rather the genius of a great improviser. When Said taught continental theory, his improvisatory flights would produce astounding blackboard notations, as un-thought-of structures took shape in white chalk. When he took on a traditional British lit survey, he loaded it with ironies and contradictions until its familiar outlines evaporated. His graduate seminars were pure inventions of the theoretical imagination, with mysterious titles like "Egotism" and "Repetition." The diagrams he wrote out in flowing longhand had intricate webs and symmetries, and we spent hours thinking over the ways they might be used. Mostly they couldn't be: his schemata were ends in themselves.

4
ACADEMOSTARDOM

CHARON: Where did you pick up this Cynic, Hermes? The noise he made on the crossing, too! Laughing and jeering at all the rest, and singing, when everyone else was at his lamentations.

HERMES: Ah, Charon, you little know your passenger! Independence, every inch of him: he cares for no one. 'Tis Menippus.

Lucian, "Charon and Menippus"

Orientalism is packed with self-contradictions.[1] The founding contradiction is that the reader cannot be sure whether Said is condemning the sources he quotes or commending them. Joshing, ragging, and jeering, Said duplicated what he criticized.[2] *Orientalism* accomplished all its goals: to erase, demolish, put to flight Orientalism as it was still practiced in 1978, when the book appeared; to provide the definitive case-study of discourse analysis going beyond the narrow borders of work by Michel Foucault; and to launch Said himself to the stratosphere of academic celebrity or what Jeffrey Williams calls "academostardom." The blow he delivered was staggering. Thirty years on, the wound still pullulates, threatening gangrene, grinning and promising an excruciating death. As recently as May 2008, the *Times Literary Supplement* led with an essay by Orientalist Robert Irwin headlined, "Edward Said still dominates the debate." Irwin reviewed two books, each naming Said in its title.[3] He points out that a great many scholars continue to fulminate against Said. These "witnesses for the prosecution"

The Case Against

Charged, that Said praises [author Erich] Auerbach fulsomely for providing the summation of Western culture at its last moment of totality, while having earlier shown how the idea of European culture as a totality under threat of fragmentation is part of the Orientalist fantasy. (O 140)

Charged, that Said objects to stereotyping but energetically stereotypes "the French" through the Orientalist Louis Massignon and "the English" by Sir Hamilton A. R. Gibb. (O 259, 263)

Charged, that Said argues that the Orient is a fiction and a representation, yet contends that the study and construction of this fictional Orient provided the knowledge instrumental in the actual conquest of territory. (O 11)

Charged, that Said denies the existence of any actual Orient, yet contends that Western representations of this non-existent entity are false. (O 12)

Charged, that Said lauds humanism (O 45, 46, 246, 266, 267, 328) and castigates Orientalism as anti-human (O 266), yet is aware that high-humanist culture produced Orientalism.

Charged, that Said reveres Western culture and ideas (O 292), yet assumes that he can separate himself from those values at will, his own "critical consciousness" having "detached itself from the dominant culture." (O 224)

Charged, that Said contends that "the realistic novel … organizes reality and knowledge in such a way as to make them susceptible to systematic verbal reincarnation" and thus that the novel shores up state power (WTC 176), but fails to acknowledge that they do so only by way of the state's educational institutions, and these he never discusses.

> Charged, that Said describes the impassive, relentless workings of discourse, with all its journals, publishing houses, conferences, links to the state, intellectual traditions, professorships, and momentum and yet insists on "the determining imprint of individual writers," resistant individuals who can stand outside that totality and successfully oppose it. (O 23)

include "Sadiq Jalal al-'Azm, Bryan Turner, Malcolm Kerr, Ziauddin Sardar, Bernard Lewis, Nadim al-Bitar, Victor Brombert, Ernest Gellner, Jane Miller, John Sweetman, John Mackenzie, and many others."

This unsmiling litany rolled off Said's back. His confidence was reinforced by the book's monumental impact. As soon as it appeared, a whole body of scholarly and cultural work began to tremble. Orientalist fiction, art, travel literature, and political analysis—all areas in which the author had little formal training and no expertise—snapped to attention and began a still-frenzied effort of self-justification. Said's book galloped into thirty-six different languages and ignited forest fires in nearly every social and human science. Orientalists were stunned, defensive, angry; some were routed, others hung on. And yet more or less the same denunciation from Anouar Abdel-Malek in an article, "L'orientalisme en crise," published fourteen years earlier in a prominent journal, caused barely a ripple.[4] Few Orientalists even bothered to answer him. So it was not the substance of Said's argument that caused its success. Something else made it powerful.

Orientalism could never have been written without the author's devil-may-care habit of inhabiting an intellectual position and vacating it at precisely the same time.[5] Only someone profoundly sympathetic to English and French colonialism could have captured the tenor and vehicle of Orientalist tradition so fully. Said had an authentic colonialist genealogy through his uncle, Charles Malik, the Lebanese Ambassador to the U.S. Said's colonialist credentials included his training at the Cairo School for American Children in the fall of 1946, at the St. George's School in Jerusalem in 1947, again the CSAC for 1948–9, and then two years at Victoria College in the Maadi district of Cairo, the self-proclaimed "Eton of the Middle East." He remained unswervingly on the Tory track when his parents enrolled him as a boarder at the exclusive Mount Hermon School in Massachusetts; during intercessions he bunked with the ambassador in Washington.[6] His tastes were Tory, too: a strict adherent of the English literary canon and classical music, this *bourgeois gentilhomme* despised jazz and found pop unspeakable. He attacked Western tradition from a very secure position inside it, much like the guerrilla students who assault their elite public school in Lindsay Anderson's late-1960s film, *If*. Once again he called upon his heritage and pulled out an ancient Western literary form called Menippean satire.

Menippean satire is designed to perform the same task as *Orientalism*: the demolition of philosophical and administrative systems through satire. Critics are often baffled by this relatively unfamiliar form: "there is hardly any fiction writer deeply influenced by it who has not been accused of disorderly conduct."[7] Any definition of the form must mention

> its origin as a mixture of verse and prose.... Its ability to satirize abstract ideas and attitudes ... the encyclopedic thrust of anatomy (encyclopedism being inherently satirical because of its stuffed, mixed, and saturated nature), and its narrative progression by means of division, digression, and detail.[8]

The form is highly intellectual since it emphasizes ideas, not plot or character.

> Menippean satire deals less with people as such than with mental attitudes. Pedants, bigots, cranks, parvenus, virtuosi, enthusiasts, rapacious and incompetent professional men of all kinds, are handled in terms of their occupational approach to life as distinct from their social behavior.

> The Menippean satire thus resembles the confession in its ability to handle abstract ideas and theories, and differs from the novel in its characterization, which is stylized rather than naturalistic, and presents people as mouthpieces of the ideas they represent.... The novelist sees evil and folly as social diseases, but the Menippean satirist sees them as diseases of the intellect, as a kind of maddened pedantry which the *philosophus gloriosus* at once symbolizes and defines.[9]

Menippean strategy was tailor-made for Said's purposes. As an obscure and as-yet-unformed person, buried in the body or mass of Orientalist stereotypes and Western ideas, he was trying to drag himself from the blurry confusion so as to establish his (and "the Arab's") distinctive identity. Yet the identity had to be constructed out of those same stereotypes and Western ideas: there were no others available for him. His solution was to create a Menippean satire, a work whose entire content consisted of the materials being ridiculed and rejected.

Said's natural kinship with this satirical mode is instantly recognizable. His insouciant self-contradictions, his hatred of systems, his Tory love of the past and his taste for the literary classics, his savage dismissals of contemporary schools of thought, his wish to remain on a high intellectual plane—all these bear the Menippean stamp. Examples of the form are comparatively rare, most of them belonging to the upper echelons of literature because of the erudition demanded by intellectual satire. The great modern examples appeared repeatedly on Said's class reading lists: Swift's *Tale of a Tub*, Flaubert's *Dictionnaire des idées reçues* and *Bouvard et Pecuchet*, Samuel Butler's *The Way of All Flesh* and *Erewhon* are a few of them.[10]

The tradition behind all these works, the Menippean form (also known more conveniently as "anatomy" from its intellectualized dissection or analysis) accounts for the wildly self-contradictory confusions found in *Orientalism*.[11] Accusations of "disorderly conduct" are commonplace when unsuspecting readers encounter this mode of satire. Reading with their traditional expectations of logic and linearity, they take on the role of straight men slipping on every banana peel the satirist throws under their inattentive feet. But contradictions are not only permitted in the Menippean anatomy, they are *de rigueur*. *Orientalism* also meets other generic requirements of this zany form—its proliferating digressions and meanderings, its ability to satirize abstract ideas and attitudes and the thrust of an inherently satirical encyclopedic anatomy, stuffed, mixed, and saturated. Said affirmed that he was studying forms that made fun of what he called the "cybernetic hope" of the encyclopedists, a long history stretching from the Greek atomists, Lucretius, Leibnitz, Descartes, Frege, and Wiener through the dictionaries, encyclopedias, anatomies, catalogs, and universal grammars of the seventeenth and eighteenth centuries, to Flaubert's *Dictionnaire des idées reçues*, Borges's *Aleph*, and ultimately to his own *Beginnings* (B 325). This list of Menippean masterworks gives notice about the genre that he had chosen and the conventions he intended to observe.

Of all the possible literary models, Swift had the most direct importance to Said as the inventor of the tactic of using a first-person presentation of himself as the very thing to be satirized. Said concurred with Herbert Read that Swift had created the greatest prose style in English. It is a style, he explained, that has efficiency and in this it resembles Orwell's style (*WTC* 74). Yet Swift's powerful prose is always flirting with the unclear. The virtuoso narrator of *Tale of a Tub* is mad, but Swift the Irishman is a sober Church of England dean. Disposed to pass his life as a normal citizen, Swift's writings show him prey to outlandish fantasies of giants, little men, talking horses, cannibalism, extracting sunbeams from cucumbers, and other futilities. If fantasies like those come from vapors rising to the brainpan, Swift has no shortage of such gas. Nor had Said. He applied terms afresh, such as traveling theory, affiliation, molestation, and extreme occasions (although he stopped short of coining neologisms, as Derrida did) and invented whole scholarly fields, such as the study of beginnings and the discipline of postcolonialism. Swift frowned upon novelty, as Said told us in class (Spring 1999): "you become an enthusiast [i.e., a fanatic] one of the great evil words for Swift." Predictably, Said's mounting enthusiasm for Swift clashes with Swift's anti-enthusiast message.

Swift was an especially stylish and charismatic model. His role as confidant of the British Prime Minister Harley and an extraordinarily powerful spin doctor who attacked—Said used the word *destroyed*—the career of the greatest English general, the Duke of Marlborough, gave him a kind of worldliness that Said especially prized. Swift served as Said's model of a worldly intellectual who manages to get some power and use it—an intellectual who can destroy with no weapon but his pen. He is aware of Swift's contradictions: "He always stood for religious conformity," yet he also "embodied the most dangerous originality"; "systems of reading" are "Swift's fear," yet he satirizes them in "this vast system-making book."[12] As expected, Said refused to resolve Swift's puzzling self-contradictions.

The appealing qualities of Menippean satire were carefully detailed in Said's classroom lectures. For example, he said that *Tale of a Tub* threatens to derail its own core narrative. The narrator, call him the Hack, offers similes for wisdom, each of which he discards like an orangutan going through a bunch of bananas. Hack says few people are willing

> to inspect beyond the surface and the rind of things; whereas wisdom is a fox, who after long hunting will at last cost you the pains to dig out. 'Tis a cheese, which by how much the richer, has the thicker, the homelier, and the coarser coat; and whereof to a judicious palate, the maggots are the best. 'Tis a sack-posset, wherein the deeper you go, you will find it the sweeter. Wisdom is a hen, whose cackling we must value and consider, because it is attended with an egg. But then lastly, 'tis a nut, which unless you choose with judgment, may cost you a tooth, and pay you with nothing but a worm.[13]

Abandoning each simile as soon as he alights upon it, this speaker closely resembles the Said who seems incapable of sticking to any given position, presenting a good example of Klein's term for Said, *dérapage*. A further resemblance exists as well. Like Said extending four points to six and then seven during his SDS speech on Palestine, he dumps his outline, violates his rhetorical symmetry, and goes back on his promise of a wrap-up, "lastly." *Lastly* goes by the board as Hack quickly overrides his own plan in order to tack a few extras onto the list, namely the Grubaean Sages (i.e., Grub Street literary hacks) who keep their messages "shut up within the vehicles of types and fables," but this leads Hack to digress on the "usual fate of coaches over-finely painted and gilt," and finally to "darkly and deeply couched" systems that he promises, in a blizzard of mixed similes, to "lay open by untwisting or unwinding, and either to draw up by exantlation, or display by incision."[14] Excess, overflowing, and stuffing the text beyond capacity are Menippean staples, and Swift, like Said, is addicted to them.

Hack's manic lists also suggest an earlier literary character, Mosca ("the fly") in Jonson's comedy, *Volpone*. Jonson gives Mosca speeches whose rhetoric and diction swoop high and low, enacting his absurd and disgusting identity. A series of just such fidgety, fussy, fluttery minds appears in *Orientalism*, but it is crucial to recall that Said was enacting the very traits he satirized.

Orientalism does not include the Menippean characteristic of verse, but neither did Braudel's *The Mediterranean*. In that book, charts, graphs, tables, and maps functioned as the prose (solid, reliable), and the prose took the part of poetry (fancy and speculation). *Orientalism* is filled to bursting. According to Said's friend Eqbal Ahmad, its strange farrago of simplicity and complexity bowed to Islamic style and the mixed forms to be found in mosques.

Orientalism moves up and down the stylistic register like the decoration of a mosque, from simple to complex and back to simple. One instance of this shift occurs early in the book. The opening section of Chapter 1 reads easily and might be mistaken for a chapter in a thriller by Eric Ambler or James Lee Burke, Jr. Readers are invited to witness a dramatic scene featuring Arthur

> **Interview with Eqbal Ahmad, Professor at Hampshire College and Weekly Columnist for *Dawn*, Pakistan's Oldest English-language Newspaper, on July 11, 1990 in Ahmad's NYC Apartment**
>
> HAV: What about a piece that Edward wrote for the travel magazine *Departures*. He makes clear there his preference for Islamic Cairo over Pharonic Cairo. A Spanish journalist friend of mine raised the question about precisely where that attachment came from, given Edward's Christian background and his atheist response to monotheism.
>
> EA: You have raised an important question. Even in terms of his style and in terms of his work. Islamic civilization has a lot to do with his work. Simple to quite arabesque, as in *Orientalism*. That's very Islamic, that shifting from the simple to the complex, stylistically. You find that in a mosque.
>
> HAV: The shift, or the complexity of the arabesques?
>
> EA: Both. The shift also. The capacity to move from very complex patterns to simple, direct symbols, telling a story, as he does in *After the Last Sky*, and to a large extent does it in *The Question of Palestine*. The style of writing.

James Balfour taking the dais in Parliament. Said tosses off a lively sketch of Balfour: "He spoke with the authority of a long-time member of Parliament, former private secretary to Lord Salisbury, former chief secretary for Ireland, former secretary for Scotland, former prime minister, veteran of numerous overseas crises, achievements, and changes" (O 31). The glamorous Balfour stands against a panorama of world-historical events:

> During his involvement in imperial affairs, Balfour served a monarch who in 1876 had been declared Empress of India; he had been especially well placed in positions of

uncommon influence to follow the Afghan and Zulu wars, the British occupation of Egypt in 1882, the death of General Gordon in the Sudan, the Fashoda Incident, the battle of Omdurman, the Boer War, the Russo-Japanese War. In addition his remarkable social eminence, the breadth of his learning and wit—he could write on such varied subjects as Bergson, Handel, theism, and golf—his education at Eton and Trinity College, Cambridge, and his apparent command over imperial affairs all gave considerable authority to what he told the Commons in June 1910.

(O 31)

This paragraph bears no resemblance to the prose of *Beginnings*, the "C+" prose of *dérapage* and the dying fall. So he can write conventional, popular prose after all: no problem! But alongside material that would be at home in a rack of quick-read novels at JFK or Heathrow—usually in alternating paragraphs—appears more challenging stuff: we are asked to analyze the way "the Oriental is *contained* and *represented* by dominating frameworks" (O 40). This rebarbative language even bears a user-warning—words italicized to notify us that we are in for an intellectual struggle. A striking shift in levels has taken place, from the potboileresque historical-novel writing of Lord Balfour's dramatic appearance in Parliament all the way to the concepts of French and American poststructural theory. Both the sumptuous glamour of Orientalism and the astringent rarefactions of French theory are stuffed into the flexible skin of Said's *Orientalism*.

The reader quickly learns that Said considers Orientalist ideas absurd and extravagant, the equivalent of the hairbrained ideas hotly pursued on Swift's Flying Island of Lagado. Like the Lagado enthusiasts, who swear that human excrement is edible and weave cloth from cobwebs, Orientalist researchers, writers, linguists, and sociologists are bursting with enthusiasm and self-interest. It is clear from Said's account that only Lilliputian minds could invent and faithfully believe such notions as the universality of lying as a fundamental Asian genetic trait. Examples of this satiric dismissal of Orientalist ideas are the fabric of the work as a whole. Sarcasm and irony infuse nearly every line: "Since these facts are facts, Balfour must then go on to the next part of his argument" (O 33). Or "How Egypt's moral prosperity was measured, Balfour did not venture to say" (O 35). By adopting Balfour's pompous phrasing, Said makes Orientalist ideas all the more absurd.

Through the centuries, Orientalists have flitted from one outlandish metaphor to another. Much like Swift's Hack in *Tale of a Tub*, they begin by ringing changes on the theme of empathy and understanding, proceed to changes on conversion and converting, move on to stages and staging and to laboratories and scientific anatomizing, and come back to the beginning with a retro embrace of empathy in the persons of T.E. Lawrence and Louis Massignon. As Said's tongue-in-cheek Menippean send-up of Orientalism unfolds, satirizing abstract ideas is his foremost occupation. His "Introduction" affirms that his topic is "not 'truth' but representations" (O 21). In reality, *Orientalism* is about the West, as has rarely been understood. "Orientalism," he wrote, "responded more to the culture that produced it than to its putative object" (O 22).

> My analyses consequently try to show the field's shape and internal organization, its pioneers, patriarchal authorities, canonical texts, doxological ideas, exemplary figures, its followers, elaborators, and new authorities; I try also to explain how Orientalism borrowed and was frequently informed by "strong" ideas, doctrines, and trends ruling the culture. Thus there was (and is) a linguistic Orient, a Freudian Orient, a Spenglerian Orient, a Darwinian Orient, a racist Orient—and so on.
>
> (O 22)

But in pricking these bubbles, he also served them up, in all their variety and profusion, for contemporary delectation: a bounteous feast for satire.

The choice of the term "Oriental" was canonical, for it had been employed by Chaucer and Mandeville, Shakespeare,

Dryden, Pope, and Byron. It designated Asia or the East, geographically, morally, and culturally. In Europe one could speak of an Oriental personality, an Oriental atmosphere, an Oriental tale, Oriental despotism, or an Oriental mode of production, and be understood.

(O 31–32)

Piling-up, enumerating, multiplying, metastasizing: techniques like these contribute to the engorged, farced effect. The Menippean mode offers a satirist the possibility of "overwhelming his pedantic targets with an avalanche of their own jargon."[15]

Writing Orientalism enabled Said to show that the West had always been preoccupied with the East, beginning with Aeschylus's *The Persians*, in which the failure to pay sufficient attention to the East causes the hero's death. "The difference separating East from West is symbolized by the sternness with which, at first, Pentheus rejects the hysterical bacchantes." Later, Pentheus is destroyed "for having incorrectly assessed Dionysus's menace in the first place" (O 57). The much-later real-life protagonist William Jones, scholar and on-site agent of the East India Company, took the East with a more appropriate seriousness. He "wrote unassumingly to Lord Althorp that 'it is my ambition to know India better than any other European ever knew it'" (O 78).[16]

The Orient fascinated "sympathetic European students," including Napoleon and Mozart, who became "genuinely interested in such matters as Sanskrit grammar, Phoenician numismatics, and Arabic poetry" (O 96).[17] But Europeans came to distrust such empathetic responses. They are allied to enthusiasm, the mental defect that Swift attributed to vapors (in other words, farts) rising to the head. After a period of empathy, Orientalists toned down their responses and began the long work of reducing their subject to familiar modes of Western classification. The table, the chart, the grid all appeared. The Orient was objectified and distanced:

Sensuality, promise, terror, sublimity, idyllic pleasure, intense energy: the Orient as a figure in the pre-Romantic, pre-technical Orientalist imagination of late eighteenth-century Europe was really a chameleon like quality called (adjectivally) "Oriental." But this free-floating Orient would be severely curtailed with the advent of academic Orientalism.

(O 118–119)

But even as Said traces this Weberian process—calling it the routinizing of Romantic Orientalism—he finds that the basically charismatic and irrational element survives. It survives even in the overly enthusiastic way the bureaucratization of Orientalism was accomplished. Said finds

> everywhere a similar penchant for dramatizing general features, for reducing vast numbers of objects to a smaller number of orderable and describable types ... a type had a particular character which provided the observer with a designation and, as Foucault says, "a controlled derivation."
>
> (O 119)

The crucial word *penchant* tells us that this phase of Orientalism was enthusiasm in Swift's sense: the result of noisome vapors reaching the brainpan. In Orientalism, the overflowing bounty of foolishness never wanes.

The sheer hugeness and immeasurability, the prodigious tombs and rocks, the millions of quick Chinese brains, the hundreds of millions of subcontinental persons of many races, languages, and creeds, all insist on the East's opulence of limitless detail and bounty. For a handful to control so many millions, that handful must be *prima facie* charismatic. Even the arch-systematizer and organization man, Renan, subject of a whole chapter in *Orientalism*, operates a kind of magical charisma.

> In his *leçon inaugurale* at the College de France (February 21, 1862), Ernest Renan proclaimed his lectures open to the public so that it might see at first hand "*le laboratoire même de la science philologique*" (the very laboratory of philological science).
>
> (O 138–139)

The East is a Career

When one travels in Judea, at first a great ennui grips the heart; but when, passing from one solitary place to another, space stretches out without limits before you, slowly the ennui dissipates, and one feels a secret terror, which, far from depressing the soul, gives it courage and elevates one's native genius. Extraordinary things are disclosed from all parts of an earth worked over by miracles: the burning sun, the impetuous eagle, the sterile fig tree; all of poetry, all the scenes from Scripture are present there. Every name encloses a mystery; every grotto declares the future; every summit retains within it the accents of a prophet. God Himself has spoken from these shores: the arid torrents, the riven rocks, the open tombs attest to the prodigy; the desert still seems struck dumb with terror, and one would say that it has still not been able to break the silence since it heard the voice of the eternal.[18]

The sky and the sea are still there; the Oriental sky and the Ionian sky give each other the sacred kiss of love each morning; but the earth is dead, dead because man has killed it, and the gods have fled.[19]

Have you ever reflected on the case of China? There you have millions of quick brains stifled in trumpery crafts. They have no direction, no driving power, so the sum of their efforts is futile, and the world laughs at China.[20]

If it be asked how the system works in practice, I can only say that it enables a handful of unsympathetic foreigners (I am far from thinking that if they were more sympathetic they would be more efficient) to rule justly and firmly about 200,000,000 persons of many races, languages and creeds, and in many parts of the country, bold, sturdy and warlike.[21]

This laboratory only *appears* to be firmly abstract and scientific: "For all of Renan's effort was to deny Oriental culture the right to be generated, except artificially in the philological laboratory," for the laboratory is "a sightless, imageless, and abstract realm ruled over by such hothouse formulations as race, mind, culture, and nation" (O 148).

> What more subtle affront could there be to "sacred" history than the substitution of a philological laboratory for divine intervention in history; and what more telling way was there of declaring the Orient's contemporary relevance to be simply as material for European investigation.
>
> (O 139)

Renan was the founder of secularism, destroyer of God and of the Bible as in any way authoritative.[22] But he was also a showman and a bit of a charlatan, someone who traded sharply on his own impressive charisma.

Said quite openly savors the elegance of Renan's insult to Christianity, and he cannot help admiring his inflated personal magnetism bordering on occult power, "the historian's capacity for skillfully crafting a dead (dead for Renan in the double sense of a dead faith and a lost, hence dead, historical period) Oriental biography." Indeed, he admits,

> whatever Renan said had first passed through the philological laboratory; when it appeared in print woven through the text, there was in it the life-giving force of a contemporary cultural signature, which drew from modernity all its scientific power and all its uncritical self-approbation.
>
> (O 146)

The arch-rationalist become occult necromancer, raising the dead: Said's intuitive depth of insight into Renan is unmatched in the literature, doubtless because it takes a charismatic to know one.

In the most erudite and creative of texts, those of Flaubert and Nerval, the philological laboratory of Orientalism regresses to the alchemists' limbic. In an uncanny anticipation of contemporary events, the poet Valéry fancied an entire alchemy that the West could use:

> The Greeks and Romans showed us how to deal with the monsters of Asia, how to treat them by analysis, how to extract from them their quintessence.... The Mediterranean basin seems to me to be like a closed vessel where the essences of the vast Orient have always come in order to be condensed.
>
> (O 250–251)

In strange ways the occult power of this image continues down to the present day. Iraqi and Saudi oil pipelines do indeed pump the Eastern quintessence, which Europe has extracted, into the closed vessels of our SUVs. In Valéry's hands, alchemy remains a living science, linked to unsavory figures such as Face and Subtle, the con artists of Ben Jonson's most successful play, *The Alchemist*. If "the very possibility of development, transformation, human movement—in the deepest sense of the word—is denied the Orient and the Oriental" (O 208), then it falls to Western mages to waken the Eastern Sleeping Beauty or Rip Van Winkle. The Orientalists' accumulated aura of mystery, hieratic power, magic, and exotic imagination begins to cling to Edward Said, the Cagliostro who has resurrected all these images and again brought them to life.

A few Orientalists went so far as to call themselves magicians, no doubt attempting to romanticize what was, as Conrad put it, the prosaic business of taking things away from those with slightly darker skin coloring than ourselves.[23] Lord Cromer, the very white Evelyn Baring, known behind his back while he ruled Egypt for a quarter century as "Over-baring" (O 35), believed Western ideas virtually changed the ionization of the air. "'The country,'" he said, "'over which the breath of the West, heavily charged with scientific thought, has once passed, and has, in passing, left an enduring mark, can never be the same as it was before'" (O 213). This is flatly arrogant, but Said, playing Hack, pretends to find it perfectly reasonable, no odder than

Swift's modest proposal to curb population by eating babies. Cromer enters the East as Pygmalion or Frankenstein or Shakespeare's Prospero. He adds the faux-classical note of divine spirit, aspiration, magical breath, and the laying on of hands.

Alongside the gothic-like gore of the philological laboratory, Said reintroduces an age-old vocabulary of the theater and the stage. Theater is another space devoted to producing charisma, as numerous studies of Early Modern kingship have amply established. Orientalism sets itself up, we learn, as a performance locale, either "the discursive place of a pedagogical tableau" (*O* 128) or an outright strutting-and-fretting Broadway playhouse: "Mohammed no longer roams the Eastern world as a threatening, immoral debauchee; he sits quietly on his (admittedly prominent) portion of the Orientalist stage" (*O* 66). This playhouse has planetary dimensions: we are close to the global world of Monty Python, specifically the Ministry of Silly Walks: Subsection, Roaming, Sitting. Said writes, "A set of representative figures or tropes are to the actual Orient—or Islam, which is my main concern here—as stylized costumes are to characters in a play; they are like, for example, the cross that Everyman will carry, or the parti-colored costume worn by Harlequin in a *commedia dell' arte* play ... [on] a theatrical stage whose audience, manager, and actors are for Europe, and only for Europe" (*O* 72–73). Immense color and pageantry help to build up the charisma attached to Orientalism. Said references Napoleon: "Egypte fut le théâtre de sa [Napoleon's] gloire, et préserve de l'oubli toutes les circonstances de cet événement extraordinaire" (*O* 86). Said's genius lay in transferring this aura of pageantry and momentousness to his comparatively humble writerly person. It was a case of charisma by association.

The illusionistic theater of Orientalism has no scientific value. But that deficiency in no way undercuts its charismatic power. Most Orientalist discoveries may well be the stuff of pantos, farce, St. George plays, penny dreadfuls, porn, tarot, and holiday horrors, a battle of images and puppets, huge papier mâché heads banging against each other, practices that fed the medieval theater—guilds, sodalities, secret societies, and brotherhoods.

In the Weberian scheme of things, Orientalism transitions to rational and bureaucratic modes, shedding its former skin of traditional and charismatic authority. "Beyond the life-span of any individual Orientalist," Said writes, "there would be a secular tradition of continuity, a lay order of disciplined methodologists, whose brotherhood would be based, not on blood lineage, but upon a common discourse, a praxis, a library, a set of received ideas, in short, a doxology, common to everyone who entered the ranks" (O 121). If the timbre and resonance of Said's critique belong to the soundtracks of music hall farce and vaudeville shorts, this notion of an Orientalist doxology—like the satiric concept of the Orientalist stage—intends to set the historical record right.

The action figures of Orientalism have an even more obvious charismatic power. Said's confessed partiality for them gives them their unscheduled *laissez passer* through his pages. His irrational liking for these figures, so evident in his teaching, apparently hung on from an early age:

> The experience of lovemaking was described in convincing detail in the World War I memoirs of Wilfred de Saint-Mandé, a British officer of whom I never learned anything at all except that he went from battle to sexual encounter for well over six hundred pages. Saint-Mandé in effect became one of the silent, secret companions of my adolescence. As a rake, bloody-minded British soldier, and upper-class barbarian he was an appalling role model, but I did not care—I liked him all the more.
>
> (*OofP* 69)

Saint-Mandé is obviously a glamorous figure—a rakehell, a dashing soldier, a ladies' man, an aristocrat. It's odd to find the founder of postcolonial criticism declaring his irrational allegiance to this Tory barbarian. And indeed the Imperial Agents who make an appearance in *Orientalism*, figures like Major Creighton in *Kim* or T.E. Lawrence in *Seven Pillars of Wisdom*, are upper-class British officers who have no real purpose in a satire of ideas. They seem rather to be present for the glamour their presence imparts to the whole project. They are not formulators of systems that are the proper stuff of satirical anatomies; they merely carry out established systems. Characters like Lawrence and Richard Burton have kinship with figures like Richard Hannay in John Buchan's *Greenmantle* and *The Thirty-Nine Steps*. They evoke another strand of charisma, that of close fellowship and military potency. They hearken back to one of the highest values in English atavism, medieval guild consciousness and secret brotherhoods. "That's feudal of you, Jeeves," Bertie Wooster exclaims, showing how close brotherly fellowship surmounts class divisions. (Kipling's poem "Gunga Din" offers another ripe example, but there military brotherhood does away with race, not class distinction.) Orientalists and the public understandably found these images appealing, with their flattering assurances that anyone of whatever class or race could enjoy the warmth of membership in the exclusive club of European empire.

But if these characters were silly, they served to camouflage a darker reality. In Said's rendering, they screened the real mechanisms of Europe's presence for the purpose of "extracting quintessences" like oil, ivory, and rubber. T.E. Lawrence is, apart from his military knowledge of guerrilla warfare, a throwback to the era of empathy. Said makes a special point of installing him within, or even after, the era of science. The already retro character of a Kim, a Creighton, or a Lawrence of Arabia is set back even further in time by virtue of his membership in a guild or brotherhood. Thus, scientific imperialism can include something quite old-fashioned, "a serious and exacting business" entrusted to a "'band,' as Lawrence called it—bound together by contradictory notions, personal similarities, great individuality, sympathy and intuitive identification with the Orient, a jealously preserved sense of personal mission in the Orient and cultivated eccentricities" (*O* 223). This makes it possible to re-characterize the nation as the band, replacing a brightly modern form of organization with an ancient one. Said brings these figures in so as to restore color to the increasingly drab and routinized fila of modern Orientalism. These nation-bands operate through their little Orientalist enclaves of scholars and soldiers, and in consequence they compete much as two rival quadrilles from adjacent Basque fishing towns will compete in rowing or sailing. The "French Orientalists were outclassed in brilliance and tactical maneuvering" by their British counterparts (O 223). Turning back time to an earlier era only enhances Orientalist charisma. The atavistic qualities that count here are individuality, determination, clubbability, reflexive courage, unwavering solidarity, brio, sangfroid, potency, and charm.

Combative, charming, contemptuous of faded monks and scriveners, Said avoided the typical academic posture of handwringing and whining complaint. He had the satisfaction of bringing human Arab form out of the chaotic and irrational congeries of myths, metaphors, and fantasies.[24] Taking on some of Orientalism's worldly political power, he ran the risk of repetition in rupture.[25] He sailed dangerously close to the wind by nearly turning into what he satirized. He succeeded because

---

Pop Quiz: Who is This Person?

As a traveler, [he] was a real adventurer ... as a scholar, he could hold his own with any academic; as a character, he was fully aware of the necessity of combat between himself and the uniformed teachers who ran Europe and European knowledge with such precise anonymity and scientific firmness.

Everything [he] wrote testifies to his combativeness, rarely with more candid contempt than his preface to *Arabian Nights*. He seems to have taken a special sort of infantile pleasure in demonstrating that he knew more than any professional scholar, that he had acquired many more details than they had, that he could handle the material with more wit and tact and freshness than they.

Answer: Richard Burton as Said described him (O 194), but his talents are the same as Said's—comprehensive learning, a taste for domination, and a generous measure of contempt.

he followed the excellent model of Swift, who became a callous economist to write "Modest Proposal," a Grub Street hack to write *Tale of a Tub*, and a John Bull Englishman to write *Gulliver's Travels*. Said became what he satirized. Performing his own acts of empathy, conversion, staging, and laboratory dissection, he bestowed on Orientalism a palpable allure. And then nimbly stepped away from it, still wrapped in his wizard's cloak.

"Smart Jewish Boys"

"Now you are with all those smart Jewish boys." My father sighed and turned around to head for the tree farm. Yeah, and unlike them, I could not write a paper.

Figure 4.1 Edward Said in Hamilton Hall (source: University Archives, Columbia University in the City of New York).

"Look," said Bruce Grill, a friend I'd met in our dorm. "Just write about Agathon. It's a great topic."

"But, Bruce, how? I mean, do what with Agathon?" Agathon was a minor figure in Plato's *Symposium*, a philosophical dialogue that all Columbia freshmen were required to read.

"Show how he fits in. Come on, man. You know. Like, why not Sophocles, you know? Why is there a dramatist in there that no plays survive? You know, Agathon didn't have any surviving plays. But he wrote a lot of hits. He's a problem, a puzzle. Solve it and you got your 'A.'"

I did as Bruce advised and got my A−. I can't recall how I solved the problem of Agathon. I never got too interested in the whole thing. What a relief to discover later that Said didn't get into such things either. Probably it would have bored him. What was it, anyway, to write about the paradox of Agathon? An opportunity for self-display. "Hey, I can find all the sources and put them in order." It was a shrewd and safe topic. But Said wasn't shrewd. He wasn't a gameplayer, a budding insect, what he called a "literary cricket." The down side was that Said's methods, if you want to call them that, couldn't get you an "A" with anybody else.

5
SECULAR CRITICISM

> A word is in order about the special role played by Swift in this book.... The reasons for this are not only that Swift cannot easily be assimilated to current ideas about "writers," "the text," or "the heroic author," but that his work is at once occasional, powerful, and—from the point of view of systematic textual practice—incoherent.
>
> Said, *The World, the Text, and the Critic*

> The establishment of a system of law which regulates the most important part of the daily life of the people constitutes in itself a moral conquest more striking, more durable, and far more solid, than the physical conquest which rendered it possible. It exercises an influence over the minds of the people in many ways comparable to that of a new religion.... Our law is in fact the sum and substance of what we have to teach them. It is, so to speak, the gospel of the English, and it is a compulsory gospel which admits of no disobedience.
>
> J. Fitzjames Stephen, in *Hunter, Life of Mayo*

Said's epochal tome, *Orientalism*, was written from a position of frank disablement, his sense that Orientalist writing had made him into a second-class, barely human, being. "The web of racism, cultural stereotypes, political imperialism, dehumanizing ideology holding in the Arab or the Muslim is very strong indeed," he notes, "and it is this web which every Palestinian has come to feel as his uniquely punishing destiny" (O 27).[1] To write from this degraded position was to create a most unusual predicament, something like that of an unreliable narrator in a postmodern novel. By 1983, the problems of debased, unreliable postcolonial narration had coalesced even further. He called the aggregate, *secular criticism*.

No one has yet fully understood Said's phrase *secular criticism*. Critics tend to read it as a euphemism and say that he really meant something else. The precise something else often matches what the commentator is working on at the time. Another tendency has been to consider it simply as a sign of negation. The critics assume that the term functions like a minus sign in algebra. Thus, secular criticism means *not*-clubbiness, *not*-professionalism, *not*-abstruse language and terms of art, and *not*- the manifold other things Said was known to oppose. A third popular way to deal with the phrase is to decapitate it and throw the "criticism" part away, making Said an opponent of religion *tout court*. This method caricatured him as the black-hooded Jack Ketch of religion, its executioner, who was calling for an end to religion as such.[2] None of these positions is satisfactory.

Literary interpretation at Columbia College (1968–72, when I graduated) was saturated by religious undertones and subplots. Only two exegetical methods were practiced, both Judeo-Christian. The Yeshivas of Brooklyn sent their best students, young men bristling with Midrashic methods and hermeneutical moves. A renowned American historian summed up the scene when he walked over from his office in Havermeyer Hall at Columbia to accept the John Jay Award 2006–7:

> The honorees waxed nostalgic about their time at Columbia College. "When I entered Columbia College, the tuition was $800 per year," [Eric] Foner said during his speech. "The large majority were Jewish students, like myself.... Contemporary Civilization, it was said at the time, was a course on the rise of Christianity taught to Jews by atheists."[3]

The other group of students came from private high schools—usually they had received a slightly better than average education, either at the hands of the Jesuits or of carefully watched prep-school masters. The WASP versus the Jew is a classic Columbia College topos. Mostly it is handled as a comedy of manners. But a more important fact is that these were the two groups with a real interpretative background. Theoretically speaking, the rest really didn't count.

Said's first pleas for a secular criticism coincided with his surprising abandonment of literary theory. Both events took official form in *The World, the Text, and the Critic* (1983). "Secular Criticism" is the title of the book's opening chapter, stationed in the breech, where no reviewer can sidestep it. And should a commentator flip to the conclusion, the book ends with a blunt chapter called "Religious Criticism," driving a final stake into something that Said apparently thought lay at the heart of American "literary cricketism." Reviewing the book, the astute Denis Donoghue registered some surprise at Said's departure from High Theory: "you see just how far, and how dispiritedly, he has removed himself."[4] This shift pleased conservatives like Donoghue and John Bayley, but younger and more radical readers like Alison Light (now a distinguished critic and a highbrow literary reviewer for the *London Review of Books*) were dismayed. "As a British feminist research student I was heartened by the trenchancy of Said's introduction" but "I became disappointed and dissatisfied as I read on."[5] Nevertheless, as Jane Gallop has shown, Said's turn away from insufficiently contextualized criticism was also part of a literary critical trend.[6] Feminism and poststructuralism were disintegrating amid cries for greater inclusiveness and demands to expand white feminism to blacks, or Eurocentric deconstruction to a postcolonial setting, or Marxism to a capacious New Historicism. Said's *démarche* might have seemed to be part of this larger trend. Yet it is also his mark and seal; the pattern of embracing some position only to evacuate it at once has a haunting familiarity.

Said assailed religious criticism in a bid to get his manifesto noticed. A swaggering, roistering exit from literary theory was one sure way to make an impression. Bruce Robbins, always canny, immediately wrote, "the mood of the book is one of militant disappointment. It begins from a recognition that theory's oppositional thrust has been neutralized."[7] The tone of this comment, its intimate familiarity with recondite debates over such matters as "Is deconstruction politically subversive?" provides an accurate feeling for the literary culture of that era. One would expect Robbins to confront the issue of defining secular criticism exactly, especially since he wrote an entire book called *Secular Vocations*, a title partly inspired by Said.[8] Yet he uses the phrase *secular vocations* to mean professional careers in literature (professors of English, mainly).[9] He has little to say about the styles and methods of religious writing. He opts for a generalizing assessment of what he considers a largely negative impulse.

> All belonging is equally "religious" and equally to be avoided. The notion of a roving, unattached criticism that both preserves its distance from its home culture and keeps free of any entangling loyalty to another social group is one of the book's ideals.[10]

Putting his conclusions bluntly in this way apparently got Robbins into some trouble with his then-friend and future colleague, Said. Indeed, he seems to miss an important subtlety: Said was not committed to the condition of being free and separate, which he considered impossible, but rather to the act, agon, and performance of separating. He clearly imagined himself in the strenuous guise of "The Captive" adorning the cover of Poirier's book.

Even the most persistent and brilliant Said scholars have stumbled or glossed over the *positive* program of "secular criticism." Paul Bové, for example, cannot find any positive content for the word *secular*, remarking simply, "Said also maintains his career-long antipathy to religious thinking."[11] As for what religious thinking might be, there, too, Bové is conventional in assuming Said must mean something entirely removed from organized religion. He takes "religious" as a loose analogy for a variety of other potential villains: the cult of expertise or any other mechanism for excluding non-experts, say, or forms of enthusiasm such as nationalism. Sure enough, soon he is belaboring "critics comfortably placed within the class-based nationalism and ethnocentrism" and affirming that these critics are just "as dogmatic as the religious can be."[12] But if "religious" is just a euphemism for nationalism and ethnocentrism, why does Said resort to the word *religion* rather than a more accurate description like *chauvinism, dogmatism, hermeticism, nationalism,* or *cult of expertise*? Any one of these terms would telegraph more efficiently the concept that Bové says *religious criticism* means. Bové has no answer. For him, Said grabs the nearest euphemism. Thus, religious has nothing to do with holy sacraments, miters, confessions, saints, gospels, patristic interpretation, Midrash, Dante's four levels of meaning, or schools of Koranic interpretation. But Said was deeply interested in emancipating literary criticism from these aspects of religious criticism. If modernity was an "unfinished project," according to some thinkers Said respected, the secularization of criticism also remained incomplete. Indeed, full modernity demanded total secularity.

Said wanted nothing less than to dislodge and replace the methods of religious exegesis and interpretation—methods that, to him, remained very much in force. Even after the Higher Criticism had de-theologized the Bible and after profane literature replaced the Bible as the chief object of textual worship and interpretative servicing, the techniques of biblical interpretation, Jewish and Christian alike, remained the governing literary critical style. Said took this as an opportunity to denounce and evacuate a gigantic interpretative system—a system much bigger than the comparatively small subset, Orientalism. He did so by mobilizing values like self-contradiction and inconclusiveness. After the vast success that *Orientalism* enjoyed, his raid on the articulate was a worthy second act.

Critics of Said have often charged him with unmannerly truculence, what I would prefer to call defiance. One of the first books about Said was Hart's *Edward Said and the Religious Effects of Culture*.[13] Its title seemed to promise some attempt to

Said Justifies Secular Criticism

[SAID]: The notion of secularism.... It seems to me that you need a secular and humane vision, one based on the idea of human history not being the result of divine intervention but a much slower process than the politics of identity usually allow. To fight around the slogans provided by nationalist, religious, or cultural identity is a much quicker thing, the formations easier to coalesce around: embattled identities that create traditions for themselves going back to the crusades, or going back to the Phoenician period or going back to the Hellenistic period. I'm actually citing cases of social and religious minorities in the Arab world, where this rhetoric of impossibly early (usually imagined) pedigrees is extremely heated, as opposed to secular interpretation which argues for historical discrimination and for a certain kind of deliberate scholarship. It implies a certain interpretive sophistication. Above all, it argues, and this is the point, for the potential of a community that is political, cultural, intellectual, and is not geographically and homogeneously defined.[14]

What one discerns today is religion as the result of exhaustion, consolation, disappointment: its forms in both the theory and practice of criticism are varieties of unthinkability, undecidability, and paradox together with a remarkable consistency of appeals to magic, divine ordinance, or sacred texts.... When you see influential critics publishing major books with titles like *The Genesis of Secrecy, The Great Code, Kabbala and Criticism, Violence and the Sacred, Deconstruction and Theology,* you know you are in the presence of a significant trend.... The cost of this shift, which began four decades ago in the ahistorical, manifestly religious

> aestheticism of the New Criticism, is unpleasant to contemplate.... Once an intellectual, the modern critic has become a cleric in the worst sense of the word. How their discourse can once again collectively become a truly secular enterprise is, it seems to me, the most serious question critics can be asking one another.[15]

define Said's use of *secular* and *religious*, especially because the author, a professor of religion, was presumably well schooled in all the differences between "religious criticism" and "secular criticism." But Hart rushes past definitions and disentanglements. Religion is his discipline, and he steps up to protect and plump for it. His defensive reaction makes perfect emotional sense, but he is mistaken to assume that *religious criticism* is a self-evident term. He takes Said to be attacking religion, period, and springs to his discipline's (and his faith's?) defense. He objects to Said because Said has allegedly "orientalized" or "othered" religion. In other words, Said has demonized religion as the weak-minded and superstitious opposite of rational thought. Hart's position is more interesting and complicated than this, but mainly he uses Said as a springboard into his own, finally unrelated, concerns. But Said is not criticizing religion; he is condemning religious criticism. Hart leaves the second half of the phrase completely out of his book-length response, and this is an error. He is correct, however, to note that Said's tone is hostile and defiant.

Closer to the target are Gil Anidjar and W.J.T. Mitchell. Anidjar conducts an elaborate reading of *Orientalism*.[16] He revives Hart's position more cleverly by equating Orientalism with secularism, carrying Hart's "othering" idea to its logical conclusion. Anidjar convicts Said of unwittingly becoming an Orientalist by virtue of embracing Orientalism's main tenet, secularism. This would be more persuasive if Said's secularism were the same as the West's secularism. But the same name means two very different concepts. Secular culture as an object of Western worship—defined as such by Matthew Arnold and all subsequent culture czars—is religion in a different guise. As Arnold made so clear, discrediting the antiquity of the Bible or even the supernaturalness of the deity in no way affected the principal social function and power of religion. Austen was duly substituted for Augustine, while all the important habits of mind, all the interpretative methods and habits of reading, remained completely unchanged. Anidjar means secularism in this sense: Western secularity-as-object-of-reverence.

But Anidjar is wrong to think that the West is secular either in fact or in its self-perception. Secular criticism is an oxymoron, an unfinished project that still has far to go. Proving that Orientalism helped make secularity an object of worship is easy for Anidjar. (Conrad did it more economically when he said that imperialism requires an idea that you can bow down in front of.)[17] Orientalism participated in desacralizing the Bible by demonstrating that Sanskrit was far older than Hebrew, so Hebrew could not have been the first language given by God. Instantly, this rendered two millennia's worth of thinking about language invalid. Secularism in turn replaced Christianity as the West's principal badge of identity and as a way to put the West above the East.[18] Until the Early Modern period, Europe had only to call itself *Christendom* to feel secure in its absolute difference from the rest of the world's peoples, who were labeled, just as straightforwardly, heathens, pagans, and idolators. Later, the picture became slightly more complicated. Christendom developed multiple sects and schisms, and trade linked and mingled some edges of the East with the West. Now Europeans and Americans pointed more often to their material and especially military superiority as their self-identifying markers. Science and technology differentiated the West from the rest. In the words of Hilaire Belloc's ditty, "We have the Maxim, and you do not." As a learned discipline, Orientalism helped to position the West as a vastly superior, scientific society that studied a less developed, amusingly superstitious, and backward lesser people.

Anidjar convicts Said of a self-defeating contradiction, namely, a shortsighted failure to see that secularism was the new "Christendom," that is, the new mark of the West's difference from the East. Secularism was the West's new religion. Enlightenment, reason, the demise of magic, the ridicule of superstition—these replaced spiritual superiority as the West's proudest boast, and this new assemblage of traits, grouped under the rubric of secularism, rotated to the center of self-justifying Western pride. Said's Enlightenment prejudices led him, Anidjar asserts, to endorse secularism without fully understanding that this meant endorsing Orientalism.

Two problems undermine this neat conclusion. First, secular *criticism* is what Said wants, not secularism as object of worship. Either way, for Said, secular criticism has failed to establish itself. Whether the West worships itself (Anidjar's view) or has never found an other-than-religious mode of interpretation (in my view), secular criticism has not yet come into existence. Second, "catching" Said in a contradiction is no more possible than catching a singer at singing or a potter at potting. One cannot catch out a Menippean satirist in a digression or a self-contradiction because digression and self-contradiction are what he *does*. Anidjar finds it odd that Said should be a closet Orientalist. But he should not be surprised, either by the presence of self-contradiction or by Said's own Orientalism. He admired and relished many Orientalists. In his earliest political essay, "The Arab Portrayed," he credited Orientalists (Lawrence, Doughty, Berque, Maspero) with being "shapers of sympathetic eastern movement" and with "enriching" and "enlivening" French and English dealings with Arabs. He showed a profound affection for some Orientalist scholars. His enthusiasm for them frequently took on the self-satirizing edge of the Hack in *Tale of a Tub*, but the affection and attachment were real. *Orientalism* enthusiastically rehearses figures as disparate as Dante, Lane, Flaubert, Renan, Massignon, T.E. Lawrence, and Schwab, and a substantial part of the book celebrates Orientalist achievements.

Orientalist Texts Resonate for Said

The great gifts of sympathetic intuition which had enabled Chateaubriand to represent and interpret North American mysteries in *René* and *Atala*, as well as Christianity in *Le Génie de Christianisme*, are aroused to even greater feats of interpretation during the *Itinéraire de Paris à Jérusalem, et de Jérusalem à Paris (1810–1811)*.

(O 174)

For both writers [Nerval, Flaubert] the Orient was a place therefore of *déjà vu*, and for both, with the artistic economy typical of all major aesthetic imaginations, it was a place often returned to after the actual voyage had been completed.

(O 180)

Whereas Aeschylus had represented Asia mourning its losses, and Nerval had expressed his disappointment in the Orient for not being more glamorous than he had wanted, [T.E.] Lawrence becomes both the mourning continent and a subjective consciousness expressing an almost cosmic disenchantment.

(O 243)

The defeat of narrative by vision—which is true even in so storylike a work as *The Seven Pillars of Wisdom*—is something we have already encountered in Lane's *Modern Egyptians*. A conflict between a holistic view of the Orient (description, monumental record) and a narrative of events in the Orient is a conflict on several levels, involving several different issues.

(O 239)

The source of the pressure is narrative, in that if any Oriental detail can be shown to move, or to develop, diachrony is introduced into the system. What seemed stable now appears unstable. Instability suggests that history,

> with its disruptive detail, its currents of change, its tendency towards growth, decline, or dramatic movement, is possible in the Orient and for the Orient. History and the narrative by which history is represented argue that vision is insufficient, that "the Orient" as an unconditional ontological category does an injustice to the potential of reality for change.
>
> (O 240)

Anidjar is correct to call Said an Orientalist, but he is wrong about why. That is, *Orientalism* is not, as he argues, a relentless attack on all Orientalist scholars. Indeed, Said recognizes his debt to Orientalism. The reflected glory and size of that field magnify his importance; it is a source of his impressive charisma.

Among all Said commentators, his influential friend and supporter W.J.T. Mitchell comes the closest to understanding what was really meant by "secular criticism." He intuitively relates secular criticism to self-contradiction:

> The strange lineage of the sacred/secular distinction in Vico, then, is I think one explanation for Said's frequent recourse to the language of uncertainty, paradox, irresolution, and what he calls bafflement in his writings. Bafflement is associated with unresolved contradictions, mysterious, labyrinthine forms, the "magic" of words, the encounter with what Leo Spitzer called "the inward life center" of the work of art.[19]

Alone among Said's critics, Mitchell correctly understands that Said actually works to convey the effect of the uncanny, working as he does in a literary tradition that prizes figures such as Beckett, Djuna Barnes, and Jean Genet. Uncertainty, irresolution, and bafflement are universally recognized as positive features of Modernist style. Only Mitchell has guessed that they might also feature in a "Modernist"—that is, a secular—criticism. At the same time that Said denounces and theoretically opposes these practices, which he calls "unthinkability, undecidability, and paradox together with a remarkable consistency of appeals to magic" ("Religious Criticism"), he practices self-contradiction and paradox with an affirmative vigor that would do any postmodernist proud. Why else do we call books about him, "The Paradox of ..." or define his style as *dérapage*? The difficulty is compounded by the presence of the word "magic" in both Said's fierce denunciation and Mitchell's symmetrically warm approbation. Even Mitchell doesn't get very far, then, in explaining exactly why secular criticism should be filled with magic.

Said was brought up and confirmed as an Anglican. His immediate family included clergymen (his grandfather founded the first Baptist church in Nazareth) and his relatives demanded the kind of upright respectability that sharply limited Said's range of possible movement. He often cited Samuel Butler's harsh anti-clerical satire that tabulated the agonies of a curate's son, who was required to "be a sort of human Sunday."[20] His identification with this tightly controlled figure, Ernest Pontifex, is palpable. Moreover, literary criticism, his chosen profession, remained deeply theological. Ancient and medieval techniques survived, undercover, as the dominant forms of American literary interpretation and criticism. Upon entering the Ph.D. program at Harvard, Said found himself in a glorified medieval scriptorium—or, alternatively, and even more tellingly, a glorified yeshiva where sages nodded and rocked before the sacred texts, and where everyone practiced textual exegesis.

To understand Said's rebellious secular criticism, we have to understand the religious criticism he opposed. Jewish, Christian, and Muslim traditions of reading share a remarkable unity of approach. All begin with a commentator locating some unexplained puzzle, some anomaly or apparent inconsistency, a "problem" in a sacred text. The game is to locate an appropriate puzzle or problem and then to solve it, a game more germane to classic Jewish (i.e., rabbinical) interpretation than to the less problem-oriented classic Christian (i.e., patristic and medieval) interpretation. A scribal humility and an acceptance of servitude seem just the opposite of Said's grandiose claims for criticism and for the exalted role of intellectuals.

A further complication is worth noting. Usually, my argument in this chapter focuses on pre-critical biblical interpretation, which emerged during the Enlightenment and was, apart from Spinoza, largely performed by Christians. Centuries later, contemporary biblical criticism, while performed by Jews as well as Christians, remains chiefly a Christian (or post-Christian) enterprise that exemplifies the "let's find a puzzle and solve it" paradigm even better than classic rabbinic interpretation, and better even than contemporary literary criticism.[21] Torah study proclaims that every verse of the Torah has seventy faces: seventy possible interpretations are available for every line of the sacred book. The more solutions are offered, the better. Stanley Fish, who best articulated the Midrashic basis for American literary criticism, always said that when debates were raging, and conferences and journals were created to assert conflicting positions, the profession was healthy and all was well. He reveled in his demonstrations that the criticism of John Milton and William Blake was an endless work, every generation of critics reversing the judgments of its predecessor.[22]

The critic most easily identifiable as a latter-day Midrashic rabbi is the one who most forcibly and destructively critiques Midrash interpretive values, Jacques Derrida.[23] He conducted a sustained demolition of what he calls "compulsive and confusionist practices—amalgam, continuism, analogism, teleologism, hasty totalization, reduction, and derivation."[24] Perhaps only a genius formed inside that tradition would dare to collide with it head-on. But if Derrida undoes textuality by boring from within, Said attacks from without. Midrashic, Muslim, and Christian exegetical problems are rigorously and pointedly excluded.

Said had little time to spare for the solving of small textual problems; indeed, he left typos uncorrected in his own work. *Beginnings: Intention and Method* includes none of the nifty little textual snags around which exegeses can begin to cling and grow. He seems unaware of what traditionally counts as a valid literary problem. Frank Kermode's book *The Sense of An Ending* was an obvious starting point for *Beginnings*. In it, Kermode drew heavily on the religious and spiritual meaning of "endings."[25] By contrast, Said's book ranged over a vast array of philosophers, novelists, poets, philologians, linguists, and others.[26] No wonder Kermode said, "It wasn't very good." To his way of thinking it appeared formless, messy, and haphazard. It violated his traditionalist, and therefore religious, preconditions.[27]

Kermode was in a position to see that every new challenge to the critical system would be absorbed or expunged. The system itself was eternal.

> The deconstruction of a text is an old figure for what exegetes *de métier* have always claimed the right to do. In the early enthusiastic stage the techniques employed may seem overbold, and attract the censure of the hierarchy—this is what happened to Empson, and to the anti-historical element of the New Criticism. But in the end the fate so much dreaded by the newest critics, who are conscious enough of history and of the cultural forces of inertia, will overtake the enthusiasts; they will be "recuperated" or, if they are not, they will be nihilated.... If [a technique] does not become institutional it falls into neglect. As it has, in not too fanciful a sense, been institutional all along.[28]

Recuperated or nihilated were not encouraging alternatives for a rebellious critic like Said. Kermode's fatalism, his resigned sighs over the inevitable triumph of the institution, suggested the dreaded and disdained passivity Said opposed. Institutional inertia, reinterpreted by Foucault as the "awesome, anonymous power of discourse," was in fact the great obstacle Said set about trying to undo.[29]

Derrida is an unlikely ally for Said, and yet one finds an explicit call for secular criticism in the French-Algerian's summa of the chief problems in contemporary literary theory. Derrida indicts a whole list of abuses in contemporary criticism, beginning with what he calls amalgam and continuism. Every one of the crimes that Derrida cites can be traced to age-old conventions of religious criticism. For example, one historian of biblical interpretation begins by insisting that continuism is fundamental:

> Biblical interpretation in this period [Scribal, mainly Pharisiac] was dominated by the scribal concept of Midrash ("interpretation"), which involved the study of a text, including its content and purpose. The rabbis who practiced Midrash believed that Scripture must be totally consistent with itself and inerrant. One part of the text could therefore be interpreted in the light of any other part and harmonized with it, and any contradictions were apparent, not real.[30]

The muscling and shoving aspect stands out. What Derrida would consider amalgam now sounds pretty rough: the text "must be totally consistent with itself and inerrant." All errancy must be stamped out.[31]

Midrash exhibits a fundamental disciplinary urge to unite the diverse parts of Scripture into a single and seamless whole reflecting the unity of God's will.[32] Interpretative boldness appears again:

> This tendency derives directly from the rabbinic ideology of the canonical Torah—Pentateuch, Prophets, and Writings—as the inspired word of God, a timeless unity in which each and every verse is simultaneous with every other, temporally and semantically; as a result, every verse, no matter how remote, can be seen as a possible source for illuminating the meaning of any other verse.[33]

Another distinguished scholar of Hebrew literature confirms that Midrash reads texts a-historically.[34] Everything is present at once in the mind of God.

Kugel explains:

> The Hebrew word midrash might be best translated as "research," a translation that incorporates the word's root

meaning of "search out, inquire" and perhaps as well suggests that the results of that research are almost by definition recherché, that is, not obvious, out of the way, sometimes far-fetched.[35]

The standard problem-solving methods are intentionally veiled and obscured in a bogus air of mystery. The Midrashic basis of most research papers in the humanities is apparent then, not only in their "find a problem and solve it" plot structure, but also in their habit of mystifying the process.[36]

Synchronizing and harmonizing all the layers was not Said's style. Innovating by producing anxiety, he brought a bead of sweat to the brow of deconstruction. As early as 1976, in a review of *Beginnings*, J. Hillis Miller, then the leading-edge deconstructionist, revealed why Said could never embrace it.[37] Secularity descends from the *saeculum*, a unit of time, a century or an age. Secularity means the messy intrusion of time, history, diachrony, a "sudden discontinuous change." Miller, who was chiefly responsible for twisting the American model of deconstruction away from any kind of historicism, argues, No, you only *think* that something has changed. You are wrong. Everything is "always present." There are no unique events. Miller lives in *Kairos*, not *Chronos*—the eternal metaphysical moment, not the world of the Timex and the Rolex. One might justifiably extrapolate that, for Miller, the accident, the *nakba*, the Holocaust, the Exodus all are "always present." Thus, he allies himself with the Jewish and Christian structure of time, in which all times are present in the mind of God.

Miller's Christian and Jewish reading of Said can be viewed charitably or uncharitably. Uncharitably, it reduces all liberation to matters of individual psychology and an abiding, a-historical synchronic "tension." For Miller to use the old-fashioned word "tension" is itself a sign of strain. The word is the bead of perspiration that appears as he strives to take the historicism out of Said's *Beginnings*. More sympathetically, Miller's reading is undoubtedly brilliant. He keenly observes that, in order to emerge, Said's work must present itself as being in the act of expressing something that remains nonetheless lodged within it. He rejects Said's diachronic narrative of progress and radical change as a "piece of story telling" that represses the presence of "what is always present," namely the eternal unchanging reality that is everywhere the same "in any moment of literary history," but he gets to the heart of Said when he says that "Derrida might be defined as the overt insistence on the 'undecidability' of those contradictions whose partial repression makes *Beginnings* possible."[38] The image of a covert suppression should remind us of the half-submerged consciousness in Michelangelo's "Captive." Partial repression and partial emergence are synonymous. Miller was the first to understand that the partial repression of something is what Said is all about.

Said managed to open up a hairline fracture within deconstruction. If Miller offers a resolute a-historicism based on the Judeo-Christian convention that in God's time, *Kairos*, everything is present everywhere at the same time, Derrida, by contrast, rejects all forms of continuism, amalgam, and eternal presence, maligning them as "compulsive and confusionist practices."[39]

Said's challenge to the assumptions of the most avant-garde literary theorists was just as destabilizing for Islam.[40] His defiance of religious criticism extends to Muslim modes. He notices and condemns the party of timeless, stable interpretation all through Islamic history. Two rival schools of Andalusian Islamic linguists serve him as examples. One school, the Batinists (sounding very much like Hillis Miller), held that every word in Arabic had a hidden meaning "available only as the result of an inward-turning exegesis" (*WTC* 36). The other school replied that every verbal performance was unique to its place and time, or, as Said puts it, "uttered for and during a specific occasion" (*WTC* 36–37). We are back to Said's preference for Swift and his inconsistencies, Swift's concern only with "local occasions." Said wrote:

> The Koran can be regarded as having an absolutely defined origin and consequently cannot be referred back to any particular interpreter or interpretation, although this is

clearly what the Batinites tried to do (perhaps, it has been suggested, under the influence of Judeo-Christian exegetical techniques).

(WTC 37)

Interpretative cautiousness transcends all sectarian boundaries: the medieval Arab linguists are literally interchangeable with the rabbinical a-historical interpreters.

The wonderfully resilient principles of orthodox scriptural interpretation survived the death of God, the debunking of biblical originality, and the desacralizing of Hebrew, as well as flaying by Jonathan Swift.[41] All contemporary interpretations of literature—high-brow, middle-brow, and low-brow—derive from these 2,000 years of weekly sermons, Midrashes, homilies, and lectures. Close readers and practitioners of New Criticism, New New Criticism, and deconstruction, reader response, and queer theory have simply exchanged their surplices and *kipas* for tweeds, black leather, or designer shades.[42] From Matthew Arnold's *Culture and Anarchy* down to the program of the 2009 MLA, secular culture has been expected to take the high road and religion to address the hoi polloi. The separation of literary interpretation from biblical interpretation was to be as absolute as the division of church and state. But things didn't work out as planned. Modernism and secularism remain abandoned blueprints, aborted or bankrupt constructions whose exposed skeletons are weathering badly before the winds of a new storm of continuist, teleological, hastily totalizing literary criticism.

Said's is the latest of the doomed attempts to raise the pagan banner. The enduring biblical tools of literary interpretation—so pervasive that they have become invisible—were the real target of his forlorn plea for a "secular criticism." He spurned most secondary literature, lauding Erich Auerbach's *Mimesis* because it was composed almost entirely without reference to secondary texts. Arguably, Foucault's spurning of secondary literature may have stimulated Said's initially fervent excitement over his work.[43] *Orientalism* attempted a similar feat of reading a variety of primary documents without supplements. Although

Said's style was not to smooth bumps, lacquer over imperfections, or secrete layer after layer of exegetical mucus around an irritant in a text, those strategies were the basis of the scholarly style of the Orientalists, who plagiarized and rewrote each other and whom he ridiculed in his anatomy. Even in his own text, he reveled in his refusal to perform that first priority of religious criticism, the reconciling of textual contradictions.[44]

Secular criticism elevates performance, opportunity, and rhetoric over logic, pure speculation, and disembodied argument. For that reason, Said is a hero to rhetorical scholar Steven Mailloux. According to Mailloux, Said is purely a rhetorician.

> *Orientalism* is self-consciously an act of persuasion at the service of rhetorical interests *opposed to* those of Western Orientalism. Idealist and realist epistemologies remain completely irrelevant here. What remains relevant is the historical context of rhetorical power that Said describes and the cultural conversation in which *Orientalism* participates.[45]

Mailloux recognizes that Said has shaken free from the rules of the religious criticism game. But if Said were to continue writing criticism, where could he go? Mailloux suggests his destination would have to be issues of power. In a way that Said's own book titles confirm, his location inside the institution of literary criticism left him very much "out of place." He had brilliantly mobilized a little-known form of criticism, the Menippean. But how could he match the fantastic rolling waves of impact that *Orientalism* had set in motion? He could not merely write a sequel; he had to begin anew.

After *Orientalism*, Said poured his energies into works of history and journalism. He also began to engage the photograph, the stage, the television debate, the question-and-answer fight, and the florid excitements of biweekly journalism. He wrote books about music, and a book-length essay to accompany photographs. He wrote short books about intellectuals, Sigmund Freud, and "democratic criticism." He gave interviews that were published as books. He wrote a memoir. But he attempted only one book of literary criticism proper, *Culture*

> **Beginning Anew: Books Published 1980–2004**
>
> *The Question of Palestine* (1979)
> *Covering Islam* (1981)
> *The World, the Text, and the Critic* (1983)
> *After the Last Sky* (1986)
> *Blaming the Victims* (1988)
> *Musical Elaborations* (1991)
> *Culture and Imperialism* (1993)
> *The Pen and the Sword* (1994)
> *Representations of the Intellectual* (1994)
> *Peace and Its Discontents: Gaza-Jericho, 1993–1995* (1995)
> *Peace and Its Discontents* (1995)
> *The Politics of Dispossession* (1995)
> *Out of Place: A Memoir* (1999)
> *Reflections on Exile and Other Essays* (2000)
> *The End of the Peace Process: Oslo and After* (2000)
> *Parallels and Paradoxes: Explorations in Music and Society* (2002)
> *Freud and the Non-European* (2003)
> *Humanism and Democratic Criticism* (2004)

and Imperialism, published a full eighteen years after his *Beginnings*. Reviewers were respectful, but they found nothing much to say: the book was traditional historical criticism, and its claims about Jane Austen and others seemed strained. And this reaction was easy enough to anticipate. He wasn't into criticism anymore. After *Orientalism*, Said's real career became a series of political performances that strove to create extreme occasions on extreme locations—the concert stage, the Lebanon-Israel border, the Arab newspaper, the TV news hour. As his reputation grew, he found himself more restive in the institutions that had given him a home. When he published late in life a collection of his early critical essays, he tellingly titled the book, "Reflections on Exile."

The Way He Taught Then

Orientalism was rolling off the presses when I attended Said's graduate seminar on imperialism. I wore a Brooks Brothers pinstripe suit, white shirt, and foulard tie, aware that Cornel West had adopted similar garb when attending the other Said class. Said looked me over and asked, "What's this!" I explained I'd been applying for a job. He shrugged as if to say, Well, couldn't you have changed? But then he put me through the usual

Figure 5.1 Edward Said in his office, Hamilton Hall (source: University Archives, Columbia University in the City of New York).

hazing, forcing me to write a little essay about why I wished to take his seminar.

Said himself was showing no sartorial restraint. His light gray, three-button check paired up with a lilac wide-collar shirt and a dark blue-gray tie with a few thin diagonal stripes—the kind of tie Paul Stuart was featuring in 1979. His pocketsquare was drawn up into a three-point white puffed design, signaling that he was an elite humanist rather than a rich banker.

His seminar performance was classic Said, beginning subdued and hunched in the chair as he summarized the day's agenda. As he got down to the substance of the lesson, his hands started working, building imaginary models of the concepts he proposed. As the theme emerged, he inspected it, held it up before him in his right hand with the fingers pointing toward the ceiling in what I called the "Yorick" position. Every idea had solidity for him even if it was invisible to us. Napoleon invaded Egypt, he was saying, not as the Spaniards invaded the New World, with soldiers, looking for loot, but also with "scientists, botanists, architects, philologists, biologists, historians, whose job it was to record Egypt in every conceivable way—not for the Egyptians"—here his hands pushed an imaginary bundle off the seminar table— "but for the Europeans." His voice rose and fell musically. "What first strikes you about the volumes they produced is their enormous size. They're a meter square." He measures this out with both hands. "And all across them is written the power and prestige of a modern European country that can do to the Egyptians what the Egyptians cannot do to the French. I mean, there's no comparable Egyptian survey of France." He gives a half smile. "You need the power to be there, and the expertise to see what the natives themselves cannot see." With this, he turned to me. "And let's see, you are reporting on something along these lines, aren't you, Harold?"

My report was about making ideas visible. "His [Macaulay's] pictorial imagination," wrote Eric Stokes in *The English Utilitarians in India*, my assigned source, "saw only in terms of black and white, and knew nothing of half tones." The new Indian Criminal Code was based "not from existing practice or from foreign law systems, but created *ex nihilo* by the disinterested philosophic intelligence." This gossamer fantasy, hatched from a public-schooled English brain, ruled several hundred million Indians for 100 years. A millennial tradition of communal possession came to a summary end. The country was diced into a checkerboard of singly owned (and taxable) lots. French and English intellectuals always pursued absolute, picture-perfect clarity, I stressed. They conjured their wildest imaginations into hard-edged realities that others had to live by. The benefits to surveillance and managerial power exactly matched Foucault's description of discipline.

When I ended my twenty-minute talk, another student asked for the floor. "This report has the usual bias in favor of Foucault's most accessible work. It's a caricature, really. Foucault's more recent work on the History of Sexuality and 'What is an author' really would correct many of these misconceptions."

"Correct his mistakes?" Said broke in. "His later work corrects his earlier mistakes? Do you really want to say that? What is so great about Foucault's later work?" he went on. "I mean he just sort of gives up on politics altogether and starts talking about 'the care of the self.' I mean, do you consider that a valuable correction?" He looked me in the eye and pointed at me. "I agree with Harold."

6
RHETORIC AND IMAGE

> At best, to judge simply from my case, we can read ourselves against another people's pattern, but since it is not ours—even though we are its designated enemy—we emerge as its effects, its errata, its counternarratives. Whenever we try to narrate ourselves, we appear as dislocations in *their* discourse.
>
> **Said,** *After the Last Sky*

> Every direct route to the interior, and consequently the interior itself, is either blocked or preempted. The most we can hope for is to find margins—normally neglected surfaces and relatively isolated, irregularly placed spots—on which to put ourselves.
>
> **Said,** *After the Last Sky*

> Our characteristic mode, then, is not a narrative, in which scenes take place *seriatim*, but rather broken narratives, fragmentary compositions, and self-consciously staged testimonials, in which the narrative voice keeps stumbling over itself, its obligations, and its limitations.
>
> **Said,** *After the Last Sky*

Said's identity as *the* American to tell *the* Palestinian story required the narrative form.[1] Thus, he found himself in the position of calling for, in the title of one of his articles, "Permission to Narrate." He was a good narrator. The colorful stories told in his book *Orientalism* directly account for that book's huge audience. Whenever he faced wider publics, such as the readers of the *New York Times* and *Harper's* or (beginning around 1986) *Al-Majallah*, *Al-Ahram*, and *As-Safir*, politics as well as populism demanded that he tell a thumping, gripping, uncomplicated story:

> Golda Meir had set the general tone in 1969 by denying that we existed at all. The first task was to get a place—literally anywhere—to say that we did exist. It hardly needs pointing out, therefore, that speaking about the Palestinian issue in the United States always has been a very different thing from discussing it in an Arab newspaper published in either Cairo or Beirut; it was even different and required more primitive rituals of assertion than what Hebrew-language papers in Israel were saying.
>
> (*PolD*, xvi–xvii)

Certainly his concession to conventional narrative modes earned him approval in the mainstream press. *The Times* presented *The Question of Palestine* as a no-nonsense contribution to the debate over Israel and Palestine, blurbing it as "a cogent and passionate exposition of the emergence of the modern Palestinian nation and its confrontation with Zionism and Israel."[2] But could standard narratives enhance Said's own charisma? Conventional narrative was the time-honored prose vehicle of realism and truth. In the book's most important chapter, "Zionism from the Standpoint of its Victims," Said explains that his aim "will be to open the discussion of the question of Palestine to a much-denied, much-suppressed reality—that of the Palestinian Arabs, of whom I myself am one" (*QP* 54). This nod to a suppressed reality reminds us that Said's problem is always that of Michelangelo's "Captive" and Vico's earliest man: the struggle to break away from a smothering, heavily repressive context.

When Said embarked on telling the Palestinian story to the world, the task seemed to call for a straightforward narration, the telling of a clear sequence of events, what seekers of a true history might justifiably demand. But he felt there were insurmountable problems with such a narration. For one, details exert a centrifugal pull that drags a narrative off its linear course. An even more intractable problem was the linear form itself, whose implications seemed to him to distort the reality of Palestinian history as a series of events that was not about single directionality but about explosive dispersion and fragmentation. "The striking thing about Palestinian prose and prose fiction," he wrote

> is its formal instability. Our literature in a certain very narrow sense is the elusive, resistant reality it tries so often to represent. Most literary critics in Israel and the West focus on what is said in Palestinian writing, who is described, what the plot and contents deliver, their sociological and political meaning. But it is *form* that should be looked at. Particularly in fiction, the struggle to achieve form expresses the writer's efforts to construct a coherent scene, a narrative that might overcome the almost metaphysical impossibility of representing the present.
>
> (*Sky* 38)

The expected, conventional form of history falsified Palestinian experience.

His handling of a passage from a novel even resembles sculpting in his effort to render the essence. For example, here he emphasizes portions of a quotation taken from a character in George Eliot's novel *Daniel Deronda*, with italics:

> [The Jews] have wealth enough *to redeem the soil from debauched and paupered conquerors*; they have the skill of the statesman to devise, the tongue of the orator to persuade. And there is no prophet or poet among us to make the ears of Christian Europe tingle with shame at the hideous obloquy of Christian strife *which the Turk gazes at* [the reference here is to the long history of European disputes about the Holy Land] *as the fighting of beasts to which he has lent an arena?* There is a store of wisdom among us *to found a new Jewish polity, grand, simple, just like the old*—a republic where there is equality of protection, an equality which shone like a star on the forehead of our ancient community, *and gave it more than the bright-*

ness of Western freedom amid the despotisms of the East. Then our race shall have an organic centre, a heart and brain to watch and guide and execute; *the outraged Jew shall have a defence in the court of nations,* as the outraged Englishman or American. And the world will gain as Israel gains. For there will be a community in the van of the East which carries the culture and the sympathies of every great nation in its bosom; there will be a land set for a halting-place of enmities, a neutral ground for the East as Belgium is for the West. Difficulties? I know there are difficulties. But let the spirit of sublime achievement move in the great among our people, and the work will begin.³

His italicizing treats Eliot's book as mere raw material from which to extract a form conceived in his own imagination. The effect of the italicized and bracketed interruptions in this passage from *Daniel Deronda* comes closer to stone cutting than to reading.

Said tells a collective not an individual tale. The six pages devoted to *Daniel Deronda* in *The Question of Palestine* express his conviction that in this novel George Eliot "revised upward" her estimate of human possibility. Eliot's previous novel had finished on a somber note.

> Dorothea [Brooke, the heroine of Eliot's novel, *Middlemarch*] emerges at the end of *Middlemarch* as a chastened woman, forced to concede her grand visions of a "fulfilled" life in return for a relatively modest domestic success as a wife and mother. It is this considerably diminished view of things that *Daniel Deronda,* and Zionism in particular, revise upward: toward a genuinely hopeful socio-religious project in which individual energies can be merged and identified with a collective national vision, the whole emanating out of Judaism.
> (*QP* 61)

Changing "Judaism" to "Palestinian liberation" in this quotation would fairly describe Said's upward revision of his own prospects. The whole discussion seems designed to explain why personal liberation is paltry, boring, and probably unattainable, whereas the collective will to liberate a whole people is noble, fascinating, and possible. Leave it to a literature professor to show that two novels give the best evidence of this position.

But how could Said write a conventional sort of history while sustaining his attack on practices such as teleologism, hasty totalization, analogism, and the rest of Derrida's strictures on religious criticism? A model for Said's history might have been the work of Leopold von Ranke, famous for his robust confidence that any historian could eventually arrive at "what actually happened" (*wie es eigentlich gewesen*).[4] Ranke's fiercely defended position that "the study of particulars, even of a single detail, has its value" was useful in a climate of *histoire moralisé*. "Ranke rejected anything that prevented the historian from seeing the historical field in its immediacy, its particularity, and its vividness."[5] Said often praised what he obliquely called the "discipline of detail."

For anyone whose theories and positions are as capacious as Said's, concrete particulars offer a stable refuge. Particulars need no cumulative meaning, so they impose no constraints. Each detail is a rock on which to stand, but not a prison wall. Details are stepping stones that lead in many directions. Thus, he urged readers to judge Swift not for his Big Ideas but for "his local performances" which is much like his frequent urgings of the Palestinians to emulate the Israelis' discipline of detail.

After the Last Sky improves matters by coupling Said's narrative with photographs. This experiment was inspired by the collaborations of Jean Mohr and John Berger, as well as influential photo-essays by Susan Meiselas.[6] After his decision to de-emphasize professional literary criticism, he turned to avant-garde forms and subgenres like the photo-essay, the preface, the music review, and the occasional essay. Later he would write prefaces and forewords to support experimental genres such as Joe Sacco's graphic novels on Palestine and his catalogue essay to accompany the work of graphic artist Mona Hatoum.[7] He sensed that narrative needed some help from the photos, that in itself it was insufficient for him. Perhaps the photo-essay was the form that secular criticism should finally take.

After the Last Sky: Secular Criticism in Pictures

1. *Structureless*, with no beginning, middle, or end. Said explicitly rejects closure for books and for life:

   "Better our [Palestinian] wanderings," he writes, "than the horrid clanging shutters of their return. The open secular element, and not the symmetry of redemption" (150). "Our characteristic mode is not narrative, but rather broken narratives, fragmentary compositions, and self-consciously staged testimonials, in which the narrative voice keeps stumbling ..." (38).

   Figure 6.1
   From *After the Last Sky*
   (source: Jean Mohr, photographer).

2. *Improvisational*. Said riffs on each photograph in turn without any apparent reason for ordering the photos in their published sequence.
3. *Formally* unstable. Text and real world circulate inseparably because instability infects both Palestinian books and Palestinian lives (38). Said's stated goal is to dramatize and clarify the qualities of alienation, discontinuity, and dispossession (41).
4. *Anarchical*. Said comments on a six-year-old darting away from an orderly seating arrangement in a school, "the child's propensity for disturbing or opposing schemes of knowledge and discipline causes him/her to leave the table, disrupt the pattern, seek unthought-of possibilities." He adds, "better the tension than the peace of passivity, or the unresisting assent to authority" (44).

continued

5. *Communicative.* Said registers chance messengers passing notes over borders (56), attaches heightened importance to the unexpected public challenge during a Q&A session (32), recalls how his grandmother "rendered with a burning fidelity" exchanges between Moses and Pharaoh, Joseph and Potiphar's wife, Jesus and Pilate as an example of the immediacy, sharp edges, and irreversibility of time (154).

Figure 6.2
From *After the Last Sky* (source: Jean Mohr, photographer).

6. *Self-contradictory.* Said values "discipline of detail," yet expresses dismay at Israelis' minute attention to any critic of Israel: "In all this vigilante propaganda, there is something truly horrendous … if you need a virtual thought police to champion a cause, something is wrong" (140). He celebrates the avant-garde and bracing "cubist reality" of Palestinian history, while condemning its formlessness: "we ourselves provide not enough of a presence to force the untidiness of life into a coherent pattern of our own making" (140).

Figure 6.3
From *After the Last Sky* (source: Jean Mohr, photographer).

As a foray into historical narrative, *The Question of Palestine* showed that he could write a coherent document with logical connectives and appropriate evidence. But the book did not allow him to do what he did best: perform. *After the Last Sky* came closer to a full exploitation of those performing talents. Improvisatory and freely digressive, it is hospitable to chance connections and rich in self-contradiction. Said's characteristic habits of *dérapage* seep back in, as *The Question of Palestine* enacts a theory of narrative fragmentation. It refuses cumulation, consequentiality, and closure. It is not truly a narrative, but it served to give Said a solid factual base for his burgeoning speaking career.

Ambition

In 1999, returning to a serious consideration of Swift after a thirty-year break, Said offered a class, "Jonathan Swift Reconsidered," to Columbia undergraduates. Always the Commander-in-chief, he made me write him a letter justifying my need to take the class. It met at the same end of Hamilton Hall where I had taken his Victorian–Modern British Lit class thirty-nine years earlier. Joining a pack of undergraduates and some despised Life-Long Learners, I slid into one of the small, scarred desk-seats nearest the window and monitored the whole room. Said entered, wearing a greenish-brown sports jacket. Some attention had been paid to dress: a custom-tailored shirt of elegant weave and spread collar, and a deftly tied foulard. And whether in haste or rebellion, he had mismatched a brown belt with black shoes.

He read aloud an opening passage from *Tale of a Tub*: "Whoever hath an ambition to be heard in a crowd, must press, and squeeze, and thrust, and climb with indefatigable pains, till he has exalted himself to a certain degree of altitude above them."[8] He spent a long time with this passage. "The problem for the modern author," he said, is that "you have to assert yourself, for in the great panorama of history [here he spread his arms] the individual is very small [here he contracted them]." It was Said's oldest theme, the single hero taking arms against the world.

HAROLD ARAM VEESER

5 April 1999

Edward W. Said, University Professor
508 Philosophy Hall
Columbia University
New York, New York 10027

Dear Edward,

Could you possibly find room for me in your short course on Swift. I would attend all the sessions as an auditor.

My reasons for wishing to attend the class are straightforward. I have returned to my project of writing a book about you and have submitted three chapters to Routledge. Attending the class would reintroduce me to your unmatched powers as a teacher, and a refreshed awareness of your teaching style will lend urgency and freshness to the text I am writing.

The course topic has some bearing on my book. Swift has always called forth your powers, and the things you have said about him gibe particularly well with the themes I have chosen to emphasize in you. Take the potential fusion of politics and the imagination. Historically, what better example than Swift? As you have argued, Swift's aim is to make people more conscious. He is an agitator of consciousness coming down to disturb perfectly contented classes of people, as have you. Consciousness has served for both of you as the radical ingredient that can disrupt unconscious patterns.

You have also placed Swift near the source of a genealogy that includes Marx and Engels, Arnold and Renan, Gramsci and Gouldner (though I don't guess you trouble yourself much about him anymore). These all share with Conrad an awareness that mind and machine gun tend to overlap. Swift seemed to you to recognize that an idea and a conquest usually arrive together. Your idea that Swift's later work is organically linked to a nascent political force (the Irish colonial community, which he played a part in creating), has evident connections to your own links to emerging Palestinian communities.

These two points—Swift as agitator and as organic intellectual—illuminate a crucial mix, in your work, of criticism and community. I think that you have tried to show the more authoritarian Palestinians that real community has to include its critics, not ban them. The American university's norms of evidence and debate should not be rejected simply because they reign in the U. S. To which Yasser Abedrabbo replies, He should Palestinize the United States, not Americanize the Palestinians. You seem to be impatient with absolute separations like Abedrabbo's and, like Swift, to have more interest in posing the more difficult and troubling questions.

Figure 6.4 The author's letter justifying his wish to attend Said's class.

In his second lecture, Said applied Frye's definition of Menippean satire to Swift: like a spider at the center of its web, he drew chalk lines on the blackboard running out to *Gulliver's Travels*, to the novelist Trollope, to "diseases of the intellect," to *Bouvard & Pecuchet*. Chillingly, he cited one of Swift's most famous lines: "Last week I saw a woman flayed, and you will hardly believe how much it altered her person for the worse."[9] Dry humor in the face of wet blood; not, I thought, a bad description of *Orientalism* itself.

After class, I walked him back to his office in Philosophy Hall. He'd been impressed with my letter of application, the one I'd just sent him to get into this undergraduate class. "Why haven't you finished the book?" he demanded. "You understand better than anybody what I am about."

Was he gaffing me? Was he confirming my insights about his resemblance to Swift? Was he saying, "We are more alike than I would care to admit?" How many others had heard the same thing, I don't know. But several attended his memorial services.

7
ON STAGE

> Great talkers obey two rules: they never sound like anyone else and they never say anything directly.
> **Edmund White,** *New Republic,* May 13, 1985

If Said were to assume the roles of activist, columnist, pamphleteer, and caricaturist that he identified in Swift, he must engage in performance, accepting all the risks entailed in adopting that role. Leaning again on Poirier, he defines performance as effort and risk: "Yet performance is not merely a happening but rather 'an action which must go through passages that both impede the action and give it form.'"[1] This arduous process involves some risk. "Thus, 'performance comes to function at precisely the point where the potentially destructive impulse to mastery brings forth from the material its most essential, irreducible, clarified, and therefore beautiful nature' (Poirier xiv)" (*ME* 2). Typically, Said pushes Poirier away as he embraces him: "Poirier's rather melodramatic ideas about brutality, savagery, and power can be moderated," he demurs. In the main, however, he thrills to "Poirier's purpose," which "is to separate the academic, liberal, and melioristic attitudes toward literature, attitudes that serve codes, institutions, and orthodoxies, from the processes of literary performance that are, he argues, essentially 'dislocating, disturbing impulses'" (*ME* 2). Thus the Weberian conundrum continues to occupy Said. The emergence of Michelangelo's figure from a block of stone, or the *Goldberg Variations* out of noise, disrupts and disturbs more than it tames and lulls. For Said, history was all about risk and irreversibility—a musician turning over two pages of sheet music and spoiling a performance, an assassin's gun backfiring and killing the shooter, or a suburban mom failing to notice the baby playing behind the car as she backs out of the driveway—some things cannot be undone. He agreed with Vico that none of this was done by chance, and yet none of it was just a given, either. He loved purely secular historians like the innovative thirteenth-century Muslim historian Ibn-Khaldun who denied the intervention of the gods and insisted on the uniqueness and irreversibility of every historical event.[2]

All of Said's careful attention to the conditions of one-time performance (for example, Glenn Gould's sawn-off piano stool and his humming along with his playing) was tied up with risk and irreversibility. The momentary nature of performance, with its demand for precipitate action and split-second decisions, could create what he called an "extreme occasion," one that bordered on trauma. "The performance of music is so momentary—it's over!" he exclaimed to an interviewer, explaining why it excited him more than the visual and literary arts. "I mean, you can't go back to it, anyway, really. And so there's a kind of sporting element that I'm trying to capture."[3] Risk and irreversibility make athletic and musical competition thrilling. Where the act takes place also counts:

> What I've picked for analysis are, first of all, the performance occasion itself, which I talk about as an extreme occasion, but an occasion with a temporality and a locale that are quite marked in the social life of the West, especially the late capitalist West.[4]

In "Performance as an Extreme Occasion," Said distinguished "the performances that concern me here" from mere happenings, athletic events, literature, and academic attitudes. These last two rejections are particularly important. Excitement and this sporting element are in danger of being lost to literary criticism. Secular criticism represents Said's attempt to revive them.

Frequently invited to lecture all over the world, Said typically gave an eloquent and thoughtful thirty- or forty-five-minute

Excerpts from Q&A Following Said's Speech Entitled "The Palestinian Perspective," Given at the University of Wisconsin, Madison, October 26, 1989 [Audio Clips Copyright Alternative Radio, Edited by David Barsamian, Sound Clips #1 and 2].

EXPERIENCED QUESTIONER (speaking softly and without pauses): Arabs in Israel have the best education, the best sanitation, the most freedom to speak out against the government's policies, the most equality and most freedom for women, of any Arabs, anywhere in the world.

SAID: Anywhere in the world? The best? Anywhere in the world? Do you really want to say that?

EQ: I tell you what. Let—Why don't you let me finish my point and—

SAID: Because I'm afraid I'll forget.

EQ: —and I won't interrupt you—

SAID: I'm afraid I'll forget your salient point.

EQ: Okay. Thank you for your question, though. Any Arabs in the Middle East—

SAID: I'm not sure about that, but all right.

EQ: You said that these problems, the human rights situations in Arab countries, have, as you put it, "been not adequately addressed." My question concerns one of amazement. I'm really surprised that a nation of four million Jews in one country can have this kind of effect on personal relations in the Arab world of 150 million Arabs —

SAID (cuts in, chuckling jovially): It does sound funny, doesn't it, when you say it that way. Of course, that isn't what I said—

EQ: Could I finish? Can I finish? Because I certainly won't interrupt you.

SAID: You can if you want. Interrupt me.

EQ: Okay, okay. Thank you. I shall.

SAID (scraping his chair on the floor as he starts to get up): Well, why don't you come up here and do the talking?

EQ: No, that's fine. I am wondering, in your masterful use of the English language, which I commend you on—

SAID (ironically gracious): Thank you. I earn my living doing it.

EQ: I can tell. I can tell. I missed an intellectually honest—

SAID: I think maybe you do, too, a little bit, don't you?

EQ: No. No, I don't.

SAID: Well, what do you, how do you earn your living, since you know my way of earning a living?

EQ: I'd rather focus it on your comments tonight, and not so much on me.

SAID: Well you don't seem to focus at all. You're just rambling on.

EQ: I'm trying. I missed an intellectually honest argument.

SAID: Oh, I see ...

EQ: That is an explanation for how Israel and the Jewish people are the cause—

SAID (cutting in instantly): I said nothing about the Jewish people. That's your importation into my—

EQ: Uh, Oh-kay, Israel.

SAID: Do you speak for Israel?

EQ: No, I don't.

(Applause from audience)

SAID: Okay. Look, I can't deal with all the, all the ludicrous distortions in what you just said. I didn't say any of what you just said. I said—(growing calmer now)—I said ... (etc.).

speech, but his genius flowered during the question-and-answer session, especially when hecklers were present.[5] The rapid-fire exchanges he performed on these occasions demonstrate critique as a fencing match, a bullfight, or a combat between rhetorical gladiators. Said would instantly recognize the Experienced Questioner, who rises from the audience with a powerful set speech that builds toward a decisive climax. Perhaps this Questioner tips his hand by using those elegant paired phrases beginning with the same word (the classical rhetorical figure of *anaphora*) or by repeating words taken from the same root that have different endings (the stylish rhetorical figure *polyptoton*). Or he may reveal his expertise through his use of irony and mock astonishment. He remains unflappable in the face of harassment to confirm what Aristotle in *The Rhetoric* calls "ethos," his self-presentation as a kindly, well-meaning, naive, innocent wronged by Said's terrible distortions.

Said immediately goes on the attack against such sure-footed and dangerous opponents, pulling no punches. He explicitly acknowledges his opponent's skill by accusing him of being a professional speaker—someone who makes his living doing exactly this kind of gladiatorial debating—insinuating by this means that the opponent is either a stooge belonging to an Israeli claque or a professional Israeli apologist. He makes no concession to reasoned argument. He calculates that the crowd will go along with any below-the-belt accusation he delivers, for they are caught up in the furious exchange of verbal punches and will have no time to weigh its validity. Winning depends less on giving the better reasons than on timing, vocal inflection, crowd-pleasing, quick jabbing, deft parrying, clinches (such as delivering a series of repeated phrases), poise, rattling the opponent, low blows, ridicule, sarcasm, and giving ruthless vent to the killer instinct. He stays on top of his opponent like a cleft stick pinning down a poisonous snake. The key is to win the point, not end in a split decision. And when he comes up with a decisively crushing remark, he delivers the *paso de muerte* perfectly.[6]

Said's final line in four-foot ballad meter produces a spectacular conclusion. Such testy, protracted fencing captures all the

On Stage • 121

> **Continuation from the Same Session [Audio Clip #3]**
>
> SAID: Let me say that your characterizations of, as you call them, "the Arabs in Israel" suggest that ... (pauses slightly) ... you know to be an Arab in Israel is ... (speaking with a rising intonation, a dose of upper-class diction, mock incredulity) ... a *f-o-r-t-u-n-a-t-e f-a-t-e.*
> (Audience applauds)
> EXPERIENCED QUESTIONER: I put no judgment on it ...
> SAID: I don't think—
> EQ: I just wondered—
> SAID: I don't think—
> EQ: That there's a contrast—
> SAID: I don't think, as a Jew—
> EQ: That there's a contrast—
> SAID: I don't think, as a Jew, that you would *want* to be an Arab in Israel. You would prefer to be a Jew.

contradictions, risk, irreversibility, aggressiveness, and theatricality of secular criticism, but it also gets modeled into beautiful verbal documents. The question-and-answer session is an Extreme Occasion because in such a live, unrehearsed event before a large crowd of mainly anonymous onlookers, one false move will expose weakness and invite disaster. Improvisation, not textuality, is the order of the day. Risk of embarrassment or humiliation looms large, captured by the ohhs and applause of the attentive and bloodthirsty audience, and must be very much on both speakers' minds. Such verbal fencing is as far from reasoned interpretation as you can get. None of the patterned protocols apply here, neither the rules of Midrash nor the wedding-cake layers of patristic meaning. As examples of the extreme occasion of secular criticism, these verbal contests are improvised, rough, and nakedly aggressive. Depending less on logic and sound argument than force of personality and the potentially destructive impulse to mastery, they represent a

> **Excerpt from the Q&A after "Nationalism," a Talk Given by Edward Said in Washington, DC, April 29, 1992 [Audio Clip #4])**
>
> QUESTIONER (speaking with a slight accent, possibly Israeli): As you spoke, I sat down to listen [sic] a number of things I hoped you might have said in the interest of dialogue or pursuing a more balanced view of the situation. Some of them are comparatively minor. In your presenting of Joe Papp, for example, you didn't mention that the following week he did turn around on his position and did re-invite the—
>
> SAID: No, he didn't. I'm sorry to interrupt you, but can I, can I just correct you?
>
> Q: Please, it's a minor point.
>
> SAID: It is a minor point, but, I mean, why not deal with the minor points first and get to the major ones later? He in fact said he would invite them at a later date when he could also get an Israeli play. That's what he did. And they were forced to put on their play at another theater. I went and attended it, and I was there, and I wrote him a letter, and I know everything about the situation.

totally different discursive universe, one tied more closely to the stage and the sporting event. In this arena, personal charisma rules.

Secular criticism means dealing with minor points first and major ones later just as it means capturing "the sporting element." It means attracting attention to the artificiality of performance. It means speaking with a mock-heroic English intonation. It means speaking against regimes even when speaking places you at risk. Said was always good at intimidation and shutting people down. When a professor berates a student publicly or a celebrated speaker makes quick work of some young anonymous questioner, the word bullying comes to mind. But in a fight, things can always go unexpectedly wrong, as Lyndon Johnson and George Bush have cause to know. Said pulled no punches, perhaps because he was training for political clashes that had a far less certain outcome.

The traits that academic critics so often bewailed in Said's writing proved effective on stage. His unexpected offer to the polite questioner above—"You can! Interrupt me if you like. In fact, why don't you come up here and do the talking?"—flusters the questioner because the offer seems to make no sense. A similar moment occurs on a national news-and-discussion television show where Said fenced verbally with one Amos Perlmutter, introduced by the program host as "an Israeli-born analyzer of Israeli politics with close ties to the Israeli government. He is a professor of government at American University here in Washington."[7]

MR. SAID: Well, I mean, unlike Mr. Perlmutter, I'm interested more in fact than I am in—
MR. PERLMUTTER: In fiction.
MR. SAID: Well, I mean—
MR. PERLMUTTER: You are a professor of English. You like fiction.
MR. SAID: Yes, yes, exactly. I don't quite know what you're a professor of, but it certainly isn't history.[8]

Said is momentarily thrown by his opponent's witty and distracting interruption. But he recovers speedily and even turns the tables. The next exchange allows him to use his own gift for non sequitur.

LEHRER: Mr. Perlmutter?
MR. PERLMUTTER: Well, I'm not going to argue now whether I am representing this point or another. I suggest that you read from time to time my piece in *Foreign Affairs* in which I discuss the need of the withdrawal of military and occupation forces from the West Bank. But you see it's not

> going to help you to argue again and again that the Palestinians are defenseless, that all of a sudden, you know, Israeli occupation has become more harsh. In fact, I was for six weeks now in Israel and the West Bank. In fact, the Peres government has demonstrated more liberalism than any other government—
>
> MR. SAID: You mean by closing the universities?
> MR. PERLMUTTER: I let you talk. I let you talk. You let me talk.
> MR. SAID: Well, why did you let me talk?[9]

Said's response leaves even this clever opponent stumbling for an answer because the opponent underestimated his skills. Both opponents abandon the rules when it suits them. Perlmutter is forced to invoke the rules in his defense; Said never does, for the rules of rhetoric are freer than the rules of reasoned debate.

As a great individual performer, Said also sought out performance occasions, from reviewing opera to publicly playing the piano at Columbia's Miller Theater. Pianist Glenn Gould and conductor Arturo Toscanini fascinated him because

> it seemed to me that both of them seemed to be musicians whose work, in a certain sense, was also about performance. There was no attempt to pretend they were doing something else, but they had sort of fixated on the notion of performance and carried it to such an extreme degree that it compelled attention on its own, and it attracted attention to the artificiality of performance.
>
> (*Wedge* interview 1996)

In the 1980s, he began to say that he was practicing intellectually what would be called counterpoint in music. He vacated the position when David Barsamian, a sort of Boswell of the Leftist great and an accomplished player of the sitar and the *oud*, began using the word "counterpoint" as a reliable key to unlock Said's complexities. In his interviews with him, Said bridled and took what appears to have been a slightly sadistic pleasure in correcting Barsamian, explaining that he now preferred to call

Interview with Eqbal Ahmad in his Apartment, NYC, July 11, 1990

HAV: You and Edward have both intervened internally, by way of the print media ["On Arab Bankruptcy," *New York Times*, August 10, 1982, reprinted in *The Selected Writings of Eqbal Ahmad*, eds. Carollee Bengelsdorf, Margaret Cerullo, and Yogesh Chandrani, New York: Columbia University Press, 2006, 357–359, a volume that includes many such pieces by Ahmad]. What are the problems and considerations before one takes a step like that?

EA: One doesn't consider. I know Edward doesn't and I know I don't. The moment you start considering, you are sunk. The Third World is dominated by minority governments.... These regimes are marked by intolerance, mindlessness, corruption, and a total determination to keep their people suppressed. When you speak against these regimes, you are taking risks.... As early as '78, [Edward] was criticizing the PLO's refusal to recognize Israel's existence. He was criticizing acts of terrorism.... When his *Al Qabas* interview came out, I was very upset.... I knew that it would produce from the PLO and some of its leaders a response of some sort. My great fear is that the Zionists could take advantage of that and kill him. I am being very honest with you.... I have been afraid for Edward's life.

HAV: I never considered that irony. Said's public rift with the PLO could doubly benefit the Israelis, permitting them to get rid of a troublesome gadfly and in the process to blame his death on the PLO and discredit them as tyrants who won't tolerate criticism and of course terrorists to boot. My other question is about the difficulties of separating the academic kind of understanding of these questions in order to reach a popular audience. A case in point is Hanan Michail Ashrawi,

continued

Said's former Ph.D. student and now an important Palestinian politician, explaining to Ted Koppel that the Israeli peace proposal was an exercise in deconstruction. Palestinian friends of mine, activists, said that she had simply gone over their heads. But she was making a point that would be understood in an academic forum. What are the difficulties of playing this dual role of a public intellectual and a literary scholar and has Edward circumvented those difficulties?

EA: The problem really is with television. Newspaper journalism and magazine journalism is a different kind of problem. And the problem is that you don't find the newspapers who are willing to publish you. It's as simple as that.... Edward and I have been a little bit luckier.... We are given the benefits of tokenism.... But if you are doing an article, you are doing the best you can do to make it readable for a general public. But you know what you don't want to compromise, it's all right. Therefore, I think that anything Edward has written for the press, he can defend, and should be able to defend it. Radio and television is a different matter. First of all, the pressure to do it is very great politically.... Because the medium has become the message and it dominates the American and Western culture as a whole. But it's a very unpleasant thing to do. You are required to say in 50 seconds something meaningful. And it's very hard to say. You do end up saying it in 60 seconds. Which of course gives to the editor at the other end 50 percent power over your work. You see what I'm saying? I have seen Edward each time he comes on television, he would telephone me if he thinks I was watching, and say, "How was it?" Because there is an anxiety about it.... It is like being at war and being supplied a single bullet to hit your target against a massive wind that is blowing to take your bullet away. If you have hit the targets, if you feel that you have come out the way you wanted to come out, it's a miracle. It's an absolute, total miracle.... So the answer to your question is, with the print media there is very little problem. One learns something about good writing. Each time I do a *New York Times* or a *Washington Post* piece I become more alerted as to how to cut more words, to make the writing more tight, more refined and less wordy. It's a good feeling even for older people like me who have been writing for decades. And I'm happy with what I see ultimately. But the media people, television and radio, it is really quite awful. Yes, you make compromises, you are not happy. You feel as if you've intellectually cheapened yourself a bit.

HAV: Do you see analogies between Said's style of handling a TV appearance and his style of handling opponents in writing? In both mediums, TV and writing, he interrupts and breaks off even the most illustrious of the opponents. If he quotes someone at length in his writing, he will often intersperse his own comments, bracketed, insisting on the alternative view, obstructing the smooth progress and momentum of the opponent whom he is quoting.

EA: Interesting, extremely interesting question.... It's very difficult to transpose something that you have learned with the image media into the structure and style of writing. It certainly doesn't affect my way of writing. I don't know about his.... What is true is that with that experience, that particular performance improves because you learn the traps, you learn the difficulties. You also, after three or four times, you realize how you are edited. If instead of 50 seconds you have spoken for one minute, then you learn to speak in 50 seconds. You are not satisfied, you can never be satisfied, but you are less ashamed.

Figure 7.1 Edward Said (source: University Archives, Columbia University in the City of New York).

his work *heterophony*, saying that he really didn't trust *counterpoint* any more because "in Western classical music counterpoint assumes the stability and centering effect of a principal theme in a given tonality."[10] Charisma depends on remaining unpredictable.

Said's secular aesthetic of negation and expulsion appears throughout his work, but a brief passage from his intriguing pamphlet entitled, "Yeats and Decolonization" summarizes four applications to political activism:

> Yeats is very much the same as other poets resisting imperialism: in his insistence on a new narrative for his people, his anger at schemes for partition (and enthusiasm for its felt opposite, the requirement of wholeness), the celebration and commemoration of violence in bringing about a new order, and the sinuous interweaving of loyalty and betrayal in the nationalist setting.[11]

In Said's interpretation, destructive force outweighs constructive force three to one. Even a new narrative is a form of negation, in that it must dislodge another narrative. The power to negate and destroy is paramount in Said's secular criticism. It followed, then, that to get close to Said was to hurry forward your own negation. Even betrayal was approved. In a controversial essay, Said noted with seeming approval that Genet regarded the betraying of causes as a positive good. True to form, Said praises "the mysteriously digressive structure" of Genet's last book. He quotes at length the section where Genet declares "the temptation to betray as something desirable, comparable perhaps to erotic exaltation. Anyone who hasn't experienced the ecstasy of betrayal knows nothing about ecstasy at all." Said then recounts how, in an earlier work, *Les paravents*, Genet's Algerian liberation fighters "exultantly betray their comrades."[12]

For the Palestinian liberationist Said to quote all this with neutrality, even tacit approval, must puzzle the reader. Said explains, "To betray them"—Black Panthers, Algerians, Palestinians—"is not to abandon them exactly, but to retain for myself [for Genet, that is: the reflexive pronoun is odd and suggests identification] the right not to belong, not to be accountable, not to be tied down." That Said here impersonates Genet and ventriloquizes Genet's own voice does nothing to dispel the reader's perplexity.

Was Said's refusal to be boxed in so overwhelming that he embraced betrayal? Was his startling recourse to betrayal a lunge to get clear of even those most attractive bonds that one's friends, allies, and ethnos have to offer? As John Mowitt has pointed out, Said theorized about the raitinization of charisma in his important essay, "Traveling Theory." There he asserts that only continued social upheaval enables theories to keep their radically upsetting impact.[13] If a theory or a critic appeared to gain wide acceptance, he put it to the sword. A political group or party could meet the same response. The leaders of the PLO must have felt persistently harassed by Said. Palestinian hardliners were frequently nonplussed. One of them, Sa'eb Erekat, whom I met in Nablus, threw down a pair of incendiary dares. "Will he come and live in a Palestinian state? Does he support the policy of armed struggle?" Said wasn't present. But it was just the sort of combat at which he would have excelled.

When Said debated former Ambassador Jeane Kirkpatrick on *Nightline* in 1988, he met a worthy opponent. She countered his attacks with the familiar rhetorical tactics of repeated interruptions and complaints that he was taking too much time to make his point. But he won by bluffing, by making her doubt for a split second the validity of the document on which she based her argument. In fact, the document was valid, but he used his authority to gain an advantage that he sustained for the rest of the exchange. Sleights of hand, to get a momentary advantage, are permissible in the political roughhouse.

Said played rough professionally, too. He met opposition with main force, and he drubbed perceived betrayers. Readers of *Critical Inquiry* and *Grand Street* were shocked by the savagery of his attacks. His vile printed remarks on Robert Griffin, Edward Alexander, Daniel and Jonathan Boyarin, and Michael Walzer were deliberate acts of intimidation.

Segment from Nightline Show, November 14, 1988

JAMES WALKER (Host): With us here in Washington is Jeane Kirkpatrick, who served as the United States ambassador to the United Nations from 1981 to 1985. She is currently a professor of government at Georgetown University, a resident scholar at the American Enterprise Institute, and a syndicated columnist. Ambassador Kirkpatrick, tell me what you think of what you've heard so far.

JEANE KIRKPATRICK: Well, what I've read so far [in the Palestinian Declaration of Principles, 1988] doesn't say anything very new, in fact. It affirms the right of—it affirms the desire for an international conference. It affirms that it may take place on the basis of resolutions 242 and 338 and all other U.N. resolutions relevant to self-determination. Now, that really means that at the same time they're affirming 242, they're also not affirming it, because some of those other resolutions call for the destruction of Israel. I also note that the same resolution calls for continuation of armed struggle. It affirms the legitimacy of armed struggle, and in relationship to what Professor Said said, I notice that the declaration of a Palestinian state affirms the injustice of the U.N. resolution that provided for both a Jewish and an Arab state in Palestine.

WALKER: Professor Said?

continued

DR. SAID: I'm sorry, Ambassador Kirkpatrick couldn't possibly have read any of the things that she said, because they weren't published. She obviously read summaries that are both inaccurate and were before the fact.

WALKER: Well, help us—

MS. KIRKPATRICK: I've read what purports to be text—

DR. SAID: If she would do everyone the kindness of listening to what in fact was said, it might enable her to form a better judgment.

WALKER: When we—

DR. SAID: It doesn't say that—may I continue?

WALKER: Please.

DR. SAID: It doesn't—the declaration—that there are two documents we're talking about, neither of which she's seen. The first document is a declaration—

MS. KIRKPATRICK: Wait a minute. I have been provided by ABC—

DR. SAID: Well, I'm terribly sorry, they just don't have the document, ma'am—

MS. KIRKPATRICK: —which purports to be a part of the resolution.

DR. SAID: —if you will just hold on a second before you leap to—

MS. KIRKPATRICK: Well, wait a minute, let—

WALKER: Mrs. Ambassador—

DR. SAID: —I will tell you what's in the document.

WALKER: Mrs. Ambassador—let me just interrupt for one second. Barrie Dunsimore, I am told, is the source of these documents. Barrie, can you shed some light on this?

DUNSIMORE: Well, I think what you have in hand is the actual translation of the declaration of independence, and you also have in hand

	a summary which was given me of the political statement.
WALKER:	Well, I—
DUNSIMORE:	I cannot—
WALKER:	If there are exceptions to this—
DUNSIMORE:	—to the fact that the declaration of independence is the English-language translation which we were given by the PNC [Palestinian National Council].
WALKER:	Fine.
DUNSIMORE:	The summary of the political document is something which was given me but is not official.
WALKER:	All right. Whatever. If there are exceptions to this, Professor Said, why don't you take this opportunity to set the record straight?
DR. SAID:	I would like to do that. First of all, the declaration of independence says nothing about the injustice of 181. It says that injustice inflicted upon the Palestinian people by virtue of depriving them of their right to self-determination and dispersion, I mean they were standing firm—
MS. KIRKPATRICK:	Following upon U.N. General Assembly resolution 181 of 1947—
DR. SAID:	No, following upon means simply that thereafter, resolution 181 was passed. And then it goes on to say that this resolution still provides the best conditions for ensuring the rights of the Palestinian people to self-determination on the basis of division of Palestine into one Jewish and one Arab state. So that second point—

continued

MS. KIRKPATRICK: Except, of course, it doesn't really say that.

DR. SAID: —let me just finish, Mrs. Kirkpatrick, and I'll—and then you can take—

MS. KIRKPATRICK: Well, you're taking a long time, Mr. Said.

DR. SAID: No, I'm not taking the time. I'm simply trying to get the facts on the table. The second item on 242 and 338, it says nothing about all the other resolutions. It says a peace conference that shall be convened on the basis only of 242 and 338. And the only conditions attached to them are that these two resolutions, which have been the two resolutions put forward by the United Nations and asserted and affirmed by the United States, that these two resolutions should be resolutions that are viewed not only as conditions, but also conditions to be implemented in the course of the peace conference. So there's nothing there—

MS. KIRKPATRICK: I'm sorry, Mr. Said, but the text which was provided me by ABC—

DR. SAID: —about any other resolution. The third point, if I may finish—

WALKER: Hold on one second. Let's just let Professor Said finish.

DR. SAID: —the third point is the renunciation of terrorism in all its forms. It says nothing about armed struggle. It says simply the state and people have the right to defend themselves against invasion, against occupation, and it says quite unequivocally that there—that it renounces,

	that the state and the political program—that there is a renunciation of violence in all its forms, whether by states or people.
WALKER:	All right, Professor Said, let me just—
DR. SAID:	So it seems to me that that is as clear as anybody gets.

Letter to the Editor: "Edward W. Said's Presidency"

With the scheduled accession of Edward W. Said to the presidency of the Modern Language Association on 1 January 1999, I regret that I must resign from the association as of 31 December 1998.... The variety of disturbing cases includes an exchange many years ago with several members of the MLA ("An Exchange on Edward Said and Difference," *Critical Inquiry* 15 [1989]: 611–646).... Said tried to discredit alternately the author's sanity, his scholarship, and his humanity. His "solemn idiocies," cried Said, "inhabit a semideranged world entirely his own." This scholar—"if that is what he is," scoffed Said—is "only, to the best of my knowledge, the author of two (or is it three?) below-average articles on Dr. Johnson." "I surmise," Said postured, that "Griffin is actually 'Griffin,' an ideological simulacrum; it could be asked 'if he is a human being.'"

(Jon Whitman, The Hebrew University of Jerusalem)

Reply:

All the comments he ascribes to me occurred in specific, extremely combative contexts in which I was attacked first ...

(Edward W. Said, Columbia University)[14]

When Verso Books, the premier leftist imprint, published a cogent, thoughtful, and accurate Marxist critique of Said's bourgeois liberalism, he ended his professional relationship with Verso. When the editorial board of *Race & Class* overruled his veto and published an article by the brilliant Marxist Aijaz Ahmad, Said resigned from the *Race & Class* collective. What was non-negotiable and constant was Said's particular form of political theater, his odd pattern of embrace-plus-expulsion. His performances were criticism at its most visceral. Indeed, they came close to physical fights.

Said's initial stutter, his Trotsky beard, his inability to control a crowd as the M.C. of the first AAUG banquet, made him an unlikely heavyweight contender. But he never stopped training. He was forever trying to score a point and win a public debate. That is why "the sporting element" counted for so much. Every jab that found its target, every "minor point," would be noted by the judges. Knocking down Ambassador Kirkpatrick was impossible, but he won over the judges: "Hold on one second," the moderator exclaimed. "Let's just let Professor Said finish." Said won that round by the judge's decision. Martial art meant not just stinging like a bee but also floating like a butterfly. It meant using his single bullet calmly. It meant getting Jeane Kirkpatrick to doubt what she knew to be true. It meant lowering the boom on writers with whom he disagreed as well as the occasional anonymous audience member. It meant scoring points. It meant winning.

"Up to the Standard"

I was stripped down to spandex and headed north on my Trek 1200, planning to cycle across the Hudson River at the George Washington Bridge and then ride with friends up the Palisades round-trip to Nyack. Leafy Riverside Drive was cool in April, but I looked forward to the sun baking the gray-pebbled concrete surface of old Route 9. As I wheeled down the gradient to 116th Street, gripping the extended triathlon handlebars, my butt high in the air, I came face to face with Edward Said about to enter a handsome late-model sedan. Every inch The Professor,

Figure 7.2 The author signing copies of his *Confessions of the Critics*.

he was dressed in a tropical worsted wool suit, a pencil-striped gray-on-white shirt with a spread collar, and a gray tie with blue dots. His elegant wife, Mariam, already seated on the passenger side, sunglasses obscuring most of her face, allowed me an enigmatic smile as she half-glanced my way. She wore a gray silk blouse over what seemed to be a white pencil skirt, no earrings, a dainty watch clasped by two black strings. They might have been heads of some diplomatic mission coming from church or a formal brunch with Kofi Annan. I considered my near-nudity and satisfied that all the symbolism was in place, I hailed him:

"Heading up to the country, Professor Said?"

"What do you call that, your pigtail?" he replied. "It's getting longer."

"But you set the standard for hair, Edward." There was some truth in it, for my first editor wanted me to devote a chapter to Said's hair.

"But, dear boy," he said, flashing me a sly, mocking smile, "you are not living up to the standard."

That ended our conversation. I knew what he was implying: eight years after getting my contract and interviewing Said and all his friends, where the hell was my book about him? I had fifty miles to think of an answer.

8
LATER VISIONS

Imagine the intellectual position of the man of the people: he has formed his own opinions, convictions, criteria of discrimination, standards of conduct. Anyone with a superior intellectual formation with a point of view opposed to his can put forward arguments better than he and really tear him to pieces logically and so on. But should the man of the people change his opinions just because of this? Just because he cannot impose himself in a bout of argument? In that case he might find himself having to change every day.

Antonio Gramsci, *Prison Notebooks*

Specific necessities can be deduced from this for any cultural movement which aimed to replace common sense and old conceptions of the world in general:

1. Never to tire of repeating its own arguments (though offering literary variations of form): repetition is the best didactic means for working on the popular mentality.
2. To work incessantly to raise the intellectual level of ever-growing strata of the populace, in other words, to give a personality to the amorphous mass element. This means working to produce elites of intellectuals of a new type which arise directly out of the masses, but remain in contact with them to become, as it were, the whalebone in the corset.

Antonio Gramsci, *Prison Notebooks*

> **CAMPUS NEWS** Columbia Daily Spectator PAGE 11
>
> ## The University Responds to Said
>
> ### Provost Jonathan Cole writes on Columbia's place in the controversy
>
> "On the Matter of Edward Said"
>
> On behalf of President Rupp and myself, I am responding to the request of the Columbia College Student Council for a statement of the administration's position in the campus discussion surrounding Professor Edward Said. I have been reluctant to do so until now because it seems to me —as it did at its inception— that the values held dear at Columbia were well known and unambiguous and did not need reaffirmation. Nonetheless, I will do so because from time to time it is appropriate to reiterate the fundamental principles on which the life of any great university depends and this may be one of those times.
>
> The rights and protections afforded faculty members are stated in Section 70 of the University Statutes - that portion that discusses "academic freedom" at Columbia:
>
> "Academic freedom implies that all officers of instruction are entitled to freedom in the classroom in discussing their subjects; that they are entitled to freedom in research and in the publication of its results; and that they may not be penalized by the University for expressions of opinion or associations in their private or civic capacity; but they should bear in mind the special obligations arising from their position in the academic community." [The Faculty Handbook, Columbia University, 2000, p. 184]
>
> Professor Said's actions, as well as those of other members of the faculty, are protected by these principles of academic freedom. We do not believe in a speech code at Columbia, nor shall we act as a speech police. As for the now famous picture of Professor
>
> Ideas expressed through public speech in or outside the classroom that may seem repugnant to us, ideas that offend our concept of "truth," that may challenge our biases and presuppositions, need to be protected unless they threaten the basic fabric of order in our scholarly community.
>
> Therefore, the recent campus discussion surrounding Professor Edward Said should not disturb us unless that discussion includes calls for fettering free exchange of ideas or for sanctioning Professor Said. The very thought of limiting the free speech of Professor Said or his critics, however unpopular each position may be to its opponents, would produce a threat to us all and to academic freedom. Such restraints on the views of our faculty could have long-lasting negative consequences for a revered feature of this University: its tolerance for what the majority may feel are opprobrious thoughts. We at Columbia did not yield —as did other institutions—to the pressure and impulse to sanction or fire professors who held unpopular political views during the McCarthy period; we will not back down from our protection of the faculty's right to express itself now.
>
> As for whether Professor Said occupies a protected position because he is a University professor, the answer is "no." No special treatment is afforded University professors in terms of their rights to academic freedom. Each of our faculty members has the same protections, no more, no less, than Professor Said. Edward Said is a University Professor because he is a giant in his field of scholarship; he has created an entire field of work. There are courses given at other universities and books published on the work

Figure 8.1 Columbia University Provost Jonathan Cole publicly defending Edward Said (source: University Archives, Columbia University in the City of New York).

Roland Barthes said that the photograph consists of two surfaces—an image and a referent; they cannot be torn apart without destroying both. The photograph and its referent "are glued together, limb by limb, like the condemned man and the corpse in certain tortures," says Barthes colorfully, "or even like those pairs of fish (sharks, I think, according to Michelet) which navigate in convoy, as though united by an eternal coitus."[1]

Said addressed the issue of the screen and the photograph in his brilliant writing about the first performance of Verdi's *Aida*. This late essay is a masterpiece of historical scholarship grounded in local knowledge.[2] Said grew up in Cairo, leaving only when

Said's pitching a stone across a border: to my knowledge, the stone was directed at no one; no law was broken; no indictment was made; no criminal or civil action has been taken against Professor Said. We have hearsay evidence and a set of assertions that have been denied by Professor Said in his own statement of the facts. Whether we believe or not that Professor Said was engaged in protected "expressions of opinion and association," the University should not intervene. Had Professor Said been indicted in another nation or our own it still might not be appropriate to punish him under University conduct rules. In short, the University might not take action against the speech or behavior of a member of the faculty even if it were the focus of civil or criminal litigation. The circumstances would govern the response. The same could be true for our students.

If this current episode were in fact about throwing a stone across a border that apparently did not threaten anyone, we might leave it at that. But this discussion is really about something more basic to the University's fabric than the tossing of a stone since, it seems to me, if it were not for Professor Said's well-known political views this would not have become a matter of heated and on-going debate. This matter cuts to the heart of what are fundamental values at a great University.

There is nothing more fundamental to a university than the protection of the free discourse of individuals who should feel free to express their views without fear of the chilling effect of a politically dominant ideology. John Stuart Mill in his wonderful essay, On Liberty, eloquently discusses why it is so important to the concept of liberty for us to support the expression of unpopular ideas that may offend or appear to threaten one's own views:

"If all of mankind minus one were of one opinion, mankind would be no more justified in silencing that one person than he, if he had the power, would be justified in silencing mankind..." [On Liberty, Chapter II, p. 23 of the Robson edition of John Stuart Mill A Selection of His Works]

and thought of Edward Said. His students and friends populate distinguished positions in virtually every major university in the world. He is one of the foremost and influential humanists and intellectuals in the world. He was named a Columbia University Professor, our highest academic title, solely based on the quality of his scholarly and teaching contributions. To have some question the value of his work and the appropriateness of his recognition at Columbia because they differ with his political views, is to lose sight of why we honor Edward Said as one of Columbia's leading scholars. The recent discussion, with a few even suggesting that Professor Said be dismissed from his position here, has reaffirmed my belief that there remains real value in the original intention of academic tenure. If we are to deny Professor Said the protection to write and speak freely, whose speech will next be suppressed and who will be the inquisitor who determines who should have a right to speak his or her mind without fear of retribution?

There are policies governing behavior at Columbia where faculty and students are treated differently. However, in matters of academic freedom involving free speech there are few protections that are offered one that are not offered the other. Were allegations made against a student similar to those lodged against Professor Said - with the same limited evidence as to intent or consequence as is apparently available in the Said case, I would work to protect the student's rights to freedom of expression and action. I would not believe that it was a matter that required University disciplinary action of any kind. Students and faculty have the right to do many things that I may think are not the right things to do, but I would never exercise the authority of the University to assure a consistent set of views to match views of those who may for the moment occupy positions of power.

Jonathan R. Cole
Provost and Dean of Faculties
Columbia University
October 18, 2000

Figure 8.1 continued.

he reached age sixteen, and he brings to this essay a resident's depth and subtlety of vision. He begins with a detailed account of the genesis of the opera, including its place in Verdi's oeuvre and his life, matters well known to Said in his capacity as a professional opera reviewer (for *The Nation*). Next comes a history of Verdi's commission from the Khedive Ismail. Ismail worked in concert with a canny French scholar who receives Said's focused attention as a worldly intellectual who also possessed superb aesthetic gifts, the archaeologist Auguste Mariette. "A wealthy Oriental potentate joined with a genuinely brilliant and single-minded Western archaeologist to give [Verdi] an occasion in which he could be a commanding and undistracted artistic presence" (*CI* 116). It was Mariette who suggested the idea of an Egyptian opera and even wrote a script that Verdi approved because it "'offers a splendid mise-en-scène'" (*CI* 115).

The financial and artistic arrangements swiftly come into focus, and Said's local knowledge of this distant event gains an almost unbelievably vivid and layered reality. Mariette partly wrote the opera's libretto and designed the costumes and sets, all this stemming from his work as chief designer of antiquities at the Egyptian pavilion in the Paris International Exhibition of 1867.[3] He excelled at façade, having stripped some thirty-five archaeological sites in Egypt, which were "rather cynically displayed as empty by Mariette, who apparently kept a bland composure in his explanations to 'disappointed Egyptian officials'" (*CI* 120). In fact, his "authentic" Egyptian mise-en-scène was derived from the scenic designs of Napoleon's monumental *Déscription*.

In Barthes' terms, this production of *Aida* was the photograph, but the referent was not Egypt. The referent was the idealized relationship Europe wished to have with Egypt.

> Cairo could not long sustain *Aida* as an opera written for an occasion and a place it seemed to outlive, even as it triumphed on Western stages for many decades. *Aida*'s Egyptian identity was part of the city's European façade, its simplicity and rigor inscribed on those imaginary walls dividing the colonial city's native from its imperialist quarters. *Aida*'s is an aesthetic of separation, for we cannot see in *Aida* quite the congruence between it and Cairo that Keats saw in the frieze of the Grecian urn on the one hand, which corresponded, on the other, with the town and citadel "emptied of this folk, this pious morn." *Aida*, for Egypt, was an imperial *article de luxe* purchased by credit for a tiny clientele whose entertainment was incidental to their real purposes in Cairo. Verdi saw in it a monument to his separate art; Ismail and Mariette, for diverse purposes, lavished on the work's preparation their surplus energy and restless will.[4]

This passage conceals an uneasy, half-conscious awareness that Said's own work is just like *Aida*, an imperial *article de luxe*, a pricey commodity destined for a tiny, privileged clientele. The creeping awareness of this fact drove him to expand his public. Said's paragraph itself embodies an "aesthetic of separation." Each of its assertions is allowed to stand in splendid isolation, linked to the others solely by their contiguous placement on the page. No "for example" or "on the other hand" could believably cement them together.[5] Reading his piercing analysis of this operatic *article de luxe*, one recalls that Said's dad was a superb retail salesman, that Said was himself no stranger to the great luxury boutiques of the Faubourg St. Germaine and Fifth Avenue and the raffiné delicacy and preciosity of the fantastically expensive "must-have" item lusted after by the dissolute and undeserving rich.

Said's fame and his essential self are like the photograph and its referent: inseparable and mutually dependent, whether it was Said the Princeton man or Said the Professor of Terror. In working so assiduously on his own façade as a key element of his career and achievement, Said anticipates the theories of screens in Jonathan Crary (his student) and Kaja Silverman. Silverman observes that "the subject relies for his or her visual identity on an external representation ... a 'screen' rather than a mirror." Using Lacanian language, she elaborates: "The subject can only successfully misrecognize him- or herself within that image or cluster of images through which he or she is culturally apprehended." For this identification to be even momentarily "'captating,'" she adds, it must be "a three-way rather than a two-way transaction, requiring a symbolic 'ratification.'"[6] "Cultural apprehension" would correspond to a mother pointing out to a child the reflection in the mirror by which the child might recognize his or her identity. In effect, the mother stages the child's image, as Verdi stages Egypt for the European (and Europeanized) elite, and as Said stages the creation of *Aida*.

According to Said, aesthetic insights were able to shape political realities. For example, in the photograph of Said as Stonethrower, the Agence France-Presse photographer served as the screen. He organized the referent (Said) and interpreted him for the viewer by composing the image along the "heroic diagonal" associated in classical Greek sculpture with "the dying warrior." Giving aesthetic objects directive force is hardly doctrinaire leftism, much less true Marxism, and it goes far to explain why Antonio Gramsci became the linchpin in Said's defense of public intellectualism. To a trade unionist, much less a Leninist, Said's cultural politics would be risible, but Gramsci, perhaps alone among radical leftists, theorized a useful role for "the intellectual." The intellectual was valuable, he said, in organizing hegemony—in persuading people to go along with a political program. *Aida* and its cluster of images might be considered in Gramsci's terms as well as Silverman's: not principally as the cluster of images through which Egyptians and Europeans are culturally apprehended and make sense to each other and themselves, but rather as a means of giving the opera's predominantly European audience an image of Egypt that would increase their sense of mastery over ancient Egyptian history as well as current political realities.[7] On this Gramscian reading, artists such as Verdi and archaeologists such as Mariette acquired a serious political role. Said sought the same power as a literary critic, although he wished to use it for and not against the Egyptians and the Middle Easterners. In each case the intellectual serves as the whalebone in the corset of his respective class.

Gramsci's respect for intellectuals was serious, imaginative, and far-reaching. And certainly Said came close to Gramsci's "new type of intellectual" when he turned his efforts to organizing Arab-American University Graduates, in the group he and Abu-Lughod founded. In Gramsci's view, philosophy itself means political activism: "The real philosopher is, and cannot be other than, the politician, the active man who modifies the environment, understanding by environment the *ensemble* of relations which each of us enters to take part in" (Gramsci 1971: 352). Gramsci added a new twist to the idea of secular criticism. The secular critic is "active and conscious"; he operates not on texts alone but rather "modifies the complex rela-

> **Gramsci on the Intellectual**
>
> Since these various categories of traditional intellectuals [administrators, scholars and scientists, theorists, non-ecclesiastical philosophers, etc.] experience through an *"esprit de corps"* their uninterrupted historical continuity and their special qualification, they thus put themselves forward as autonomous and independent of the dominant social group. This self-assessment is not without consequences in the ideological and political field, consequences of wide-ranging import. The whole of idealist philosophy can easily be connected with this position assumed by the social complex of intellectuals and can be defined as the expression of that social utopia by which the intellectuals think of themselves as "independent," autonomous, endowed with a character of their own, etc.
>
> (Gramsci 1971: 7–8)[8]
>
> The traditional and vulgarized type of the intellectual is given by the man of letters, the philosopher, the artist. Therefore journalists, who claim to be men of letters, philosophers, artists, also regard themselves as the "true" intellectuals. In the modern world, technical education, closely bound to industrial labor even at the most primitive and unqualified level, must form the basis of the new type of intellectual.... The mode of being of the new intellectual can no longer consist in eloquence, which is an exterior and momentary mover of feelings and passions, but in active participation in practical life, as constructor, organizer, "permanent persuader" and not just simple orator.
>
> (Gramsci 1971: 9–10)

tions of which he is the hub" and has the intellectual's power "to transform the popular 'mentality' in a cultural battle" (Gramsci 1971: 352, 348). This is a pretty rousing brief for the role of an English professor and it also extends its sphere of activity beyond the solitary act of writing articles.

Retrospectively, Gramsci's endorsement of the intellectual as organizer would seem to undercut Said's pursuit of individual charisma. After all, organizing is more than a matter of gaining attention, of having presence, of asserting one's superiority of judgment and intellect. In this respect, Gramsci would not have picked out, as a probable leader of organic new movements, the young Said who coveted his fellow students' striped socks and loved to wear his new watch because it made him feel decidedly dressed up; who preferred English accents and French conversation and dropped the occasional consular or royal name. Abu-Lughod, inventor of the AAUG who returned in his final years to help organize the new Palestinian "state," would have been the likelier candidate for Gramsci's praise. Said was more of an observer. His childhood prepared him to become an intellectual *de luxe*. From age seven or eight, he sat in his parents' box at the theater, taking in the French opera, visiting orchestras, the *Comédie Française*. He bought and obsessively played the vinyl records of all that he had heard. He always had a room of his own.[9] Money for these records, tickets, piano lessons, and box seats was no object. At the age of ten, when most are playing with tops and yo-yos, Said was tearing open his most coveted Christmas gift, an eight-record set of "The Barber of Seville." It was Said as *article de luxe* that hypnotized his upwardly mobile clientele, the striving middle-class cadres in Columbia College and the postcolonial émigrés who founded a school of thought in Said's name. This background enabled him to be a more powerful critic of his class.

Said's presence, physical as well as intellectual, served as a kind of persuader in the Palestinian cause. To Israel, Said's presence—his clothes, oboe-like voice, and aristocratic manners—had the potential to do harm. He was on the radar, like a Gramscian cluster of MIGs or F111s. His photographs helped to confirm his popularity, and he was a welcome guest on *Charlie Rose* (five appearances), *Nightline*, MacNeil-Lehrer, and other programs. He tried to explain the power of the image to more consistent Marxists, such as his interviewer Michael Sprinker:

Later Visions • 147

In the case of Palestinians, where the picture that's presented is incomplete, you can try to complete it, or you can take advantage of the deep contradictions in the society. Such a process would produce somebody like myself, who is a committed Palestinian nationalist on one hand, and yet through education and certain kinds of intellectual affiliations, a member of the elite. The conjunction of these two makes it possible for me to appear on television to intervene ...[10]

Scrambling the cultural codes was Said's strategy. As Silverman argues, "What is determinative for each of us is not how we see or would like to see ourselves, but how we are perceived by the cultural gaze." We can neither choose how we are seen, nor can

Figure 8.2a Ronald Reagan (source: Collection of the Ronald Reagan Library and Museum).

Figure 8.2b William Jefferson Clinton (source: Robert McNeely).

Figure 8.2c Edward Said (source: University Archives, Columbia University in the City of New York).

Said's Style[11]

more than anything he enjoyed introducing me to the best Cuban cigar, the finest single malt, and the only car I should consider buying.

(Nicholas B. Dirks: 35)

He loved asserting his superior taste in almost everything, from clothing to cigars and shaving brushes (I remember an elaborate excursion across town to purchase such a brush, following a particularly conspiratorial lunch, and then a fierce argument in French with the shop assistant from Paris about the relative qualities of bristle). Thus Edward lightened the burden of our more serious conversations.

(David Freedberg: 44)

For Edward—and this is important—made resistance attractive. Much has been made of his charm, his civility, his love of life, his interest in clothes and cuisine. But who says that intellectual rigour and moral clarity have to come with sloppy cooking or a badly cut suit?

(Ahdaf Soueif: 90)

Edward was, among many other things, an athlete of extraordinary ability and grace.... Edward invariably turned up in crisp cotton whites with state-of-the-art racquets. (I once took a friend to hear him speak on a panel about music at Columbia's Miller Theater; the conversation was, predictably, brilliant, but the singular feature of the evening, according to my friend, was Edward's exquisite English shoes.)

(Jean Strouse: 99)

we spirit a new screen into place, but we can "struggle at the collective level to substitute another image for the one through which we are conventionally seen, or, to deform or resemanticize the normative image."[12] Said plainly opted both to deform and to resemanticize Arabs and thus to re-form the "screen." Just as his elegant image had made him exceptional yet at the same time completely at home in the intellectual environment of the Ivy League institutions, he was able to thrust his unclassifiable self as a spanner into the stereotypic perception of "the Arab man." Said well knew that the achievement of celebrity goes some way to making a subversive message tolerable.

Taking secular criticism into the realm of visual representation means confronting a world of cliché and *idées reçus*. For Said, it offered a means for creating seductive new visions of the real. If the camera's non-match with the spectatorial look gave it the power to prove to ordinary vision, against all appearances, that a horse in motion gets all its feet off the ground, Jonathan Crary has shown how other nineteenth-century inventions, such as the stereoscope, humbled the viewer even further. The bipolar apparatus of the stereoscope—one image presented to each eye—produces a "referential crisis" because the viewer no longer can believe that the eye simply sees what is "there"; unaided, natural human perception is already an elaborate exercise in crafted illusions. Crary argues further (showing his formation in the freshman cabal of Columbia's SDS) that such devices function more like machines than tools. Marx contended that, in the factory, the workman who once made use of his tool is used by the machine, which subjects him to a relation of contiguity, of part to other parts, and of exchangeability.[13] In the realm of vision, the stereoscope turned apparently passive observers into machine operators who produced the apparition of depth. The routine of moving from one card to the next and producing the same effect, repeatedly, mechanically, "transubstantiated" the mass-produced cards into a compulsory and seductive vision of the "real" (Crary 1990: 132). Thus, by demolishing the assumption of classical vision that what is seen is what is there, capitalist modernization generated "techniques for imposing visual attentiveness, rationalizing sensation, and managing perception" (Crary 1990: 24).

Complicated interpretative machines, such as Orientalism, also impose attentiveness and manage perceptions: contiguity links the fledgling Orientalist to the machinery of academic accreditation and self-reproduction. Said, who attempted to insert himself somewhere between this grinding machinery and the product it spat out, pointed out that seemingly independent artists and creative individualists were predictable cogs in an apparatus devoted to producing the same image over and over: "Every major Arabist in Europe during the nineteenth century," he wrote, "traced his intellectual authority back to" the first president of the Société asiatique, Silvestre de Sacy (O 129). In the visual-apparatus-as-factory, Orientalists and journalists are all busy with the rote labor of "converting" and "staging" the East. Thanks to Said's intelligent appreciation of Foucault, Canguilhem, and the other anti-humanists, he knew the propensity of machines to use the user.

Said began carving himself out of the bedrock of historical events by taking action. He translated a key speech at the U.N., marqueed as "a committed Palestinian nationalist … and a member of the elite," gave television interviews, and appeared in BBC documentaries about Palestine. And finally, when he had some memorable performances as a public actor in the can, he offered himself as exemplum and imitable type. What disarms the reader of *Out of Place* is that, swooping across this global field of action, is the *beau sabreur* who garbs himself in capes and velvets, gilds his reputation, pursues titles and honors, cherishes the opera and expensive pens, and sketches graceful amateur reviews. His original stroke was the *combinatoire*: Amilcar Cabral in a Savile Row suit. A new Swift, then, gnashing imprecations against empire, but mincing toward us in spats.[14]

But the costuming was a disguise, a political strategy designed to short-circuit the stereotype. In this period, his critical work began to focus most fruitfully on issues of disguise—façades, screens, feats of impersonation. Two influential essays from

Culture and Imperialism, his discussions of Kipling and of Yeats, follow the pattern of his essay on *Aida* by focusing on artists who wield political potency because they project identity onto the skcrim of public awareness. In a career devoted almost entirely to interpreting India for an English audience, Kipling projected himself in a variety of guises including a line soldier in "Gunga Din," a white supremacist ideologue in "The White Man's Burden," and even a mongoose in his children's story, "Rikki Tikki Tavi." In his novel *Kim*, which Said defended as one of the great English classics, he carried this method to its full extreme. Native, English, and liminal characters all receive detailed and sympathetic elaboration that reflects, as Said establishes, the lavish resources of local knowledge that Kipling brought to his task.[15]

Said highlights the presence of local knowledge scientists in *Kim*: two of the prominent characters are ethnographers. The top-ranking male in the book is a colonial official and a scholar who gives Said excellent evidence for saying that *Kim* is a study of the union of knowledge and power, the great Foucaultian theme. He pushes on to explore the relationships between ethnographers and imperial institutions, and here he explicitly takes up Weber's ideas about exchanges of power between bureaucracies and the individuals who work for them. His elaboration of Weber's ideas offers the view that

> societies can be neither rigidly run by "structures" nor completely overrun by marginal, prophetic, and alienated figures, hippies or millinerians; there has to be alternation, so that the sway of one is enhanced or tempered by the inspiration of the other.
>
> (*CI* 141)

This description fits Said's own position as an alienated (even a prophetic) figure inseparable from the rigid structures of the university, the AAUG, or the PLO.

The essay on Yeats touches the same compelling issues. Said identifies Yeats as a national poet, "who during a period of anti-imperialist resistance articulates the experiences, the aspirations, and the restorative vision of a people suffering under the dominion of an offshore power" (*CI* 220). He shows that even in an ostensibly non-political poem like "Leda and the Swan," Yeats tries to understand colonial violence and resistance. In this poem, Said argues, the colonial power—disguised as usual—rapes Ireland. But the question Yeats poses in his final line ("Did she put on his knowledge with his power/Before the indifferent beak could let her drop?") expresses the enduring problem of passivity that infuses much of Said's work, in part because it is endemic to the colonial situation. Yeats's final lines recognize the limits of enforced passivity in the possibility that some useful transfer of knowledge can occur. The charismatic and fully sexualized male figure is closely identified with the exercise of power, while other moments in the poem, such as the reference to Helen (the issue of this rape) and the burning of Troy, endow Leda with more agency, suggesting that her legacy will have some historical impact.

Autobiography reinforces such a reading: Said's fertile engagement with the captivating power of Orientalism shows that the object of transgression can turn the tables, refuse to be passive, and emerge the stronger for the encounter. To entertain his allegorical reading for a moment, just as Leda can never erase the experience of having been seized, Said cannot emerge free and clear from "a web of racism, cultural stereotypes, political imperialism, dehumanizing ideology holding in the Arab" (*O* 27). Both will have their identities mixed up with and bound to those of the aggressor. But the new mixture will have its own destiny.

Here and in other late essays, Said follows out to the end some of the most exciting directions suggested by theory. Using historical research and biography, he takes up the suggestions of the New Historicists and Marxist criticism. Using Weber and other interpretative sociologists (Victor Turner, Bourdieu), he makes fascinating the charismatic intellectual who exists fruitfully in the mechanized guts of impersonal routines and bureaucracies. Again, local knowledge, charisma, and rhetoric (especially memory and delivery) provide his ultimate critical power and direction. It does Said no service to exaggerate the value of his late critical works. He had small talent for the intricate, convoluted debates that increasingly ruled literary criticism. The point is that he grasped his limitations and refused to mannerize them. His best late works achieve the old brio and bolts of insight. The lesser ones often seem predictable, and *Culture and Imperialism* too often resembles a rapid-fire bibliographical round-up. But when he moved into more flamboyant venues and found he could use force of personality, the laws of charisma made up for his halting logic, and from then on, there was no grace he could not claim.

By the end, Said was managing his aura pretty well. His final project, the West–Eastern Divan Workshop for young Palestinian and Israeli musicians, epitomized his cultural elitism, his political idealism, his anti-professionalism, and his status as an *intellectuel de luxe*. It defied professionalism since he was an amateur while his partner in the venture, Daniel Barenboim, was a renowned Israeli conductor. It defied separatism because it brought together kids on opposite sides and caused them to collaborate—a word that in this context lost its deadly political connotation. It contained elements of Tory anarchy—Tory because they played, after all, classical music, and anarchic since the whole operation took place without state auspices or Establishment sanction.

Romanticism scholar Peter Manning has drawn attention to the oddity of Said's public identification with music, even though he was merely an amateur musician.[16] Said's purpose in doing so belonged to his ongoing political strategy of the image, his efforts to frustrate the Arab stereotype by moving from the top down. He politicized music by making sure he appeared often with Barenboim. This carefully cultivated relationship was presented as Barenboim and Said in concert, in all meanings of the word. Showing the Israeli master conductor and world-renowned pianist arm-in-arm with Said, the Palestinian amateur, created an iconographic tableau that proved Palestinian and Israeli could coexist and flourish together, at the highest level. "Personal example is very important." In addition to

Figure 8.3 Edward Said and Daniel Barenboim (source: Associated Press and Ruth Fremson).

demonstrating this favorite dictum of Said's, the collaboration implied a further lesson: just because you are an amateur, not an expert, you need not sit quietly in the back. Participate as an equal partner. Don't succumb to the bluffing and intimidation of the cults of professionalism and expertise.[17]

The orchestra was also a rebuke to any creeping suggestion, in Said's own mind, that as an *article de luxe* he was merely appeasing his own private desires or catering to an imperial elite. His West–Eastern Divan Workshop youth orchestra presented a calculated riposte to *Aida*'s aesthetic of separation. Here was a musical organization dedicated to dissolving barriers, not erecting them. It served as a "screen" on which both Palestinian and Israeli audience members might project their own visual identities. Here was Said playing the mother who points the child out to himself: Look! It's you! And the image of the two partners fused Palestinian with Israeli as a microcosm of the bi-national state that Said proposed. Viewed in this way, Divan could be described as a "struggle at the collective level to substitute another image." And he even met Gramsci's requirement for the new intellectual: he was an organizer of something at last.

Abu-Machiavelli

My grad school girlfriend told me that a friend of hers had criticized Said, in his absence, during a student–junior faculty party. The next day Said called the hapless junior faculty member who'd said the careless thing and delivered a savage diatribe, sparing no profanity or threat. I used to wonder whether such outbursts were involuntary or Machiavellian-calculated. The question arose with new urgency after I returned from my third West Bank research trip. A PLO heavyweight had badgered me about Said.[18]

"Does Said support the armed struggle?" the Palestinian heavy needled. "How come Said never sends us an article for the people of Jerusalem?"

Figure 8.4 Zeyad Essa, the author, and Sa'eb Erekat in Nablus, West Bank.

"Professor Said's not fixated on recovering his property," I said, defending my mentor. "He thinks that exile lets you see events more objectively."[19]

"Will he come and live in a Palestinian state?" he shot back, shading his eyes and squinting into the distance. "Said's so far away," he concluded with a flourish. "Our think tank is so full, we don't need more."

I checked in with Said from Kennedy Airport as soon as I touched down. "Edward? This is Harold."

"I know what you've been up to," he exploded, without ceremony. "Why have you been saying terrible things about me all over the West Bank and Gaza? Sa'eb Erekat told me the whole story."

"What?" I was dumbfounded.

"Look," Said cut me off, "I may be in New York, Harold, but I know what's going on. Erekat told me he met you and you demeaned me to his face."

Surprisingly often, strength and insecurity go hand-in-hand. Said was vulnerable and thin-skinned. But his short fuse and pyrotechnic moods were keys to his charisma. You had to watch him, in every sense of the phrase.

9
MARQUEE INTELLECTUAL

[T]here remain but three methods that I can think on; whereof the wisdom of our ancestors being highly sensible, has, to encourage all aspiring adventurers, thought fit to erect three wooden machines for the use of those orators who desire to talk much without interruption. These are, the pulpit, the ladder, and the stage-itinerant.
         Jonathan Swift, *Tale of a Tub*

There's only one way to anchor oneself, and that is by affiliation with a cause, with a political movement.
         Said, *The Politics of Dispossession*

Wherever you live, it is probably Egypt.
         Michael Walzer, *Exodus & Revolution*

The place from which one speaks can matter more than what one has to say. On one hand, geography is the gritty, ground-level fact of life, the object of territorial ambition and political lust. A socio-political class can be such a "place," and so can a political movement. Gramsci considered like-minded groups as territories that had to be won in a war of position; Said pursued the conquest of blocs of thought and people.

As a boy, Said skidded among three locations. He was taken repeatedly from Cairo to Jerusalem to Beirut. Exactly where he grew up became an issue; an investigator egged on by *Commentary* magazine and an Israeli foundation, loudly proclaimed that Said had not grown up where he claimed.[1]

Said's middle years were spent in constant travel between the U.S., where he lived, Beirut, where his mother lived and where his wife was born, and Europe, where he knew the languages. Trips to Africa, Egypt, the Gulf States, and all over the Americas lent a bit of variety to the itinerary. His own "exile" and "transcendental homelessness" were constant themes throughout his writing. He reminded interviewers that he didn't even own his apartment, a fact that to him proved he had killed off any lingering attachment to places.[2]

As a gifted performer of improvised dialogue, Said preached a secular gospel of "the best that is thought and known" on a campus built like a Roman amphitheater. Columbia University's Low Plaza, a quarter-mile square bounded by Hartley, Dodge, Furnald, and Livingston dormitories and stoppered at one end by the august domed and pillared edifice of Low Library and at the other by Butler Library with its classical frieze, formed a virtual Roman theater some 300 yards square. Even striding across this vast and populous arena, his green Loden cape flapping behind, Said attracted the curious gaze. "The whole world is watching," chanted SDS activists like me and the French students of 1968, and with reason, because Paris and New York were natural theaters housing the national headquarters of television networks. He was favorably placed to talk much without interruption.

In Said's terms, Palestine is not so much a place as a displacement. One could take this insight in two directions. One is trauma and lamentation, the option he rejected. The other is the theater and other cocoon-like enclosures in which ordinary time and space disappear, identities are temporarily suspended, and the world forks into two distinct classes: performers and observers. Palestine seems to be a sort of natural stage that is blessed/cursed with heightened visibility and many more column inches than it deserves in proportion to its population. Actively reinforcing his personal geography and providing Said with heightened visibility, Palestine was a great asset.

Interview with Edward Said in his Apartment at 448 Riverside Drive on August 1, 1989

EWS: Do you know what you should do? You'll do me a big favor if you can do this. Go to St. George's School, which is in the old Jerusalem, which is where I went and where Father went. And my father—do you know the English system? Do you know what the first eleven is?

HAV: The cricket team.

EWS: And the soccer team. They're both eleven. My father was on both of them. It must have been before 1910. And in the main hall of St. George's, in what used to be the refectory, the dining hall—I don't know what it is now—but I saw it in the 40s, when I was a student there (in 1947 I left), they have the lists of the first eleven. In those days, before they had last names like Said, he was called Wadie Ibrahim. Wadie like my son. I-b-r-a-h-i-m. If you could just photograph the boards, you know, the rolls of the first eleven.... We wanted to take our son last year when they wouldn't let us in. And one of the things I wanted to show him was the house where I was born. I wrote about it in *After the Last Sky*.... But I mean, I've never seen it. I haven't seen it in forty-five years. But you can see it. I'll be very curious to see if it's still there. There's a cathedral, St. George's Cathedral. It's an Anglican mission to Palestine. And next to St. George's Cathedral is a little parish church, understand? I was baptized in St. Paul's Church.

Interview with George Khadder, CPA, in Jerusalem, August 1990

K: Edward Said, son of Wadie Said, was born in Jerusalem. The family Said is originally from Nazareth. Now Wadie Said was a partner with his cousin, Boulos Said, in a well-known stationery shop in Jerusalem.... They say *muktobit Said* [(كتبة)] "the library of Said"; they don't call it the Palestine Educational Company, but that's the exact name of it.... Boulos Said is married to the sister of Wadir Said, the father of Edward, you see. That's where the "cousin" comes in. Wadir Said emigrated many years ago to the [United] States and then came and lived in Jerusalem and married in Jerusalem.... Then, in 1948 they had to close down in Jerusalem. They moved to Cairo. They opened the Standard Stationery Company there, in one of the central locations in Cairo. I visited the place many times. Then something happened with the nationalization there and all that sort of thing; they moved to Beirut. They opened that store in Beirut for some time. Thereafter they moved. They left Beirut and migrated to the United States.

HAV: Do you know of people in Jerusalem now who might have been classmates of Edward Said?

K: Well, you have to ask the headmaster of St. George's School—that's where he was educated—Mr. Basaroui. He is the headmaster, Ativim Basaroui.... Whether [Edward] continued and then left the school afterwards when they went to Cairo—I don't know anything about that, you see. To my recollection, I have never seen the boy except when he was a little boy, and then thereafter I've never met him, except through his articles that we read every now and then

continued

through the Arabic newspapers. He writes beautifully, I must say, with proper arguments and analysis, with excellent ideas that he gives, excellent. I really feel that a man like this should be proud amongst our Palestinian people. He's a real Palestinian, between you and me. Inwardly he is a good Palestinian.

HAV: Do you feel that he's a good Jerusalemite?

K: A good Jerusalemite in the first place, of course!

HAV: Is there anything that I should pursue while we are here together?

K: Well, I don't think I can say more about Edward Said except from just faint recollections of his family. And of his father, whom I knew very well, of course, Wadie.

HAV: What kind of man was he?

K: He was one of the best salesmen in the area, you know, one of the best salesmen. You would go into the shop and you could never get out without buying something, you know, the way he treated the customer, the way he presented the case. He was an excellent salesman. And he was very active in the shop. He didn't rely entirely on the employees that he had, but he personally met the customer himself, the way—you know how it is in business—to meet the customer and to talk to him and make him interested, if he is a little bit ... not inclined entirely to buy it but he'll buy it when his father talked to him, you know. That I noticed.

HAV: Was he very personable?

K: Undoubtedly. Very sociable, and the way he talked was ... excellent language. He talked English beautifully well. He must have been great when he was a young man there and then.

HAV: Were you and Wadie at St. George's at the same time?

K: No. The father was not a St. George's boy, but at Bishop Gorbet's School, it used to be called Bishop Gorbet's School. It also belonged to the Anglican church. It's on Mount Zion. They call it in Arabic مدرسة صهيون—the Zion school—but both schools belong to our Anglican church, our diocese.

HAV: Edward Said has a strong interest in music. He almost became a concert pianist.

K: Really. I didn't know that.

HAV: Did the father, too, have some kind of interest in the arts or in music?

K: I don't know about that.

HAV: Is there any other distinguishing feature of the father that you can remember?

K: Actually, I bought *my* [first] stamp album through his interest in stamps. He made me buy it, although I couldn't buy it at the time. But he said, "You must buy it." And then I bought my first stamp album from his store.

HAV: Edward Said is a collector of pens.

K: Pins?

HAV: Pens. Fancy pens. As soon as you told me that it was a stationery business, the pens made sense.

K: That's right.

HAV: So the father was a stamp collector.

K: I don't know, but he made me interested to buy the album, when I was starting collecting stamps. It's a pity that I lost it in our house in Talbeya. We left in 1948. We left everything in the drawers and just took the keys, hoping that we'd be back in a couple of weeks. Since then the house has been occupied by Israelis. We don't get a penny out of them and we don't get a single cent of rent out of the house now.

HAV: Just stolen!

continued

> K: They occupied it and there in the house—what they call the Absentee Property Commissioner, or whatever his name is. They had a beautiful house, the Saids, in Talbeya.
>
> HAV: Does the house still stand?
>
> K: It stands, but it is occupied by Israelis. The best way is to take a taxi. Tell the driver to take you to Talbeya. But then there is an offshoot road across King George Street.... I don't know if anyone will be able to locate the house. It's difficult, you know.... Talbeya is one of the most beautiful colonies, built mainly by various Christians, practically all Christians.
>
> HAV: You may be happy to know that Edward Said is a good athlete and that he continues to play squash and tennis.
>
> K: Really? Would you like to have a smoke?
>
> HAV: No, thank you. I don't smoke.
>
> K (disapprovingly): Hmmm.

The vivid physical setting of an old hall, with its mounted cricket lists and the boards bearing his father's name, the old family house, the Cathedral, the little parish church—all these physical remnants of the past are specific and local. They suggest a Proustian recovery of the past through its material remnants, but they also suggest a global stage. I returned to Palestine three years before Said did and by lucky chance found George Khadder, an American University of Beirut graduate with an English accent. He had worked for the Said stationery business as an accountant. "It is just this sort of figure that Said would never have become," I thought, "even if he had stayed on in Palestine." And in Khadder's eyes, Said was nothing really remarkable, either, just another English-educated Palestinian and one who lost any real significance once he left the center of the world, Jerusalem. Indeed, the unmistakable lack of wonderment in Khadder's voice makes it seem as if he might suddenly turn and say, "Edward Said, *c'est moi*."

Charismatic father, charismatic son. Said was a chip off the old block, a bit of a salesman, an image-maker who could sell you on Gramsci, or Gerard Manley Hopkins, or his own theory of the day, as surely as the dad could sell you a stamp album. Jerusalem and Egypt took on uncanny, almost magical powers: they remained the birthplace of charisma, the site of his father's extraordinary success.

After the Last Sky is of course about the magic of a place that was, according to Said, denser than any other with cultural symbolism. At the beginning of the book, he cites a 1979 UNESCO Commission report bearing Willy Brandt's name.[3] It estimates that the impoverishment of the South—not just countries below the equator, but also southern regions within prosperous states, such as Italy—"seems destined to continue for the foreseeable future."[4] Since 1948, Palestinian history has consisted of a chain of displacements. Palestinians are chased from the land to the camps, from the camps to Amman, from Amman to Beirut, and from Beirut to Tunis. Said entitles one book about them *The Politics of Dispossession*. His own memoir bears the title *Out of Place*.

Geography gained unexpected importance from other factors, too. Said, geographic theory, and phenomenology came of age together during that thirty-year French theoretical renaissance he so much admired. In Gaston Bachelard's *Poetics of Space* and *Poetics of Fire*, in the Annales school, and of course in Foucault's *Discipline and Punish*, spatial analysis became a principal technique for studying the humanities. Edward Soja argues that space has replaced time as the dominant armature for philosophic and historical study.[5]

Extreme location was Said's original idea and his great contribution to phenomenological method. The "consciousness of consciousness" had to include the mind's surroundings. In his eyes, both Gramsci's and Foucault's views of things were at root spatial. The geographic emphasis so evident in his article about *Aida* inspired a new tradition of secular scholarship.

A fine example is Timothy Mitchell's analysis of starkly unfamiliar Berber spatial meaning in his seminal book, *Colonising Egypt*. He writes that the dividing of space broke down life "into a series of discrete functions—sleeping, eating, cooking, and so on—each with a specific location."[6] The difference between the two poles, which are the dark, nocturnal, uncooked, reproductive, lower part of the house, and the high, light-filled, noble, human, utensil-stocked, cultural upper part of the house, is not absolute but "an always unstable deferring or differing within."[7] Said writes secular criticism against the practice of making such differences absolute, against rationalizing and neutralizing other, non-European spaces, and thus subduing them to Western "religious" methods of interpretation.

Said's geographical interest connects to his prose. An "unstable deferring or differing within" nicely describes what we have seen to be his skidding slippage or *dérapage*, his defiance of rationalizing Western norms such as consistency, linear progression, stability, resolution, and decisive closure. Attention to "third space" in the work of Homi K. Bhabha, Gayatri Spivak, and Edward Soja, in the journal *Third Space*, and across a swath of radical geographic writing demonstrates how relentlessly critics after Said have challenged the Western method of organizing space and prose. Since Bhabha and Spivak also violate the conventions of traditional academic prose style, a relationship begins to form between extreme location, secular criticism, and off-putting prose. For each of these writers, prose becomes an extreme location in which cultures clash, penetrate, and emerge from each other. Each performs the failure of neatly conventional English to match a fractured postcolonial reality.

Real property excites terrible jealousies, longings, and delusions. Often nostalgia for place is a primitive, voodoo-like, hocus-pocus of quasi-religious intoxication. When I interviewed Mr. Ahmad el-Nahas about his days at Said's fancy private high school, Victoria College of Cairo, he was transported by glassy-eyed memories of his fabulous youth.[8] Khadder's effusions over Jerusalem ("a wonderful city, one that has a magnificent history, you know") obviously were reflected through rose-tinted cigarette smoke. Said's longing to revisit his birth house and his father's high school sports trophies partakes of a kindred nostalgia. Sentimentalities like these beg to be patronized. Even a hard-bitten war correspondent such as Gloria Emerson, whose Vietnam journalism won a Pulitzer Prize and who ought to know better, attributed to Palestinian Gazans "an attachment, deeper than any known to most Americans except for those of native Indian blood." This attachment "pushes the Palestinians to go back and look at their land where the Israelis have lived for more than four decades."[9] From one angle, her well-meaning words could be seen as the purest Orientalism. But mystic spirituality is unnecessary to explain the refugees' longing to get away from leaky shacks and open sewers—their actual situation for the last sixty years.

A further madness inherent in place is apparent in Foucault's notion of "heterotopias." That which is *heteros* (other) about *topos* (space)—such as a cemetery or a museum—represents the collision of moments or cultures that were not in fact coexistent. Perched between the real and the representational, places such as the Cairo opera house where Verdi premiered *Aida* and the location in Tangier where the crew of Italian–Jewish cineaste Gilles Pontecorvo's *The Battle of Algiers* filmed real Algerian revolutionaries playing themselves, are larger versions of the internally bisected space of Barthes' photographs. The divided city—another *topos* that is *hetero*—is everywhere, from colonial Algiers to Johannesburg to Laredo/Nuevo Laredo. It is the founding myth of postcolonialism, exciting authors from Fanon to Edward Said to Timothy Mitchell, from Lord Curzon to Abdul JanMohamed.

In a 1986 interview with Jonathan Crary, Said confirmed that Fanon was the original, important postcolonial intellectual—to the point of defining the field. A secular politics of interpretation finds an ally in Fanon's spatial thinking. One passage had special importance for Said:

> The zone where the natives live is not complementary to the zone inhabited by the settlers. The two zones are opposed, but not in the service of a higher unity. Obedient

to the rules of pure Aristotelian logic, they both follow the principle of reciprocal exclusivity. No conciliation is possible, for of the two, one is superfluous. The settlers' town is a strongly built town, all made of stone and steel. It is a brightly lit town; the streets are covered with asphalt, and the garbage-cans swallow all the leavings, unseen, unknown and hardly thought about.... The settler's town is a town of white people, of foreigners.

The town belonging to the colonized people, or at least the native town, the negro village, the medina, the reservation, is a place of ill fame, peopled by men of evil repute. They are born there, it matters little where or how; they die there, it matters not where, nor how. It is a world without spaciousness; men live there on top of each other, and their huts are built on top of the other.... The native town is a crouching village, a town on its knees, a town wallowing in the mire. It is a town of niggers and dirty Arabs. The look that the native turns on the settler's town is a look of lust, a look of envy; it expresses his dreams of possession—all manner of possession: to set at the settler's table, to sleep in the settler's bed, with his wife if possible.[10]

Marxism had its intellectual blocs; Colonialism had its Manichean cities. Foucault theorized uncanny places as placeless heterotopias; but Said anchored his extreme locations in a political history of force and domination. They had exact coordinates on a planetary map, and pinpointing them made him the Magellan of the postcolonial globe.[11]

To Said's religious opponents, the Promised Land spreads itself everywhere with oppressive weight. "We still believe, or many of us do, what the Exodus first taught," wrote Michael Walzer:

first, that wherever you live, it is probably Egypt; second, that there is a better place, a world more attractive, a promised land; and third, that the way to the land is through the wilderness. There is no way to get from here to there except by joining together and marching.[12]

A crisp, efficient brevity informs Walzer's short, entertaining book, which projects the heroic story of Moses leading his people out of bondage in Egypt onto many later liberation movements, and he gives examples of anticolonial movements that have cited the Exodus as their inspiration. The flesh and blood creatures living in Egypt and Canaan never enter into Walzer's discussion.

In a response to Walzer, "An Exchange: Exodus and Revolution," *Grand Street* (Summer 1988), Said initiates a new method of literary criticism. It is the same as the method used in his critique of *Aida*. In both cases, Said adduces a thick description of the political and historical factors at the moment of composition. Stepping behind the polished surface of *Exodus and Revolution*, Said links Walzer's innocent fable to the current situation in Israel/Palestine. By suppressing the Palestinians' reality, their side of the story, he argues, Walzer has surreptitiously justified Israel by obliterating its victims.[13] He asserts that the motives for writing such a book are clear and present—Walzer wishes to justify Israel's current occupation of Palestine as a kind of liberation struggle. Said takes the opposite position and gauges the impact of this Jewish arrival in Palestine on the Canaanites. He reminds readers that Walzer's book is written now and has an impact on the present. The mythic and historical distance notwithstanding, in reading Walzer's account one feels that in destroying the native inhabitants, the Jewish settlers were—and are—simply carrying out a divine edict. By setting the scene a few millennia back, Walzer can support colonial conquest and retain his liberal political credentials. Said summons his hallmark charismatic anger and demands that Walzer defend, not his assertions about the Israelites and the book of *Exodus*, but its allegorical political implications and its surreptitious, implied political effects in the present. Said's attack forged a new kind of cultural criticism. The analytic that can unpack the political implications in "Leda and the Swan" can also discern, in an ostensibly objective essay about some topic remote in time and place, a virulent polemic aiming to win advantages in current political struggles.

> **"Palestine, Then and Now: An Exile's Journey Through Israel and the Occupied Territories,"** *Harper's Magazine*, December 1992
>
> Mine was the generation raised in an Arab world that accorded the Jewish state no recognition at all; even the idea of Israel was anathema. This odd proposition, that Israel did not exist, made possible a policy of non-knowledge, a void that erected a wall around itself, allowing both Israeli and Arab leaders to get away with literally everything in the name of security. Until 1967 the Arab world, including the millions of Palestinians floundering in exile, nearly forgot about their compatriots who remained in Israel after 1948. Until 1967 it was nearly impossible to use the word "Israel" in Arabic writing. All this was supposed to cost Israel in legitimacy and resolve, so that if we didn't acknowledge its presence it would go away. Of course it didn't, although even those many of us whose passports and safe jobs made it feasible to return needed a long time to make the trip, cross the barrier, confront the difficult reality.
>
> (48)
>
> Four days after finding the house I took my family to St. George's to visit the old "Bishop's School," as it is known among Jerusalem's Arabs. There I showed my son, Wadie, his grandfather Wadie's name on the cricket and soccer First Eleven boards for the years 1906 through 1911. In the assembly room, where morning prayers used to be held, a seventy-year-old caretaker asked us shyly whether we'd like to see old school pictures. He went to the cellar and brought up a number of them—a class picture from 1942, the staff in 1927—one of which riveted my attention. It was signed "Kh. Raad," for Khalil Raad, Palestine's most famous photographer, a nervous but gifted man whom I remember would fussily arrange and rearrange us

> for group pictures during weddings, confirmations, and the like. There, seated on the floor next to a young man carrying a soccer ball with "1906" written across it, was my father, age thirteen.
> So many histories, starting and ending in Jerusalem. A fitting accompaniment to the ebbing of my life on the one hand, and, on the other, a concrete reminder that just as *they* had started and ended, I did and would too, and so also would my children, who could now see for the first time the linked narrative of our family's generations, where that story belonged but from which it had been banished.
>
> (50–51)
>
> I would find it very hard to live there, I think: exile seems to me a more liberated state, but, I have to admit, I am privileged and can afford to experience the pleasures, rather than the burdens, of exile. Yet I also feel that, as a family, the four of us need the connection, need the assurances that Palestine and Palestinians have really survived, and this we now have. I think I needed the chance metaphorically to bury the dead, and, what with the large number of funerary associations for me, what had been Palestine was indeed a mournful place. But I can feel and sometimes actually see a different future as I couldn't before.
>
> (55)

In *After the Last Sky*, Said writes with dismay about Palestinian aimlessness and untidiness. He accuses his people of not caring enough about their own status, history, and level of organization. In 1992, seven years after this book was published, he returned to Palestine for the first time in four decades. The article in *Harper's Magazine* brings Said and Palestine geographically, spatially together: they are one. Fed by this two-way root system, he and Palestine grow bigger.

172 • Marquee Intellectual

"I'm Very Upset"

I called Said's cousin, Sylvia Nasser, from my hotel room on a hillside in Amman.

Sylvia picked up.

"Yes, I am at the Ambassador Hotel."

"And did you have a pleasant trip?"

"Yes. In fact I even met an interesting person, a man from the U.N."

"Oh, that is nice."

Figure 9.1 Staff of the Ambassador Hotel, Amman, Jordan.

I waited for her to continue and when she said nothing, I added, "I was hoping that you would find some time to see me."

"But, Aram, does Edward know you are here? I have just received a telex from him in which he asks me not to see anybody."

"But I just saw him and told him I was coming. He knows I'm coming to see you."

"Then, Aram, I am quite puzzled and I do not know. Because he writes in his telex that he would not wish for me to have discussions about him with anyone."

I was speechless.

If I had come just to see her, she continued, "then you must come to see me. I will not talk about Edward—anything that I know of Edward is very personal and I wouldn't discuss that in any case."

Very personal stuff is just what I want to hear! I did not say that. "I don't want to compromise you," I told her, imagining myself in a white pressed shirt smiling her towards the forbidden topic while the two of us sipped sweet coffee. Then, I had a cowardly urge just to skip the whole thing. "Perhaps I should talk to Edward."

"Yes, talk to Edward," she replied. "But you will come to see us. We have a heart, after all. You should not have to be in this country all alone, without friends. So come tomorrow."

I wrote a fax to Said on the Marriott Hotel's English-script typewriter. He wrote back. It was a classic Said performance, a back-and-forth samba of positions forcefully taken and then decisively withdrawn.

He was "very upset" although he reported chuckling over the list of questions I had proposed to ask Sylvia. These questions would be "silly and inappropriate in the extreme," for she was a "friend in the family" whom he rarely saw and was "as connected to my intellectual life as the man in the moon." He went on to add, "Intellectual biographies are all very well, but when they stray into miscellaneous and by no means crucial family connections they seem to me to have been diverted altogether.

I can't obviously prevent you from seeing her, but I wish I wasn't made to cooperate in this effort. I very much appreciate your sincerity and the good things you have to say about me, I really do: but I can't seriously be made to accept the idea that I should vet various expeditions into my past via miscellaneous family members." He ended with a typical embrace and repel statement: "I don't want to get caught up in a weird Rashomon type thing, with me as subject, and as referee. I hope all is well. Please rest assured that I am sympathetic to what you are doing and that I am genuinely fond of you, of course. But I hope you understand my own feelings too. Yours, Edward."

Edward Said counseling passivity? Rest assured, my ass.

10
POLITICAL ROUGHHOUSE

In these pages the history is not of the Arab movement, but of me in it. It is a narrative of daily life, mean happenings, little people. Here are no lessons for the world, no disclosures to shock peoples. It is filled with trivial things, partly that no one mistake for history the bones from which some day a man may make history, and partly for the pleasure it gave me to recall the fellowship of the revolt. We were fond together, because of the sweep of the open places, the taste of wide winds, the sunlight, and the hopes in which we worked. The morning freshness of the world-to-be intoxicated us. We were wrought up with ideas inexpressible and vaporous, but to be fought for. We lived many lives in those whirling campaigns, never sparing ourselves: yet when we achieved and the new world dawned, the old men came out again and took our victory to re-make in the likeness of the former world they knew. Youth could win, but had not learned to keep: and was pitiably weak against age. We stammered that we had worked for a new heaven and a new earth, and they thanked us kindly and made their peace.

T.E. Lawrence, *Seven Pillars of Wisdom*

There is always something peculiarly impotent about the violence of a literary man.

Oscar Wilde[1]

Said had his academic following. He had the readers of *Raritan* and *Wedge* and *Third Space* and *Interventions* and *Critical*

Inquiry. He had some readers of *Harper's* and *House and Garden* and *The Progressive*. His liberal academic audience thrilled to discussions of exile, identity, the "politics of interpretation," the role of the intellectual, and primacy of the individual over the system. The dependable audience for these topics topped out, he liked to complain, at 2,000 people who bought each other's books. Even branching out to the wider audience of *The Nation* and *The Progressive* (about 93,000 readers by 1996) was an exponential improvement. Said was a master of the liberal politics so well suited to his educated American and European audiences. He had the further advantage that he could offer himself as Exhibit A. He could point to himself and prove that individuality was never dissolved back into the hot tea of group identity. As "the most recognized Palestinian in the United States," he was the perfect case study for academic woolgatherers who loved to debate whether "the subaltern can speak."[2] He was happy to take his lumps and fight back. He complained that he was being made a spokesperson for terrorism, as when some ruthless Palestinians killed an old man at sea or an obscure academic labeled him a "Professor of Terror."[3] Said also enjoyed correcting Arab chauvinists who made him their champion, misreading *Orientalism* as an anti-Western polemic.[4] But the charisma he exerted on professors and pundits had negligible effects on the PLO.

When we pick up the story, in late March 1988, the Palestinian *intifadah* had been raging for over three months. It had transformed the world's opinion of Palestinians and Israelis. The Israelis suddenly assumed the role that only months before had been firmly assigned to Arabs: the role of violent bullies and Goliaths. Meanwhile, the face of the Palestinian was no longer the stubbly Arafat but instead a bunch of cute twelve-year-old boys—valiant little Davids, right down to the slingshots—overmatched but refusing to back down.

> Thousands of young children and teenagers—what the locals and later the international press called the *shabab* (young men)—donned the *kuffiya* emblem of Palestine and,

Interview with Ibrahim Abu-Lughod, Sheridan Avenue, December 29, 1991

A-L: Because for the most part [Edward] has lived in this country, he is known to the Arabs only through translations, not through his actual creative work in Arabic. Now when he appears there, he is now better in Arabic than he was before. But he couldn't give a lecture in Arabic. Now he can. He does not speak in the National Council or in any of these meetings. He simply sits there. So they don't feel that he is really interested enough, involved enough. He is not part of any particular group. So he is part of America! That's how they think of him.

HAV: When you speak of the reception of Edward Said in Tunis or his keeping silent in meetings of the Palestine National Council, it's difficult for me to imagine that. He dominates every assembly that I've ever seen him in, and in literary circles he's treated as a major figure whose presence could never be ignored in any way. It's a humbling thing, then, for him to participate in Palestine National Council meetings?

A-L: Sure. In most Arab things he feels, I think, just a slight discomfort, because he is not as fluent in Arabic, in oratorical Arabic, as these guys in the National Council. I mean, I feel inhibited. I've spoken I think once in the National Council, because I feel ignored for one thing. It's an insult to me.... Now, I have no doubt that they would listen to Edward. If he decided to speak, they would listen—or at least at the beginning they would listen. That is, we pay attention when George Habbash [leader of the Popular Front for the Liberation of Palestine—a Palestinian branch of the PLO that competed with Fatah and

continued

> other groupings within the PLO] speaks, when Yasir Arafat speaks. There are a few people because we know they are the ones who have power. The others have nothing. So if we want to have influence, we don't want to influence these guys, because these guys have no power. You influence the leadership, and with the leadership, Edward speaks. That is, if you sit with Arafat and a few of his cronies, then he speaks, because that's what he went for, that's where power is.
>
> HAV: When he went to the United Nations in 1974 during the famous visit by Arafat, was he translating?
>
> A-L: Edward was translating the speech that Arafat made. That's all. He was not yet very involved in the movement.
>
> HAV: Was that a risky thing for him to do, in the sense that it hurt his image? Given the time at which this happened, 1974, shortly after the Munich killings, was it the equivalent of Yasir Arafat embracing Saddam Hussein? Did it have that kind of [negative] impact on the public last August?
>
> A-L: At that time probably not. Nevertheless it was risky. I was, frankly, surprised. I didn't know that he was working on the translation.

raising their fingers in a V for victory sign, engaged the most successful army in the Middle East in an unequal confrontation which dazzled the world. The children were angry, determined and fearless. The Israeli soldiers lacked the proper training to put down the *intifada* and overreacted. The story perpetuated itself dramatically.[5]

At first, the *intifadah* was directed through weekly samizdat leaflets signed by "the Unified National Leadership"—an ad hoc coalition whose members rotated and who represented all the major Palestinian liberation organizations.[6] "This means that the left organizations have almost equal weight with Fatah," as opposed to the Palestine National Council (of which Said was a member): there, Fatah dominated.[7] The leaflets included no reference to the PLO, Yasir Arafat, or the notables, patrons, and Big Shots who were by now identified with Arafat's old Fatah group. Of course Fatah was alarmed.

> While firmly adhering to the slogan that the PLO is the sole legitimate representative of the Palestinian people, activists here have taken the initiative on the ground. The voice of this leadership is communal and anonymous; clandestine leaflets have replaced the press conferences of former days. In the process, some traditional nationalist leaders have been overwhelmed by events.[8]

Even the most cautious and expert specialists were inspired to feel that the torch was being passed. "Part of any new generation of Palestinian leadership which does emerge will probably come from occupied Palestine, where new forms of organization are already appearing," wrote political scientist Rashid Khalidi. "More subtle in its approach and strategy," this new indigenous leadership "will be unlike the current leadership, which is located entirely in exile and knows its enemy primarily from being on the receiving end of Israeli bombing raids and assassination attempts."[9]

To a degree, the PLO as much as the Israelis was the target of *intifadah* rage. The most famous *intifadah* poem drew a repellent picture of Arab men sitting all day in cafes—like mussels, the poet wrote, in his most brilliantly demeaning line. "In fact, the intifada was an open-ended rebellion, an attempt by children to destroy everything which had surrounded them and left them without hope, the PLO included" (Aburish 1998: 206). The famous Woodstock-era generation gap was a pinhole compared to the Palestinians':

> It was a revolt against local conditions by children who claimed greater knowledge than their elders and who viewed their fathers with derision while hating the Israeli occupier. There was anger against a leadership-in-exile which had grown comfortable and corrupt.[10]

> **"Children Bearing Rocks"**
>
> With stones in their hands,
> They defy the world
> And come to us like good tidings.
> They burst with anger and love, and they fall
> While we remain a herd of polar bears:
> A body armored against weather.
>
> Like mussels we sit in cafes,
> One hunts for a business venture
> One for another billion
> And a fourth wife
> And breasts polished by civilization.
> One stalks London for a lofty mansion
>
> One traffics in arms
> One seeks revenge in nightclubs
> One plots for a throne, a private army,
> And a princedom.
>
> Ah, generation of betrayal,
> Of surrogate and indecent men,
> Generation of leftovers,
> We'll be swept away—
> Never mind the slow pace of history—
> By children bearing rocks.[11]

The Unified National Leadership of the *intifadah*, a revolving body of anonymous West Bank and Gaza leaders, suddenly had taken over the Palestinian liberation struggle. Just as suddenly, the U.S. Secretary of State, George Pratt Shultz, flew on emergency visits to the West Bank. But no Palestinian would agree to meet with him. Next, Shultz called and asked Said to come to Washington, D.C., for a meeting. Said dutifully checked with Arafat, who directed him to meet with Shultz. In the memorably scornful wording of UNL communiqué number six, dated February 2, 1988, "these little yellowed leaves who go off on pilgrimage to meet with the representatives of the unholy trinity [Jordan, Egypt, and the United States]" are enemies of the *intifadah*.[12] Other UNL communiqués hammered the message home. On April 2, 1988, the leaflet cited "the uprising masses' rejection of Shultz, the secretary of U.S. imperialism." Another called for a "comprehensive strike in reply to the Zionist Shultz' visit." May 28's leaflet denounced "George Shultz attempt to resume the conspiracy aimed at aborting the uprising." Another, published on the same day, called for a "full-scale strike to mark the visit of Shultz." The message was clear: "The popular and national committees of the uprising stress their firm condemnation of any meetings with any US and Zionist politicians" (Communiqué no. 19, June 6, 1988).[13] In spite of these insistent prohibitions issued from the very streets of Gaza and the West Bank, Said flew from New York to Washington and met with Shultz.

When Said met officially with the Secretary of State, George Shultz, who greeted him as a fellow Princeton man, the conversation was cordial, even chummy. Most striking is the shared universe of political assumptions. One could not imagine such a conversation between a Secretary of State and Noam Chomsky or Alexander Cockburn or Terry Eagleton. But as Said went into the meeting, he knew the *intifadah* has been boiling for three months, that Shultz had been unable to find a single Palestinian in the territories who would meet with him, and that Arafat was threatened by the *intifadah* and its implicit challenge to his leadership.

For a brief moment, the UNL had unobstructed freedom. Everyone involved—internationalists and NGO workers, professors and sociologists, the leaders of Fatah, and the youths and women actually fighting the *intifadah*—all considered it a potentially fatal challenge to the old-line exiled leaders and Fatah hegemony in the Palestinian liberation movement. Unfortunately, these hopes were extravagant: the PLO proved cagier and more ruthless than the *intifadah* youth imagined.[14]

"The PLO was stunned by what was happening but remained afraid to commit itself" (Aburish 1998: 202). A month passed

Interview with Ibrahim Abu-Lughod, Sheridan Avenue, December 29, 1991

A-L: Edward called, I would say, probably around 11:30 at night. And it's not usual for Edward to call people at 11:30 because by then he's—

HAV: He's a morning person.

A-L: In any case, he said he'd just come back from either the ballet or a theater of some sort—that's why he's calling late—and that he has a message on his machine, in which Richard Murphy, the Assistant Secretary of State for Middle East Affairs, says ... "Mr. Shultz wants to see the two of you to discuss the general situation in the Middle East. You can call me at any time," and he gave him two, three numbers. So he [Said] said, "Well, we have an invitation. What should we do?" I said, "Well, in principle we are interested. But I want to ask a couple of questions." And Edward said, "Okay, what questions?" I said, "Number one, is this a private meeting, secret, or public? If it's secret, I will not go. You should know that. I will not go to a secret. If it's public, I'll go. And second, what topics does he want to discuss with us?"

HAV: Do people like Shultz realize that you are members of the PLO?

A-L: Oh, yeah! They told us that ...
[Here Abu-Lughod's pony-tailed grandson came in for a cookie. Abu-Lughod gave it to him and continued.]

A-L: Then we went to see Mr. Shultz. Mr. Shultz, I would say this. He entered in a green jacket. It was St. Patrick's Day and, as he carefully explained to us, his wife is Irish. I think he was being sporty. I mean, literally, he was being sporty. He was very, very courteous. Really, maximum courtesy. And exuding politeness, joviality, and so forth. And also, [inaudible]. I call it a policy of systematic cooptation. That's what I call it. He told us both, be seated. I mean, he decided where we'd both sit. Edward took one chair, I another chair, he there, Murphy to his left. And [April] Glaspie was taking the notes. The woman's role: secretary.... So, we gossiped a little bit about that, about what was happening, and this and that, and then he said: "You know this is not a negotiating session. I invited you because you are very distinguished authorities on the subject"—no mention of the National Council—"you are eminent scholars and this and that, and American citizens. And you know, I'm an academic, too. I'm really anxious to finish this job because I have a chair at Stanford, and my wife has gone already there to set up the house, and, I mean, we are set. So, we should view this as a seminar, this session. So we talk openly, because we have an important problem that is on your mind and on my mind. So this is in the nature of a seminar. We give and take. We are trying to understand the issues. That's how I want this meeting to be. So it will be very informal." And this and that. "Oh, sure. This is a seminar. It has nothing to do with politics. Nothing, of course." This duplicitous behavior on the part of all the parties. We share an illusion, as it were. And then he started. He revealed for the first time, then, that he is going to Jerusalem within a couple of weeks, which is one reason that he invited us. And, "you know, the last time I was there I invited the leaders from the community to come to a meeting because I wanted to explain to them how serious we are in our effort"—all very gentle, much gentler than he comes across on television—"that when I invited the leaders, they didn't come. Had they come, they

continued

would have found out how serious we are about finding a fair solution to their problem of occupation. We are very serious about that. And had they come, they would have heard me say the following." Then he pushed the button and the secretary came. He said, "Would you get me the text of my speech to the people of Jerusalem." And of course she came with this nice, fancy paper—I don't know what it's called, but very fancy paper—and of course they gave us each a copy. "If you notice here—this is the speech—if they had listened to it, they would know how serious we are. What we want to do"—and this is as if we had never seen it: of course we knew the speech: it was published in the *New York Times*. Oh, yeah! Oh, Yeah! [laughter] "We want the Palestinians to have greater economic and political control over their lives." And he looked at us: [this is said in an intense stage whisper] "Do you understand what that means? Control." "Oh, yeah! Oh, yeah!" [laughter]. Then he went a couple of steps down to show us that he is really talking about the exercise of power by Palestinians over their affairs. "Is that independence?" "Oh, no, no." So we let him talk, I mean he allowed himself to talk for about twenty minutes, about the objectives. Pre-empted the possibility of independence and of course, "We need authentic representatives to negotiate with." No word about the PLO. Then after he finished, Edward took over, and he spoke for probably, I would say, fifteen minutes. Edward talked about nationalism, about the unique place of Palestine. And then I took over—again, for another fifteen minutes. I emphasized the role of the PLO, self-determination, and of course, independence. So. And then we went into these areas. He said, "We can't support self-determination. We can't

> support independence. We cannot. But a negotiating process, we are anxious to have a negotiating process between the two." So we said, "We are all for negotiating." And Edward there caught him.... "If you believe in the efficacy of the negotiating process, then why do you exclude independence a priori? ... That is, you can't say that the two antagonists, whatever they agree on, we will support, if you already exclude independence. Then the independence cannot be negotiated!" And Edward caught him there. And he said, "You might be right. But we don't think it's practical, we don't think it's—" You know. "The land is so small, and the age of communication—" and so forth and so on. He was not going to accept independence. He was not going to accept the PLO as a negotiating partner. And we went on. Obviously there was a deadlock. But he is arguing, and we are arguing. In the end, I gave it to him. As Edward says, "He began to hit him with the hammer." [laughter]

before the PLO issued a statement in support of the *intifadah*.[15] Although the Arab media loved the images coming out of the territories and ordinary Arab audiences excitedly praised everything the Palestinian women and children were doing, Arab leaders privately feared the spread of a new populist movement. The leaders were and are dictators and strongmen. "Overall, the Arab governments had no interest in a new populist movement succeeding and infecting their people," continues Aburish. "Arafat did not threaten them, but a genuine rebellion did" (Aburish 1998: 205). Conversely, the Arab leaders backed Arafat and the PLO old men—the mussels—against the upstart *intifadah*.

By April, the *intifadah* had been co-opted, reigned in, and made to serve Fatah's diplomatic program.[16] Now a pious formula from the Koran was affixed to each UNL message, the PLO was always named as the sole representative of Palestinian people, and Arafat himself was signing the communiqués. "But even with their acceptance of the PLO umbrella," writes Aburish, "the UNL still represented a threat to the PLO leadership" (1998: 208).

Quickness in debate was Said's great strength but when the political crisis arrived, he proved too slow. His Waterloo was the *intifadah*. He made a terrible political error; during the first crucial months—before Arafat and Fatah wormed their way back into control—he helped the PLO co-opt the *intifadah*. He repented this mistake soon enough. By late 1988, he was writing a slightly satirical human-interest piece about PLO chairman Yasir Arafat, emphasizing his outlandish habits, such as eating tea-soaked cornflakes.[17] In October 1989 he launched an open attack on the PLO, charging Arafat and the others with corruption, ignorance, and bad leadership. He publicly criticized Arafat in a daily newspaper, *al-Qabas*, that was read throughout the Arab world. This "surprise criticism by an insider," as *Mideast Mirror* put it, brought an instantaneous reaction from the PLO. Within two days, the PLO spokesperson in Tunis, Yasser Abedrabbo, answered each of Said's charges, going so far as to call Said "opportunistic." The opportunism charge stung: Abedrabbo was making it seem that as soon as the *intifadah* leeched glamour from the PLO, Said had decided to switch sides. Within eighteen months of this exchange, which was never patched up or resolved, Said had resigned his thirteen-year position as a member of the Palestine National Council, an advisory body that voted on PLO policy.

The politics Said chose to enter were anything but abstract and remote. At home, he lived in a setting—New York's upper west side—where the survival of the Jewish people and the creation of the State of Israel mattered more than global warming or the U.S. national debt. Abroad, the realm of real-world liberationist politics was a truly intolerant landscape. Whole peoples were exiled, housed in camps, sent away. Millions were starved and gassed. Killing a radical in his house or car was considered a reasonable act. By 1987, most of the founding members of the PLO had died violent deaths. One historian offers the following sober assessment:

> Many of the most dynamic individuals who had founded Fateh, and who had dominated the PLO for the first decade and more after the mid-1960s, as well as other competent PLO leaders, had disappeared by the mid-1990s. Most of them were eliminated as a result of assassination by Israeli or Arab intelligence services or by others acting for them, like the Abu Nidal organization, while a few of them died of natural causes or were otherwise disabled. PLO leaders who were assassinated between 1968 and 1991 included Abu 'Ali Iyyad, Ghassan Kanafani, Sa'id Hamami, Abu Yusuf al-Najjar, Kamal Nasser, Kamal 'Adwan, Majid Abu Sharar, Abu Hassan Salameh, Brig. Gen. Sa'd Sayil (Abu al-Walid), 'Isam Sirtawi, Abu Jihad, Abu al-Hol, and Abu Iyyad.[18]

Said got very close to this bloody and terrifying world. He dined at home with Kamel Nasser an hour before the latter's assassination. That is just one example.

The embrace–expel maneuver reappeared once more. Said drew charismatic wattage from the PLO but rejected the essential ethnic identity that seemed to be required of him in return. "The national identity becomes not only a fetish, but is also turned into a kind of idol," he told interviewers, "a kind of desperate religious sentiment."[19] Bored with questions of identity, he voiced incompatible opinions about it. Identity never can or should stabilize, Said once exclaimed. "I am—as we all are—a sort of hybrid."[20] He could imagine no stability or anchoring that would not become a loathed prison. Even nationalist struggle against European colonialism, which was a good thing, according to Said, had the downside of glorifying national identity. "The idea that there is a kind of redemptive homeland doesn't answer to my view of things," he told Salman Rushdie.[21] But in the roughhouse of actual political and military struggle, he tried to have everything both ways in his usual nonchalant and self-contradictory fashion. He reversed, for example, all his claims of never having joined the PLO and stated:

> I am part of the PLO and I have taken part in this long struggle which led us to the Algiers Declaration [in which the Palestine National Council endorsed a two-state solution in historic Palestine in November of 1988]. My intention is to indulge in criticism from within, not from without.[22]

In this luminously self-contradictory passage, Said refutes everything he ever said or was going to say about the responsibilities of the intellectual. "I refused all inducements to join one of the groups or to work in the PLO, largely because I felt it was important to preserve my distance. I was a partisan, yes, but a joiner and member, no" (*PolD* xxiv). Elsewhere he declares that he never committed himself completely to a cause or party: "I simply have not been able to do it, preferring to retain both the outsider's and the skeptic's autonomy over the, to me, vaguely religious quality communicated by the convert's and the true believer's enthusiasm" (*RI* 108).

Belonging or being part of something had no place in an intellectual's life. The intellectual, he claims, should be "an anarchic and yet highly concentrated figure," a "deeply confrontational intellect" (*RI* 14–15). How could this *set-apart* being be construed as "part of the PLO"? His only loyalty was to his liminality.

> The intellectual as outsider is best exemplified by the condition of exile, the state of never being fully adjusted, always feeling outside the chatty, familiar world inhabited by natives, so to speak, tending to avoid and even dislike the trappings of accommodation and national well-being.
>
> (*RI* 63)

Half-in, half-out of the PLO, he further resembled the half-formed human figure attempting to make itself within the rocky morass of Michelangelo's "Captive." The Palestinian liberation struggle endowed him with global charisma yet threatened to consume him, like his very own cloak of Nessus.

Figure 10.1 Adapted from *Captive* by Michelangelo (source: Scala/Art Resource, New York).

> Interview with Robert Siegel, "All Things Considered," National Public Radio, January 11, 1999)
>
> SAID: Since it's virtually impossible to imagine that they're going to be separated surgically, the two populations, and since the population of the Palestinians is growing so that, by the year 2010, there's going to be parity between them and the Israelis, the only way, in my opinion, that it could possibly work is that there be some arrangement whereby they live together as equals.
>
> SIEGEL: This idea of having a single, bi-national democratic state would require both sides to give up something that's different from territory, and even different from political power, but to give up the idea of having a nation-state that expresses Jewishness or being a Palestinian, through the existence of that country.
>
> SAID: Yes and no. In other words, I see no difficulty for Jews in such a state to live as Jews, and Palestinians to live as Palestinians. What it requires, I think, is the giving up the notion that Israel, for instance, is not the state of its citizens, but the state of the whole Jewish people, wherever they are.
>
> Similarly, Palestinians dream of a Palestine that is Arab and that is part of the Arab homeland. So it requires a limitation on, you might say, romantic ideas of the nation that simply fly in the face of the actuality, namely that, for Palestinians, there are Israelis there, Jews, and for Israelis, that there are Palestinians there who are Muslim and Christian Arabs.

Political Roughhouse • 191

Said remained a hopeless idealist, despite fitful attempts at Machiavellian realism, as in belatedly jettisoning the PLO.[23] So extreme was his idealism that he actually thought

> what has enabled Israel to do what it has been doing to the Palestinians for the past 54 years is the result of a carefully and scientifically planned campaign to validate Israeli actions and, simultaneously, devalue and efface Palestinian actions.[24]

On this view, the victory of Israel in Palestine was simply a result of "the immense diffusionary, insistent, and repetitive power of the images broadcast by CNN, for example."[25] Reading Gramsci one-sidedly, he found justification for his self-aggrandizing conviction that images, not material forces, ruled people's actions.

The question forces itself: how effective could such a limited political vision be?

"Partial Credit"

Said admitted me to his apartment on 448 Riverside Drive in Manhattan and led me to his dining room for breakfast. The Persian carpets layered one on top of another and the Chippendale furniture in this spacious aerie declared that nothing has been allowed to enter without severe inspection and hard-won approval—though approval from a rather conventional designer. The rooms were gracious but not egregious—a little bigger, perhaps, a little more cosmopolitan than your average upper-middle-class enclave. Only the grand piano was exceptional. It was a working instrument, not an ornament.

"Did you see Shahak?" he asked me. I laid my spotless Coach portfolio on the table. Said looked at it with distaste. "Let's get this off the table, then," he said, taking it over to the sideboard. "We have to eat here."

Touché, I thought. Now it begins. "Yes. I interviewed him for hours. He was very forthcoming. And he admires you this side idolatry."

The TV on a counter near the table was off. The telephone rang occasionally. His wife, Mariam, was about the house, but not the two kids, Najla and Wadie.

"What was his apartment like? I've heard it's quite a sight."

I told him about all his friends whom I had visited, and about my visit to Gaza, and the *intifadah*.

"Yes, the conditions there are worse than Soweto, worse than the South Bronx," he said proudly, "and still the Palestinians won't give up."

I wanted to talk about the battered Ford Cortina coughing its way through the deep wadis as we moved through flooded Jabaliya Camp in Gaza. But here, sitting between Persian carpets and grand piano, it would have been gauche.

"Now you're going to have a real Palestinian breakfast," he announced. He laid out the *lebneh* (a cheese of dried yoghurt), *zaataar* (a tangy greenish, oregano-like mixture used dry as a condiment), pita bread, and oil-cured black olives. "This is what I have had for breakfast every day of my life." I raised the willow-patterned coffee cup. He dabbed the corners of his lips.

Said began telling me how he'd come to commit himself to the Palestinian cause. "But in '72 I was married to a Lebanese," he said. "For the first time I had a real connection with a real society. And I was working on *Beginnings,* essentially rewriting and putting it together, which I finished a year or so later. So I took the time to sit down and work on my Arabic. I mean, of course, it was always my first language spoken. But reading, writing, my whole education was European, it was English, right?"

I admired his apartment and especially the trapezoidal, book-lined writing office.

"Did I tell you, Harold, about the English psychiatrist; she was here in New York for a Freud Society event? Well, she was desperate to come up and see me, here, in this apartment. She didn't stay, just looked around and then got ready to leave. 'Why?' I asked her. 'Well, I'd heard you lived this way and I wanted to see for myself.' Harold, she couldn't believe that an

Arab Palestinian, a barbarian after all, could live with a touch of comfort and a piano."

The bourgeois setting impelled me to ask him why he had condemned the trendiest movements in literary theory. He tensed, drew back, and peered at me under scowling brows.

"Wait! Harold. Are you one of those theory people who think I have nothing to say?"

I peddled back furiously. He took a parting jab at new historicism and moved on.

11
DROPPING THE PLO

What I was doing—this is something that I learned from Foucault—was producing things that become a box of utensils for other people to use.... The whole theoretical dimension is completely absent in Middle East studies. A historian would never think of turning to a Middle Eastern history journal to try and understand what general lessons might be. Why is there a conscious or unconscious consensus against theoretical work in Middle East studies? That could be political. It could be the formation of people. There could be more immediate stakes here: jobs, patronage, money.

Edward Said[1]

He [Nelson Mandela] paused for a moment and then said something that I shall never forget as long as I live. "Every victory that we registered in London, or Glasgow, or Iowa City, or Toulouse, or Berlin, or Stockholm gave the people at home a sense of hope, and renewed their determination not to give up the struggle. In time we morally isolated the South African regime and its policy of apartheid so that even though militarily we could not do much to hurt them, in the end they came to us, asking for negotiations."

Said, *The End of the Peace Process: Oslo and After*

Although Said was a grand man of British letters, in every respect he is closer to Spivak and Bhabha than to even the least doctrinaire Marxist critics, such as C.L.R. James, Antonio Gramsci, and Raymond Williams.[2] His insistence on every true

Interview with Eqbal Ahmad in his Apartment on 92nd Street, July 11, 1990

HAV: Could you have foreseen earlier in Edward's career that he would have such a tremendous impact in forming a movement among North American literary critics who would make space for the serious academic reception of Third-World literary texts?

EA: Frankly, no. Not that clearly. I told you the story of the first article that I read of his, "The Arab Portrayed," I had at that time a feeling, and I've said this to my colleague, Ibrahim. I impulsively called Ibrahim Abu-Lughod and said, "This man can do extremely good work if he can sustain his dissent, his anger." He has sustained his anger and his dissent. But I had not anticipated the impact he would have in the field of literary criticism. I understood that only after the publication of *Orientalism*.... This book broke new ground. And so much new ground that its faults were forgotten. *Orientalism* had come out and by the time I had read half of it, I thought that something important had been done. After that it was easy to foresee that Edward would have an important influence. Look, he tapped something very important. He tapped the roots of modern Western Civilization, which they had been unwilling to acknowledge. And the primary argument that *Orientalism* is more about the Occident than about the Orient was a very hard [case to prove]. And he did that with a theoretical sophistication that goes beyond what he acknowledges, namely the debt to Michel Foucault. It was putting Foucault to a use which Foucault may not have anticipated himself.... I saw Foucault six months after *Orientalism* had come out and I asked him, "What do you think?"

continued

> I said, "He says that he is using your categories in *The Archaeology of Knowledge*. He says that in the 'Introduction'." [Foucault] said, "Yes, but it is beyond my own imagination the uses to which he has put it." So *Orientalism* was a very major work, so far the most major work he has done.

critic's need to sustain absolute sovereign independence, unwillingness to join any organized political group, and occasional celebration of betrayal as a guarantee of critical honesty, all these positions mark him as significantly different from more identifiably "Left" political intellectuals. Despite protests to the contrary, he fits into the set of themes and methods that today bear the name of postcolonial theory.[3]

Said was both a poststructuralist and a postcolonial.[4] He united the excitements of radical politics and radical theory.

Few paid much attention when Said condemned terrorism and the "maximalist nationalism" encoded in the Charter of Fatah, which forbade "all solutions which are substitutes for the total liberation of Palestine." In *The Question of Palestine*, Said condemned what he called "the conservative version of the Palestinian quest," by which he meant the desire to push Israel into the sea and other such bluster.[5] He dismissed as theological the position that demanded a return of all land expropriated, bought, or abandoned in 1947–8. He asked the 1983 PNC to "accept the realities of Israel" and asserted that "the liberation of Palestine was neither possible nor really our goal, so why maintain so ludicrous a formula?"[6] As Bruce Robbins once observed, the point of the story Said tells is "the point of 'no return.'"[7] The pun specifies both Said's position on return and his view that history is irreversible.

PLO officials predictably shrugged off Said's remarks as the precious mutterings of an unworldly academic, and they were mildly shocked that a previously good soldier would now be speaking up. The Arab press reported a "'surprise criticism by

Surprise Criticism (in October 1989 Said Went Public: He Criticized PLO Policies and PLO Corruption)

I am worried because we have started to lose the things we achieved and for which we sacrificed. This worry prompted me to say what I want to say. My intention is to indulge in criticism from within, not from without.

It is time we wondered about Palestinian activity in America. Why has the United States become an arena where small Palestinian "stores" are vying for the spoils?... Why is it allowed that this should be an alternative to the formidable political and national task of representing the Palestinian cause in the United States in a clever and logical manner? Because at the end of the day we will succeed if we do this properly.

There are many segments of the (American) public who support us totally, but they haven't been mobilized, they haven't been used, they haven't been asked to do anything. Everything is arranged in small corridors between Tunis and America. They (PLO officials) come and go and that's the end of the story.

We are incapable of effectively using the achievements of the intifada. It's our fault. The Israeli and American governments are our enemies and are acting as such. We must act in a commensurate manner. We cannot say "please talk to us" ... We are weaker and we do not have a strategic ally or armed forces to speak of. What we have is a courageous and creative people whose commitment to the struggle against occupation in the West Bank and Gaza knows no bounds. This is our main resource ... and we must have representatives and a representation that reflect this in a fair and just manner, so that this truth is conveyed to the American arena. This has not happened to date.

What the PLO has not (yet) understood is that the United States as a government, and as a society in general, is hostile to us and that dealing with the United States and American ... institutions requires a knowledge of how these institutions operate and the use of available resources.[8]

an 'insider'" and a "surprise attack on the organization's [PLO's] performance in the United States." PLO officials made some polite concessions. Chairman Arafat invited Said to Tunis to discuss the criticisms. One of Said's intended targets, Hasan Rahman, the ranking PLO dignitary in the United States, was dispatched briefly to Canada, and a few other PLO officials

> **"The Leaders of the PLO are not Sociologists" (The Sharpest of the PLO Intellectuals, Yasser Abedrabbo, was Assigned the Task of Answering Said's Charges)**
>
> Professor Said is not presenting us with a new discovery, but reiterating something that has been obvious to our people for over 40 years.
>
> What is required is the "Palestinization" of the Palestinian community in the United States, not the "Americanization" of the Palestinian leadership in Tunis!
>
> [Said's demand for] "technocrats" [who have] detailed knowledge of American society [are all too easily twisted to undermine the PLO's representative status and] present the PLO as unqualified to hold a dialogue with the U.S. in the first place, and therefore unqualified to represent its people in other forums.... Presenting the matter from the viewpoint that the PLO's problem in its dialogue with America stems from its lack of detailed knowledge of American society can serve goals which may be diametrically opposed to the aims of those who adopt such a position. The leaders of the PLO ... are not sociologists specializing in the American social structure and its decision-making processes, neither are they required to be ... technocrats.
>
> The main lesson of the intifada has been the importance of having confidence in the abilities of our people and their organized forces, and the necessity of nurturing the people's various communities and forces wherever they be in support of the intifada and its aims.[9]

were told that they might be reassigned. For the most part, however, nothing changed. Said was speaking in the tones of the *intifadah*, and the old men in the Tunis-based PLO turned a deaf ear.

A chasm divides the PLO man from the charismatic critic Said. By claiming that Palestinians could gain power in America without bothering to amass knowledge about America, Abedrabbo denied the basic axiom of postcolonial theory. All postcolonial critics agree that power depends on knowledge and vice versa. Said himself brilliantly explicated the power/knowledge dependency, beginning with his account of Napoleon's invasion of Egypt, where the scholars were sent in before the troops.[10] Political realism also places a premium on knowledge. Machiavelli insisted on a leader knowing more than his opponents. The "high degree of unpreparedness of the Palestinian side for what they found at Camp David" in 2000, when U.S. President Clinton tried to force an agreement, "was a problem that has plagued the Palestinians in their international negotiations since the very beginning in the 1920s."[11] PLO ignorance was a fact that no amount of bluster could disguise.

Conversely, the PLO's charge that Said was too subjective is instantly recognizable and entirely correct. His most astute critics, Aijaz Ahmad, James Clifford, Catherine Gallagher, Bart Moore-Gilbert, Dennis Porter, and Robert Young, are as one when they say Said overvalues the unstoppable power of the individual.[12]

The PLO agreed with Said's colleague-poststructuralists: that he wildly overvalued his own individuality.[13] The U.S. Secretary of State turned out to be much shrewder than Said perhaps anticipated. Shultz "knew perfectly well that he had Arafat mesmerized with his carrot of recognition, but he wanted to squeeze out of him an even clearer, sharper and more precise support for the U.S. conditions."[14] Despite his Princetonian-Old-Boy backslapping with Secretary Shultz, charm and force of character were insufficient to change U.S. strategic goals, which were to compromise Arafat, further split him off from the young *intifadah* radicals, and make him entirely dependent for power on

U.S. and Israeli hand-outs. If Said thought he could change all that, then he had too much faith in his charisma.

In short, the PLO seems to have thought that Said was: (1) too far away from the struggle; (2) too ready to believe that he personally could change the course of U.S. policy; (3) acting like an American, not like a Palestinian; and (4) acting like an academic, not like a worldly person. From the PLO's point of view, he had underestimated the science, the magnitude, and the principles of international politics. To the extent they were right, it was a crushing indictment.

More important than the rightness or wrongness, or even the morality, of the parties, Said's showdown with the PLO offers a rare insight into the limits of Said's charisma. The PLO forced three challenges upon Said, and his resolution of each one fashioned an essential plank of postcolonial criticism. First, he showed that identity was a political and historical fact of great moment. Ultimately, he had to decide whether he was a Palestinian or an American, an *intifadah*-supporter or an Arafat-supporter, a young turk or an old bureaucrat. These were tough decisions since, in each case, he was both, born with an American passport and also born to Palestinian parents in Jerusalem. He felt rebellious and "younger" than Arafat "the Old Man," but he also loved dealing with ambassadors and ministers of state. He admired youthful courage but despised youth's callow melodramas and cluelessness. He despised the *shabab* who sat around a dingy apartment waiting for some imaginary deliverance. Second, he came up against his own geographical limits. He objected that the PLO's America Committee had never been to America and did not speak English. The PLO shot back that Said had never lived in Tunis or visited Gaza or Nablus.[15] They despised each other's geographical limitations, which were as undeniable as mailing addresses. That *they had never been here* stoked his anger and frustration. They in turn loathed him because, as Abu-Lughod paraphrased them, "How does he know what kind of crummy place Tunis is?" Ultimately he was forced to admit that he could never live in Palestine ("Perhaps I would find it hard to live there: exile seems to me a more liberated state").¹⁶ For their part, Abedrabbo and Arafat snorted that they had no interest in being sociologists of America. Third and last, his humanism came face-to-face with his Foucaultianism, and they mutually annulled each other. Said's humanistic idealism received its most stunning rebuke when events revealed that no single individual (in this case, himself) can be the agent and instigator of history.¹⁷ By contrast, the PLO asserted an almost Foucaultian view of historical determination. The PLO's worldly realism yielded a more accurate and cynical reading of the limitations on personal initiative and power, and of the Americans' profound material commitment to anti-Palestinian goals. The heroic and charismatic outsider failed to redirect the plodding, anonymous bureaucratic System.

Said's belief that charisma could negate the rules of *realpolitik* proved unfounded. He had been drawn to the PLO in the 1970s when Palestinians "had in some very fundamental way unsettled Lebanon's identity."¹⁸ Now it fundamentally unsettled his own identity. By meeting with the U.S. Secretary of State, by estranging himself from the truly revolutionary Palestinians and helping to co-opt and roll back their tragic and original rebellion, he became like T.E. Lawrence, someone whose heart was in the right place, but whose actions had stolen the victory from youthful fighters and handed it to corrupt old men. The photograph of Said posed as an *intifadah* stone-thrower poignantly illustrates his change of heart—about a decade too late. The tragic irony is that he arrived at the site of the *intifadah* in 2000, not in 1989. By contrast, Fabrizio del Dongo's arrival a day late to Waterloo is a model of timeliness. That the commemorative photograph should pose Said in the heroic diagonal—the classic figuration of "the dying warrior"—is almost unbearable in its historical sarcasm.

Yet in purely academic terms, Said's contradictions, including even the tragic irony of his politics, have proved remarkably productive both for other scholars and for himself.¹⁹

He held fast to his belief in charismatic politics and his rooted loyalty to human rights. Although he fought for these, he could not toughen or coarsen himself to face the real political world.

202 • Dropping the PLO

In his hands, charismatic criticism went as far as it could go. The marriage—strenuous by definition and great because utopian and mad—of literary imagination and practical politics, reached dissolution in the later Edward Said.

"Wonderful Cheeses"

The PLO was profoundly unpopular in the United States, nowhere more so than in New York. This notoriety gave it a louche glamour. Said was heckled or challenged often. The Jewish Defense League vandalized his office. Around that time, while traveling in Spain after graduate school, I impulsively purchased a wheel of Flor de Escueva cheese—dense, delicious, and demurely sweating. It was the size and weight of a bocce ball. I wrapped it to the specifications of the Spanish Officina de Correos and shipped it off addressed to Edward Said, 90 Morningside Drive, relieved that I had expressed my feelings. Long after summer was over, while back teaching in Salina, Kansas, I learned from friends that the arrival of my cheese had caused,

Figure 11.1 A wonderful cheese!

not the expected appreciation for a mildly exotic gift, but perplexity and consternation. The NYPD was duly called, the suspicious object removed by the explosives unit, and my cheese detonated in an armored vehicle. As the years passed, my shame diminished, and I hoped that my thoughtful gesture had been long forgotten. But recently when I reintroduced myself to Mrs. Said, she said, "Oh, Harold. Yes, of course I know you. You are the one who sent those wonderful cheeses."

12
SAID IN HISTORY

The religious or political prophet always preaches to the converted and follows his disciples at least as much as they follow him, since his lessons are listened to and heard only by agents who, by everything they are, have objectively mandated him to give them lessons.

Bourdieu and Passeron, *Reproduction*

Soon after [Said] died, Mariam told this story to me and my wife: "When we first set up house together, my parents' Lebanese housekeeper asked me (this is a traditional question), 'Is your husband a doctor or an engineer?' I told her that he was a teacher. When Edward heard that, he flew into a fury at me. 'I am not a teacher,' he yelled, 'I am a writer, a theorist, a critic.' Then the other day at Columbia, they showed Ric Burns's film about the university and toward the end of it Edward says, 'In the end, that's what I am …'" Here Mariam paused to catch her breath. "A teacher."

Ben Sonnenberg in *Remembering Edward Said*

"Said wasn't even boring." That was the judgment delivered in 2007 by Walid Raad, a young professor and writer wearing a black tee-shirt for his television appearance. It registers a catastrophic loss of Said's personal charisma—perhaps equal to the corresponding rise in his institutional charisma. The verdict may be just. Consider how completely Said's name has become shorthand for righteous resentment and a proud banner carried by scholars determinedly building postcolonial reputations.

Further attrition of personal glamour can be laid to journalistic over-exposure and simplification. Overuse is bound to take the shine off a reputation. But perhaps it is time to amend the familiar view of Said as a gifted critic deformed by the needs of propaganda. Sometimes his work was too openly polemical and coarse-grained, too attached to empty platitudes like *oppositional intellectual* and *speaking truth to power*. These portentous banalities offended the etiquette of post-humanism as well as the canons of clear thought. Too bad! He was still an inventive dynamo and an engine of vitality. He could not hold a coherent political line, but at least he never became a conservative. His liberation politics were as instinctive and anti-totalitarian as Pete Seeger's, but more deeply rooted in the intellectual culture of Europe and the United States. Then why has such a great gap opened to part the live rebel from the dead bore?

Said's career as a provocateur is partly at fault. As an expert inciter, he turned himself into one of the few visible figures of late-century literary culture. By 1970, little in American public life could have been more alien, remote, and irrelevant than literary criticism. Said grasped that the way to attract notice was to generate fresh copy. The papers and newscasters wanted to run sensational pieces on tenured radicals and nutty professors, not orotund rehearsals of intricate semiotics. A brilliant rabble-rouser who had been annealed by years of public conflict, he took his cues from avant-gardist promoters who knew how to get the public worked up about art. He brilliantly combined the American public's appetite for weirdness with its fixation on health and self-help. Thus, when he declared Orientalism to be a silent, creeping disease of the West, the diagnosis tripped a thousand alarms. The Tehran hostage crisis of 1979 suggested that he might have been right in 1978 about Western incomprehension of the Middle East.[1] For the next twenty-five years he remorselessly goaded the one demographic that more than any other comprised the vital center of serious American culture. By egging on the most refined and sensitive intellects in the land, and by flushing out certain liberals' covert double standards, he caused uproar after uproar. No provocateur ever had a better target than Israel: every pebble he threw released an avalanche of rejoinders. The yield of his criticism was easily ten-fold.

But Said became a historic figure in ways that mere controversialists cannot be. Engaging in "particular struggles of a very limited sort" (*WTC* 83) means that these "occasional" (*WTC* 77), "marginal" (*WTC* 77) and "sporty" (*WTC* 77) writings will soon have "disappeared or lost their significance," "will not survive their occasions," and "can pray for no transcendence."[2] Although pouring his energies into ephemera appeared self-defeating for Said's long-term literary reputation, it nonetheless augmented his institutional stature. The university and its society required someone with his academic pedigree at his precise historical moment, for as Said finished Princeton and Harvard and began teaching at Columbia, the institutions of higher education had toppled into social revolution. He had just the right profile to take a commanding role.

In that sense, Said's life offers one of the most vivid narratives of class in the history of American academia: a humanist—and a very great one—inventing the university as it invented him. His revolution was social, symbolic, and permanent. The American university of Woodstock, SDS, and Black Panther rallies may have gone, but a Said-sponsored worldliness remains a defining feature of contemporary departments of English and Comparative Literature. The result is that today one cannot enter an English department without seeing Saids on every hand. The made-to-measure English shoes and the Loden-green cape have gone; the courses on repetition and molestation have been replaced by hybridity seminars and subalternity studies. But to see a young professor range freely across a spate of disciplines is to experience déjà vu and glimpse Said drawing his far-flung parallels and defying the cult of expertise. His scorn of disciplinary border-fences has become the expected transgression underlying all Cultural Studies. A talk on "Instant Global Distribution and the Future of Thought" or "Literary Studies as a Symptom in the Pedagogical Space" recalls Said's demand for a more worldly perspective.[3] A book such as Andreas Huyssen's

Other Cities, Other Worlds or Chenxi Tang's *The Geographic Imagination of Modernity* summons up the macaronic variety of Said's *Beginnings*, just as Laura Winkiel's *Modernism, Race, and Manifestos* or Frederic Spotts' *The Shameful Peace: How French Artists and Intellectuals Survived the Nazi Occupation* will make some remember Said's *Politics of Dispossession* and *Representations of the Intellectual*.[4] Whether Said initiated this change or an institutional need produced him is unimportant. What matters is that he was among those who restored charisma and gave direction to the departments of English and Comparative Literature.

Said entered the disciplinary fray just at the moment when donnish, well-mannered English departments decided to become insurgent enclaves of interdisciplinary raiders. A helpful simplification would be to say that Said allied himself strategically with mutinous post-structural French-trained theorists and then, once the tottering *ancien régime* had succumbed to their joint assault, turned against his erstwhile deconstructive allies. The issue of that subsequent contest now is clear. In the words of one prominent historian of criticism, Said's position has won:

> Could it be that Said is out of touch with the fact that his side in the struggle for hegemony in the profession has won? Can he not know that his legions—the partisans of experience, particularly when the experience is of dislocation, alienation, and the exile occasioned by differences in identity and the politics derived therefrom—are in power?[5]

The social revolution he helped bring about could be shown in an unflattering light. One radical critic, Aijaz Ahmad, who left the American academy in protest, accused Said of strangling the incipient Marxist revival of the 1970s in its cradle. "The subalternist project," as Said defines it, Ahmad wrote, is "an upper-class émigré phenomenon at odds with its own class origins and metropolitan location."[6] In other words, those who gave lip service to subalterns flew business class. Ahmad argued that Said had prepared academic careers-in-the-waiting for "typical upper-layer bourgeois" professors from abroad. The professors and many of the graduate students who entered the field begun by Said all tend to possess the same cultural capital: "the class privilege, the presumed oppositional and beleaguered situation, the technical ability to collaborate as well as compete, the professional location—of the more privileged sections of the incoming immigrant in the United States" (Ahmad 1992: 210–211). Minus Ahmad's sarcasm, however, this is a rousing brief for Said as Gramsci's organic intellectual—an honorable category assigned to those who articulate the self-awareness and political program of the emerging social group to which they belong. The problem for Marxists like Ahmad is that Said was organic to a revolutionary cadre that was, by third-world standards, filthy rich.

Part of its wealth was the cultural capital attached to language fluency. Said earned the right to represent this class by giving language proficiency glamour and symbolic value. Whereas a command of multiple languages hardly raised the social status of a Levantine merchant in, say, Tripoli, Said persistently made "many languages" his rallying cry and an absolute standard of academic excellence. Now cultural capital was to rest principally in a student's or a professor's command of multiple languages. The banner of "many languages" was raised as early as Said and Maire Kurick's translation of Auerbach on *Weltliterature*, and again when Said posted a notice as a preface to *Beginnings* that reads, in part:

A NOTE ON TRANSLATIONS
I must explain my policy on translation. Every text not in English (with the exception of those in Russian) I have studied in the original language. Wherever possible, however, I quote from an already published English translation, which I have checked against the original. In instances where there is no translation available or where the translation in my opinion is inadequate, I have made my own (sometimes mainly literal) translation. The reader is therefore to understand that unless otherwise indicated translations are my own ...

(B xvii)

As the first text in an avant-garde book, this note had the air of a manifesto. Today, one of the principal markers of academic status is proficiency in a variety of languages; the more global and the further from English, the weightier their symbolic value.

Why was Said able to convince his students of the unlikely proposition that he was subversive, someone who was barely getting away with his sabotages under a cloak of bespoke tailoring? Simply this. We wanted to be outsiders. Said convinced us that we were. Along with languages goes worldliness, particularly an exile's sense of always being on the move, with a packed bag under the bed and a passport—real or faked—sitting on the dresser. Ahmad mordantly calls this "the presumed oppositional and beleaguered situation" of the post-colonial critic, a pure affectation in so spoiled and privileged a cohort (Ahmad 1992: 210). But it should not be dismissed so casually. Critics are beleaguered, if not economically then as members of English departments "bleakly marooned," as Terry Eagleton put it, in the "extravagantly philistine, money-obsessed society" of the United States.[7] Instead of a forced migration, this sort of "exile" is affective and intellectual. But it is in some sense real.

The class in which I first heard about Gramsci in 1977 was assigned to meet in 620 Hamilton Hall—the Amsterdam Avenue end, opposite the campus-quad where Said's classes usually met. "*This* is the way they get back at us," he exploded as he walked into the room:

> They put us in an impossible room, the worst in the building. It's because they know what we're reading—Gramsci, Fanon, black men, liberation thinkers and poets. Is that so intolerable? The University wants the fire trucks to drown out the lectures!

This diatribe was presented to the assembled class, which included the future academostar Cornel West, sitting in his vintage three-piece pinstripe suit with a toddler on his lap. Said convinced me that we stood on the front line of some sort of battle.

Against all the odds for 1977, Said sustained a 1968-level of excitement by pretending that we were all holding an imperiled, vaguely clandestine cell meeting, although in fact it was an ordinary class offering spelled out in IBM lettering in the Registrar's list of courses. The clandestinity was an illusion; the excitement was not. The samizdat handouts and the extempore quality of the lectures and blackboard work all confirmed the underground sensation, as did the fact that we—at least I—had never heard of Gramsci and never read Fanon. Said's vivacity of argument matched that of the revolutionary readings.

Said made his impression, converted his ephebes, and sent forth his newly minted troops to fight his battles not in the guise of a controversialist, but in his capacity as a university teacher, one whose charisma was personal and institutional. He wasn't just another journalist or pundit. The power of performance that distinguished him was better seen in the class- or seminar-room. His stuttery, free-style expositions of his own terms like *beginning, originality, inauguration, authority, molestation, affiliation, late style,* and *extreme occasion*—each term sprouting links to the others—suggested Coltrane or Jackson Pollock. Such performances sounded well in a closed room filled with rapt students. They were inconceivable under the static glare of polemicists and the press. But even under Kleig lights, he was a personage, a physical presence that evoked responses from one's own body. Louis Menand once wrote that Said was like Cary Grant: both would have cut a figure anywhere. Said was neither a film idol nor a coolie rebel. He was a teacher.

A professor addressing a classroom of students: can local knowledge ever be more occasional, transient, and throwaway? Said's principled embrace of mobility had its geographical form in his refusal ever to buy an apartment; intellectually he embodied it in his devotion to writing occasional essays and teaching. "Above all, neither pianist nor essayist can offer final readings, however definitive their performances might be," he observed; "[t]he fundamental sportiness of both genres is what keeps them honest, as well as vital" (*RoE* 229). Just as he never owned an apartment, so also he never acquired title to a theory. For him theory was just another notation to be realized in performance—exactly like a playscript. His pessimistic essay "Traveling

Students Remembering Said[8]

Edward was an extraordinary teacher in class, as he spoke, folding and unfolding his bifocals, opening and closing beautiful pens, glancing at discussion notes written out in hotel stationery from his latest journey. He made his students feel that we were in a world in high definition, that we were at the lucid heart of something.... Despite his overwhelming and charismatic presence, he helped you think and to think that intellectual work mattered urgently.
(Ann Dopico: 38)

Even if you ran into him on the street altogether by chance, he induced the sense that you must not let your mind atrophy by irrelevant or superfluous thinking, inspiring you with the pleasure of every moment.
(Stathis Gourgouris: 48)

Among the Orthodox Jewish students like myself at Columbia College, studying with Edward Said, a man so identified with the Palestinian cause, had the added allure of verging on an encounter with the Other. Yet Edward's Otherness quickly dissolved under the force of his intelligence with its appealing directness, lack of pretension, and the unexpected generosity with which Edward engaged students without a hint of condescension.
(David Stern: 95)

He had the extraordinary ability to be perfectly comfortable around power, to consort chattily with the Columbia brass, hang out at Ivy League campus clubs, or rub shoulders with dignitaries, and then turn around and act with me or his other students with a disarming boyishness marked by the genuine and unguarded excitement of debate. He was very playful, charming, prodding, and had an impish sense of humor.
(Timothy Brennan: 17)

Theory" shows ideas losing their force as they "travel" further from their point and moment of origin. Lukács and Genet have their thoughts diluted by later thinkers. Mutability molests all things under the moon. No theory has a fixed address; all are prey to the deformations wrought by changing societies, not to mention internal debates amongst the theory's practitioners.

If what attracted Said was the sportiness and for-the-nonce quality in theories and essays, he must have felt the same magnetism in teaching. Teaching is perhaps the most transient of intellectual genres, the one that leaves the least material or visible traces. After every class, you wipe the blackboard clean. These conditions render it all the more exciting, spendthrift, and aristocratic. It is truly the intellectual equivalent of royalty throwing money out of windows.

The question imposes itself: how good is this lesson for notably non-aristocratic students? If a local critic, a Said or a Swift, cavalierly throws away hope for transcendence and pours all energy into passing, soon-to-be-forgotten events, what sort of toolkit or blueprint does such a role model pass along to students and followers? In part, it must be a self-destructive one. Said left a considerable dossier on the topic, not only in the interviews conducted by former students, who always seemed to be coming back for more, or the indirect homages paid in books by former students and colleagues.[9] His views come up continually in his published commentary on other critics. The French philosopher Kojève's "famous lectures and seminars on Hegel seemed to have formed an entire generation" (*RoE* 188) and—admiringly—Foucault's "courses at the Collège drew large audiences, to whom he returned the compliment by actually preparing his lectures, always researching them exhaustively, delivering them with appropriate formality and respect in the best tradition of the *cours magistrale*" (*RoE* 193).

Said left his own solid legacy of sorts. He planted the postcolonial argument before the Reagan/Thatcher times ever began. But for the most part his students misunderstood or distorted his work. He had his disciples and knights errant, and he spoke of leaving a toolkit for others to use. Certainly his students and his readers have produced extraordinary works. Bruce Robbins' *Secular Vocations* and *Upward Mobility and the Common Good*, for example, develops and transmogrifies Said's theories about the social and political meaning of a scholarly career. But it would be more correct to say that for Robbins, Brennan, Viswanathan, and Wicke, the work of Said functioned just as Oscar Wilde thought prior work should: as the starting point for a new creation.

Indeed, how could it have been otherwise? Said's blueprints resembled M.C. Escher's drawings of impossible objects. His maps and directions were contradictory and blurred, and he pushed acolytes away as much as he drew them to his breast.[10] Robbins detected something important when he wrote that Said, the fierce public defender of anti-professionalism, was devoted to professional ideologies of local action and absolute practitioner autonomy.[11] Said's interest in locations and local effort seemed to oppose his support for the placeless, universal "oppositional" intellectual.[12] I would take this idea further: just as professions form an enclave of independent actors cradled within larger institutions that demand obedient conformity, so English departments form a still more unfettered zone within the already relatively autonomous profession of professors. Said admitted that "literary departments play a necessary conservative or curatorial role," but he pressed the English department to attend "at least as much to the discrepancies and dissonances of human experiences, as it [does] to its routinely compartmentalized stabilities" (*RoE* 169). The oldest Saidian dilemma, that of autonomy within institutions, returns with redoubled force. However monitored or state-mandated or committee-decided a course syllabus might be, a teacher amidst students behind closed doors is finally on his or her own. Said relished the classroom as the last redoubt of perfect autonomy.

Predictably contradictory, Said, the most visible campaigner against professionalism, became president of that great turbine of professionalization, the Modern Language Association of America, 38,000 strong and the professors' equivalent of the American Medical Association and the American Bar Association. He fought to obtain the crown, as it were, even as he demanded an end to monarchy. Robbins tells us that, like other literary critics, Said is "used to playing with the possibilities for indeterminacy and polyphony," but in his case an "unlikely complicity" occurs: "the duplication by the critic of an object strenuously criticized."[13] Robbins is spot on. The critic who duplicates the object he criticizes collapses the self into the self's satiric target. The eternal model is Swift, who leeches energy from the satiric victim on whom he has vampirically battened—and recall that Count Dracula gave his victims perpetual life. Said received powerful transfusions from the utterly new books and authors he introduced. Students prefer what is new to what is old, and he won lasting loyalty from Michael Sprinker and Bruce Robbins, for example, by alerting them to the very existence of the thinkers (Lukács, Gramsci, Althusser) who would shape their politics, fuel their careers, and transform their lives.

It bears repeating that, for quite a few years, Said was all alone in transmitting the continental theory revolution. Students from the late 1960s and 1970s routinely refer to "Edward Said, at the time the only tenured member of Columbia's English department on speaking terms with French theory."[14] And it bears remembering that English departments were quick to grab the mantel of revolutionary leadership, proclaiming themselves the safe-house of resistance and subversion. Theory identified itself as "a technique of trouble," and Said repeated that phrase in his essays and in class: a supposed adjunct, supplement, parasite, or frame becomes indispensable, central, substantial.[15] Deconstruction even pretended to have the kind of historical inevitability that used to be claimed by Marxism: deconstructive reading of any given passage "has to go against the grain of what one would want to happen in the name of what has to happen" (de Man, *Critical Writing*, 221–222; in Guillory 1993: 231). Said made the classroom into an extreme occasion, the ultimate example of local knowledge. Its ephemerality was the essence of the experience. "The time period for killing a bull should never extend beyond fifteen or twenty minutes," he had learned from Hemingway, "for after that the bull learns to distinguish between an artfully deployed cape and the solid reality of a man's body" (*RoE* 236). Approaching every class like a torero, Said made the lesson "an extremely limited site of intensity, irreversible in its processes, precisely calibrated in its space for maneuver" (*RoE* 236). The bulls, needless to say, always went for the cape.

Just as Said placed himself—sympathetic, ironic—inside and outside the MLA and the profession, or inside and outside the PLO, he taught his students to operate in the same way. Those who would understand and profit by his example must take up positions inside and outside the charismatic presence of Said himself. He provided no models to follow, and if you aped him you were bound to get him wrong. The price of admission to Said's search for liberation was pretty high. You had to live with a kind of instability, an extraordinary volatility, the sinking sensation of falling through traps. You groped methodologically in the dark. You abandoned all known ways of doing scholarship. You had to write in unacceptable styles. It was a heavy tax to pay for self-respect. It was what quite a few students wanted, however, and Said stepped forward to provide it.[16]

One of Said's lessons involved the dignity of teaching. Research is serious. Writing is serious. Even giving invited lectures is serious. But teaching is merely the machinery of academe. It belongs to the NCTE, the CCCC, and the AWP—acronyms that, like the unintentionally eloquent WAC, suggest the populist anti-intellectualism of that branch of the profession. Said reversed this proportion. He undid the antithesis between pedagogy and performance.

His personal glamour was somehow transmitted over to the space of teaching. Said's charisma dazzled the "Generation of '68," my generation. He was already an impressive master of public personality, a moneyed, prepped, polished, upper-crust American prince. Mercurial to the point of instability, he was making and remaking himself before our eyes, now an intense cerebral theorist, now a sidekick of guerrillas, statesmen, and thugs. The gears screamed as he slammed into reverse and

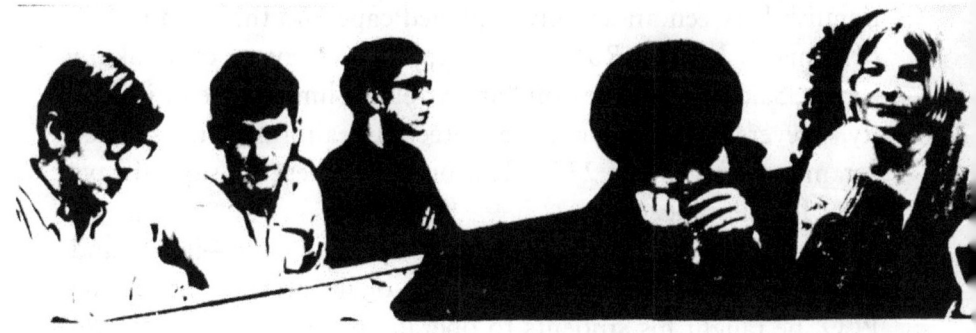

WMHT proudly presents Generation '68 for your entertainment and edification. This series of 15 one-hour programs will premiere Monday, February 5, at 8:00 p.m. Generation '68 is a unique idea in local programing as it will be the product of teenagers, for teenagers. Forty-eight high school students from Channel 17's signal area have joined forces to script, staff, and star in a show featuring both serious discussion and showcased talent. The student team feels that they have something important to say about life from their perspective — about their peers, their problems, their hopes and dreams. The series was conceived as a way in which WMHT could partially fulfill a desire and a need to serve the potentially large 12-20 audience with significant programing.

The project was launched at an information-discussion session held on Thursday evening, October 26, ı the auditorium of the Channel 17 facility in Riverside School, Schenectady. The three staff members present — Erik Van de Bogart, Manager of School Services; Cora Jane Hurlburt, Assistant Manager of School Services; and Jack Finch, Program Manager — were prepared for the unexpected and were met with youthful enthusiasm and a wide variety of talents. The following school districts have chosen to involve students in the experiment: Amsterdam, Averill Park, Ballston Spa, Berne-Knox, Bishop Gibbons, Burnt Hills-Ballston Lake, Cardinal McCloskey, Cohoes, Colonie, Columbia, Duanesburg, Draper, Guilderland, Heatly (Green Island), Johnstown, Linton, Middleburgh, Milne, Mohonasen, Mont Pleasant, Notre Dame, Perth, Schalmont, St. Columba's, St. Joseph's, Scotia-Glenville, Shaker, and Troy.

Meetings during the next three months familiar-

Figure 12.1 The author in 1968 (source: *The Albany Times-Union*).

ized the group with various aspects of a television production and helped to develop ideas concerning the direction of the series. A three-day workshop session held during Christmas vacation gave our budding entretreneurs an opportunity to work with staff professionals in graphics, writing, the studio and control room before the brushes, cameras, and switchboards were turned over to them. The group was also split into two complete production teams so responsibility could be divided and programs prepared on an alternate-week basis. Flexibility has been assured by allowing students with multiple interests or talents to play dual roles, such as writing and directing, or graphics and talent.

Video taping began on the morning of Saturday, January 13, with a three-hour rehearse, tape, and critique session that yielded the opening program. It is devoted to an introduction to the idea behind Generation '68 and its metamorphosis with segments taken from pre-production meetings and workshops, plus comments from key members of the team. Among them are Eugene Beaudoin of Shaker, Steve Tocco of Mohonasen, and Harold Veeser of Guilderland who will explain how they feel about being involved in the series and what they hope to give as well as gain. The final half hour of the show will be live, using the phone-in technique of Telecon. The teens of Generation '68 invite their viewing audience to telephone both questions and comments to the panel which will be present on their debut evening. Two succeeding programs, already in various stages of completion, spotlight changing teenage values and mores, and the use and misuse of drugs among teenagers. Tune in "17" for an hour that will really turn you on.

Charisma in Performance[17]

After Edward died, I could hear his voice, the cut and thrust of it; I still can. He was such a striking figure to look at that it took his disappearance from the field of outward vision to make plain to me how vivid and compelling he was simply to listen to.... The tune of Edward's thought, as it came down the telephone or across a table or a sofa, was a kind of passionate musical interrogatory: he drew you utterly into the key of his mood, the tenor of his argument, the fascination of the words' sequence and pattern.

(Marina Warner: 105)

All utterances seemed confidences, I felt (even when he broke off for an intermittent word with his apparently numberless friends and acquaintances), that I was in the privileged realm of knowing and being known. I can't imagine that this experience was mine alone.

(Allen Bergson: 11)

With his handsome elegance, his fierce and competitive intelligence, his famously demanding theoretical rigor, he already exuded the kind of charisma that drew disciples. Even then, before he became an international celebrity, there was something about him larger than life.

(David Stern: 95)

Edward was not a politician. He was charming and articulate, gentlemanly and courteous, but it did not come naturally to him to be politic or diplomatic. He spoke his mind, even if what he said was sometimes wounding or harsh. It was this frankness and candor, his hatred of hypocrisy and cant, and the lucidity of his mind, that made generations of young people love him.

(Rashid Khalidi: 60)

transformed the Princeton man into a Palestinian Arab. Because he did nothing halfway and was an essentially amiable and sociable man, he invited us to tune in and see what would happen. His students demanded to be in an exclusive club of outsiders and rebels, and Said replied, "Look how shiny, how intriguing you are, not because of what you have been up till now, but for the infinite possibilities of what you might become." It was a thrilling message, and a lot of Said's students took it deeply to heart.

Abjuring the macho temptations to preen and dominate, Said's real impact lay in his humility. My favorite passage in all of his work is a brief sketch of a college friend, Hanna Mikhail, whom Said defines as "always an exceptionally decent, quiet, and intellectually brilliant man."[18] We learn that Hanna (John) was almost a double of himself. He was exactly Said's age and Palestinian by birth, his family being "firmly rooted in the Quaker community of Ramallah [on the West Bank]." Like Said, he went to America, in Hanna's case to attend Haverford College. Then he became, in quick succession, a professor at the University of Washington, the chief information officer for the PLO in Beirut, and a bullet-filled corpse on a Lebanese street. In a powerful, understated passage, Said describes how Hanna ran a meeting he had arranged for him with the canonical Modernist writer, Jean Genet.

> Hanna remained fairly quiet throughout; he later told me that he had wanted to let me feel the full force of Genet's special vision of things without distraction, and hence his—Hanna's—relative withdrawal. Later I was able to read back into that gesture some of the forgiving permission that Hanna had given everyone around him, and how that permission to let people be themselves was the true focus of Hanna's search for liberation. Certainly it was clear that Genet appreciated this aspect of his companion's political mission; it was the deep bond between them, that both men in effect had united passion and an almost self-abnegating tolerance.[19]

I gasped when I read this, thinking, "Said is Hanna." The anarchic threat lightly concealed by the phrase "let people be themselves," the setting as a protected, semi-secret enclosure, the anti-corporate drive behind any "search for liberation," the avowal of deep bonds, passion, and self-abnegation—all this may hearken back to the early Christian cells and Weber's version of Jesus Christ. But it was also the terrifically appealing magic of academic life. Here one might walk into class hungover and picking sleep from the eyes, trudging through a daytime routine, and walk out like St. Paul headed for Damascus, consumed with sudden excitement and mystery. All the themes of this book come through in Hanna: the humanism defined as letting people be themselves; the inseparability of personal and political liberation; the love of excellence and the spirited encounter of superior minds; the crucial role of the enabler. Tolerance and permission occupy the center of this portrait. Charisma is small as well as big, and in this passage, the murmur of intimacies displaces the grand standings and combats that seemed the heart of Said. No less than his mocking comebacks and his relish for life in the big arenas, Said's acquaintances remember him as a kind of Hanna, someone selfless enough to drift quietly into the background, who steps aside and takes pleasure in another's self-fulfillment.

Notes

1. The Charisma of Edward Said

1. Max Weber, *On Charisma and Institution Building*, ed. S.N. Eisenstadt, Chicago: University of Chicago Press, 1968.
2. John Gillory, *Cultural Capital: The Problem of Literary Canon Formation*, Chicago and London: University of Chicago Press, 1993, 244. All references are to this edition.
3. The title of Barbara Johnson's essay about the disheartening decline of one inspired critical method ("Nothing Fails Like Success") conveys her acceptance of the Weberian assumption that institutional success is the end of charismatic excitement.

   > As soon as any radically innovative thought becomes an ism, its specific ground-breaking force diminishes, its historical notoriety increases, and its disciples tend to become more simplistic, more dogmatic, and ultimately more conservative, at which time its power becomes institutional rather than analytical. The fact that what is loosely called deconstructionism is now being widely institutionalized in the United States seems to me both intriguing and paradoxical, but also a bit unsettling, although not for the reasons advanced by most of its opponents.
   >
   > (*A World of Difference*, Baltimore: Johns Hopkins University Press, 1987, 11; quoted in Guillory 1993: 241)

4. Describing this "immense enterprise of *symbolic alchemy*," Bourdieu notes

   > [t]he constitution of an unprecedented ensemble of institutions for recording, conserving and analyzing works (reproductions, catalogues, art magazines, museums acquiring the most recent works, etc.), the growth in personnel (full-time or part-time) dedicated to the celebration of the work of art, the intensification of the circulation of works and of artists with the great international exhibitions and the multiplication of galleries with many branches in various countries, etc.—everything combines to favour the establishment of an unprecedented relationship between the interpreters and the work of art.
   >
   > ("The Market for Symbolic Goods," in Randal Johnson, ed., *The Field of Cultural Production: Essays on Art and Literature*, New York and Chichester, West Sussex: Columbia University Press, 1993, 170)

5. Bourdieu, "Market for Symbolic Goods," 167.
6. Bourdieu, "The Literate Tradition and Social Conservation," in Pierre Bourdieu and Jean-Claude Passeron, *Reproduction: In Education, Society and Culture*, tr. Richard Nice, London and Beverly Hills: Sage Publications, 1977, 125.
7. Norman Finkelstein, interview by Harold Veeser. Finkelstein is author of *The Rise and Fall of Palestine: A Personal Account of the Intifada Years*, Minneapolis: University of Minnesota Press, 1996, among other works on Palestine, Israel, and the Jewish Holocaust.
8. Weber, *On Charisma*, 29.
9. In matters of magic it is not so much a question of knowing what the specific properties of the magician are, or those of instruments, operations, and magical representations, but of determining the foundation of the collective belief, or, better, of the *collective misrecognition*, collectively produced and maintained, which is at the source of the power that the magician appropriates.
   ("Market for Symbolic Goods," 169).
10. Chapter 5 of *Beginnings* is devoted to Foucault and Derrida, as is "Criticism Between Culture and System," first published in the criticism flagship journal *Critical Inquiry* and later revised as Chapter 9 in *WTC*, 178–225.
11. At first glance, Vico might appear to confirm Marxist determinism. In *The New Science*, abridged translation of the Third Edition (1744), eds. Thomas Goddard Bergin and Max Harold Fisch, Ithaca and London: Cornell University Press, 1970, paragraph 238, p. 36, he avers that "the order of ideas must follow the order of institutions," a statement close to the most notoriously deterministic and materialist passages in Marx's oeuvre. Yet Vico considered language a material force that mediated between economics and culture. In this perception he was original.
12. Vico's example is thunder, which the first men and women designated as angry speech uttered by some gigantic invisible man. Syllogism and sorites were two types of chains of reasoning Vico knew from classical thought, and they had no part in the "poetic logic" of primitive humanity. See Hayden White, *The Tropics of History: Essays in Cultural Criticism*, Baltimore and London: Johns Hopkins University Press, 1978, 204. "Sorites: 'A series of propositions in which the predicate of each is the subject of the next, the conclusion being formed of the first subject and the last predicate' (Mansel)" (*Oxford English Dictionary*, 446).
13. Edward Said, "Michel Foucault, 1927–1984," *Raritan: A Quarterly Review*, 4.2, Fall 1984; rpt. *RoE*, 196.
14. Edward W. Said, "Vico on the Discipline of Bodies and Texts," *Modern Language Notes*, 91, October 1976, 814–826; rpt. *RoE*, 85–86.
15. Said even preferred Vico's radically negative account of reason to that of his other favorite thinker, Jonathan Swift. Swift's satiric formulation of humans as merely animals capable of reason (*capax rationis*) preserved the high status and beneficial power of reason, but Vico proposed an extraordinarily radical reversal of Enlightenment prejudice, which had elevated reason to godly heights. For him, human language, specifically

human speech, caused reason to evolve out of feeling, humans out of beasts, and society out of chaos. But the active agent was poetic, creative, imaginative, and irrational human speech, not rational abstract thought.

16. The parts [of rhetoric], as most authorities have stated, are Invention, Arrangement, Expression, Memory, Delivery. Invention is the discovery of valid or seemingly valid arguments to render one's cause plausible. Arrangement is the distribution of arguments thus discovered in the proper order. Expression is the fitting of the proper language to the invented matter and words. Delivery is the control of voice and body in a manner suitable to the dignity of the subject and the style.
(Cicero, *De Inventione* I, vii, 8)

17. Guillory 1993: 264, draws a telling parallel between Theory's "supplementing of the literary syllabus at the level of graduate school and composition's practice of displacing it at the entry level of university study."
18. Said's many studies of Palestinian politics differ insubstantially from Clifford Geertz's thick descriptions. Certainly, he was familiar with literary approaches using interpretive anthropology, including those that became literary New Historicism. He read Stephen Greenblatt's seminal New Historicist essay, "Improvisation and Power," in 1978 and introduced it to The English Institute, an organization of scholars self-described as "a major resource for recent developments in criticism, theory, and scholarship, without neglecting traditional fields of interest and modes of literary analysis."
19. When the West–Eastern Divan, the Arab–Israeli youth orchestra that Said and Barenboim assembled in 1999, played again in August 2008 in Paris, its performance of Schoenberg Opus 31 and act one of *Die Walkyrie* stood at an immense remove from the grinding political realities that have worn down the residents of Jabaliya, Jenin, Shatila, and the other refugee slums.
20. Edward W. Said, *On Late Style: Music and Literature Against the Grain*, New York: Pantheon, 2006, 8.
21. Hippolyte-Adolphe Taine, qtd. *Norton Anthology of English Literature, Vol. 2*, 4th edition, ed. M.H. Abrams, *et al.*, New York and London: W.W. Norton, 1979, 506. Taine is speaking of Byron.
22. The type recurs in Trilling's early fiction. He appears as Hettner in "Impediments" (*The Menorah Journal*, 1925), and in a later story, "Of This Time, of That Place" (*Partisan Review*, 1943), we have "Tertan"—a near-anagram of Hettner.
23. The critic Morris Dickstein, "Foreword," *Lionel Trilling and the Critics: Opposing Selves*, ed. John Rodden, Lincoln and London: University of Nebraska Press, 1999, xxiii, writes that, as Trilling's student, he was simply "too Jewish" for Trilling.
24. Lionel Trilling, "Impediments," *The Menorah Journal* (1925), rpt. in Lionel Trilling, *Of This Time, Of That Place, and Other Stories* (1979).
25. His memoir, *Out of Place*, revealed that he was in fact ill at ease but learned to disguise it, for example, by looking at the bridge of the nose rather than into the eyes of his interlocutors and students.

26. Edward W. Said, "Cairo Recalled," *House and Garden*, April 1987, 20, 24, 28, 32.
27. Op. cit., 32.

2. Beginning Again

1. Samuel Weber, "The Intersection: Marxism and the Philosophy of Language," *diacritics* 15.4, 1985, 111; quoted in Young, *White Mythologies*, 129. Joseph Conrad, letter to Robert Cunninghame Graham in G. Jean-Aubry, *Joseph Conrad, Life & Letters*, 2 vols., Garden City: Doubleday, Page and Co., 1927, I. 216.
2. Walid Raad and Jalal Toufic, "The Withdrawal of Tradition Past a Surpassing Disaster," United Nations Plaza Broadcast: Seminar 3, opening lecture, January 31, 2007 (http://unp.kein.org/v2v?page=1).
3. Timothy Brennan, "Places of Mind, Occupied Lands: Edward Said and Philology," in Michael Sprinker, ed., *Edward Said: A Critical Reader*, Oxford: Blackwell, 1992, 75.
4. Said's political ally and mentor, Ibrahim Abu-Lughod, told me outright in my interview with him, Evanston, Illinois, December 29, 1991, "Edward is very impatient."
5. Edward Said, "Swift's Tory Anarchy" and Said, "Swift as Intellectual," *WTC*, 54–89.
6. *Interviews with Edward W. Said*, eds. Amritjit Singh and Bruce G. Johnson, Jackson: University Press of Mississippi, 2004, 231, 90. Comparable examples appear throughout the interviews: "I'm interested in people who are unsystematic" (*Interviews* 31); "[I'm] trying to maintain a certain kind of tension without resolving dialectically" (*Interviews* 158); "I responded to [James] Clifford that inconsistency was very important, because I hate systems" (*Interviews* 237).
7. Bill Ashcroft and Pal Ahluwalia, *Edward Said: The Paradox of Identity*, London and New York: Routledge, 1999.
8. Later, in *The World, the Text, and the Critic*, Said extended the idea of imprisonment to encompass the notion of repetition as a kind of bondage. Quoting from Conrad's novel, *The Secret Agent*, a description of the mentally disabled boy Stevie drawing "a coruscating whirl of circles" that effectively bound him to the page, he added:

   > I think it entirely likely that Conrad imagined Stevie as a kind of writer viewed *in extremis* who, in being taken for a sort of pointless idiot, is limited terribly to two poles: inscribing a page endlessly or blown to bits and without human identity.
   >
   > (*WTC* 97)

9. Edward Neill, "Critical Condition," *Times Educational Supplement*, October 12, 1984, 32 (review of *The World, the Text, and the Critic*).
10. *The Edward Said Reader*, eds. Moustafa Bayoumi and Andrew Rubin, New York: Random House, 2000, 3.
11. The true ambivalences of Conrad, however, seem to me to lie in questions of form rather than abstractable political content.... I'm just an old-fashioned product of the Cambridge English School. Just as

Edward Said was an old-fashioned product of Lionel Trilling's Columbia.

(Terry Eagleton, "Edward Said, Cultural Politics and Critical Theory (An Interview)," *Alif Journal of Comparative Poetics*, 25, 2005, 262)

12. Gayatri Chakravorty Spivak, "The New Historicism: Political Commitment and the Postmodern Critic," in Veeser, ed., *The New Historicism*, New York and London: Routledge, 1989; rpt. Gayatri Chakravorty Spivak, *The Post-Colonial Critic: Interviews, Strategies, Dialogues*, ed. Sarah Harasym, New York and London, 1990.
13. Theory passivity cast doubt on the knowability and controllability of human motivation (Freud's id, Marx's class, Nietzsche's discourse, etc.). Biographical passivity (a tough father, confusing mother, bullies at school) caused fear and self-doubt. National passivity meant exile, estrangement, disgrace, and defeat. Thus, Said's work is riddled with extermination of the subject by post-structuralism, childhood experiences that only psychoanalysis could (and did) competently deal with, and various deterministic systems invented by people on the left.
14. I can't identify with a Marxist party here. I can't identify with a Marxist rhetoric here.... It would therefore be presumptuous for me to say, well, I identify with the Marxism of Lukács, or the Marxism of Adorno. They all strike me as interesting, perhaps historically important texts, but no more than that.

("Interview with Edward Said," *Edward Said: A Critical Reader*, ed. Michael Sprinker, Oxford and Cambridge, MA: Blackwell, 1992, 261)

15. Edward Said, "Traveling Theory," in *WTC* 234.
16. Georg Lukács, *The Theory of the Novel*, trans. Anna Bostock, Cambridge, MA: MIT Press, 1971.
17. Hayden White, *Metahistory: The Historical Imagination in Nineteenth-Century Europe*, Baltimore and London: Johns Hopkins University Press, 1973, 160.

Michelet grasped the essential point that Vico had made about any specifically historical conception of human reality—namely, that the forces which are overcome in any advance in society or consciousness themselves serve as the materials out of which the new society and consciousness will be fashioned.

18. Said, *PolD* 128.
19. "[H]e put his son up to something basically illegal ... [M]y father's ostensible indifference to my fate ... led to my being banned from the one city in the world in which I felt more or less at home" (*OofP* 288).
20. "My own first marriage was a short-lived and unhappy one" (*OofP* 255).

3. Emergence
1. Introduction to Michelet's translation of Vico's *The New Science*.
2. Northrop Frye, *Anatomy of Criticism*, Princeton: Princeton University Press, 1957, 163.

3. The theorists Said evokes make their brief or lengthy appearances only to be superseded, set aside, as if he were saying, "Well, I dealt with that one. Who's next!"
4. *The New Science of Giambattista Vico*, eds. Thomas Goddard Bergin and Max Harold Fisch (Abridged Translation of the Third Edition, 1744), sec. IV, paragraph 408, Ithaca and London: Cornell University Press, 1970, 90.
5. *New Science*, sec. II, paragraph 400, in Bergin and Fisch, 85.
6. *New Science*, sec. II, paragraph 386, in Bergin and Fisch, 80.
7. Jeffrey J. Williams, "Name Recognition," *the minnesota review*, NS 52–54, 2001, 185–208.
8. Richard Klein, "That He Said That Said Said," *Enclitic*, 2, 1, Spring 1978, 85–86.
9. Klein, 88, considers Vico "less used than venerated" by Said.
10. David Gorman, "The Worldly Text: Writing as Social Action, Reading as Historical Reconstruction," in Joseph Natoli, ed., *Literary Theory's Future(s)*, Urbana and Chicago: University of Illinois Press, 1989, 185.
11. Gorman concludes that

    this self-production is the image of all intellectual activity for Said.... Moreover, though it is the foundation of culture and the source of spiritual values, the mind is a product of one material process—namely, its own self-creation—among others. It is to be understood not as a result of divine ordination but as arising from poor, uncertain, and indeed accidental circumstances. Moreover, before it becomes anything so sophisticated as intellection, consciousness is an affair of will (Vico's *conatus*); and, no matter how rarefied its activities become, its permanent condition remains one of struggle.

    (Gorman, "The Worldly Text," 185)

12. Richard Poirier, *The Performing Self: Compositions and Decompositions in the Languages of Contemporary Life*, London and New York: Oxford University Press, 1971, vii. All references to Poirier's work are from this volume. Poirier was more important to Said than anyone has supposed. He was an English professor at Harvard while Said studied there, and Said dedicated his last book, *Humanism and Democratic Criticism*, to his "dear friend, great critic, teacher." At different points in his career, Said repeatedly designated him as the best literary critic in America. This unusually high estimate of Poirier remains unexplained.
13. Britain made its commitment in the form of the Balfour Declaration of 1917 "to facilitate the establishment of a homeland for the Jewish people ... in Palestine." Ibrahim Abu-Lughod, "Territorially-based Nationalism in the Politics of Negation," in Edward W. Said and Christopher Hitchens, eds., *Blaming the Victims: Spurious Scholarship and the Palestinian Question*, London and New York: Verso, 1988, 194. "Al-Naqba Day, which commemorates the beginning of the suffering and exile of the Palestinian people," Yasir Abed Rabbo, "Land and the Intifada," *New York Times* Op-Ed, May 16, 2001.
14. Interview with Harold Veeser, December 29, 1991. Abu-Lughod considers himself formed more by the Arab world than Said. Not only had he

worked professionally in Cairo for three years as director of UNESCO's department of social sciences research immediately after receiving his Ph.D. from Princeton in 1957, but also, earlier, he had been involved in the Syrian Ba'ath and left-wing parties. In 1992 he returned permanently to the Middle East, where he was professor and vice-president of the Palestinian flagship university, Bir Zeit. He kept up a heavy speaking schedule throughout the West Bank, Gaza, and Arab sections of Israel and was active in Palestinian curricular reform.

15. The best-known Armenian-American writer, William Saroyan, depended on *Hairenek Weekly* and ethnic readers after his initial celebrity faded. When I wanted to break into print, my neighbor in Salina, Kansas, Dimitrios Sapounas, said, "You're part Armenian! Find the Armenian journals, and they will publish you." I appeared in *The Journal of Armenian Studies* and *Ararat*. Said's famed senior colleague, Lionel Trilling, published his first work in *The Menorah Journal*.

4. Academostardom

1. Robert Young has catalogued them conveniently in "Disorienting *Orientalism*," *White Mythologies: Writing History and the West*, London and New York: Routledge, 1990, 119–140. In *Postcolonialism: An Historical Introduction*, Oxford and Malden: Blackwell, 2001, 384, he added:

    in fact you could argue that postcolonial studies has actually defined itself as an academic discipline through the range of objections, reworkings and counter-arguments that have been marshaled in such great variety against Said's work. Who among postcolonial critics, struggling to emerge from the half-life of traditional disciplines ... has not begun their postcolonial new life with a critique of Said? The production of a critique of *Orientalism* even today functions as the act or ceremony of initiation by which newcomers to the field assert their claim to take up the position of a speaking subject within the discourse of postcolonialism. It goes without saying that, as Eagleton has remarked, the statutory requirement of this initiation rite is that the newcomer denounces one or preferably several aspects of the founding father's text, [Said's *Orientalism*], criticizes the very concept of the postcolonial and then asserts that he or she stands outside it in a position of critique. This ritual has now even developed a *mise-en-abyme* repetition effect, whereby the new critic makes his or her intervention by criticizing not only Said, but all previous commentators as well, conflating their texts with Said's and then accusing them of either repeating or not recognizing the very problems that they originally located in the ambivalences of Said's text ... and so on. Only by doing this do you demonstrate that you are discursively in the true.

    Young's amusement conceals a disturbing truth.

2. Bruce Robbins, *Secular Vocations: Intellectuals, Professionalism, Culture*, London and New York: Verso, 1993, 158: Said has an "unlikely complicity" with the objects of his criticism, which complicity is evident in "the duplication by the critic of an object strenuously criticized."

3. Robert Irwin, "Lured in the East: Tricky with Argument, Weak in

Languages, Careless of Facts: But, Thirty Years On, Edward Said Still Dominates Debate," *Times Literary Supplement*, May 9, 2008, 3–5. The books were Daniel Martin Varisco, *Reading Orientalism: Said and the Unsaid*, Seattle: University of Washington Press, 2008 and Ibn Warraq, *Defending the West: A Critique of Edward Said's* Orientalism, Amherst: Prometheus, 2008.

4. Anouar Abdel-Malek, "L'orientalisme en crise," *Diogène*, 24, 1963, 109–142. The critique continued in A.L. Tibawi, "English-Speaking Orientalists: A Critique of Their Approach to Islam and to Arab Nationalism," *Muslim World*, 53, 3–4, 185–204, 298–313; Talal Asad, *Anthropology and the Colonial Encounter*, London: Ithaca Press, 1973. Said told interviewer James Paul, "Anouar Abdel-Malek's article in *Diogenes* [sic], which meant a lot to me, may have been read by a few hundred people. But *Orientalism* was read by many thousands." *Interviews with Edward W. Said*, eds. Amritjit Singh and Bruce G. Johnson, Jackson: University Press of Mississippi, 2004, 47.

5. The writers I like most are not sermonizers or pronouncers of undying truths, but those who puncture other people's pronouncements—like Swift, who is a great favorite of mine, or Conrad, where what seems to be clear really isn't so clear because it is surrounded by doubt and uncertainty about what you've seen. I like that very much.
(Edward W. Said, "Cultures Aren't Watertight [interview with the *Guardian*]" in Singh and Johnson, 231)

6. Said left Egypt in Fall 1951 (via the luxury ocean liner the *Nieuw Amsterdam*) for his "American banishment" at Mount Hermon (1951–3). He graduated from Princeton (Class of 1957), and Harvard (Ph.D. 1963).

7. Hans Kellner, "Disorderly Conduct: Braudel's Mediterranean Satire," *History and Theory*, 18, 2, May, 1979, 197–222.

8. Kellner "Disorderly Conduct," 205. The lost works of Menippus were interpreted by Varro and other Romans, including Apuleius and Petronius. Lucian's satiric dialogues claim Menippean ancestry, as do Erasmus's *Praise of Folly*, Robert Burton's *Anatomy of Melancholy*, the French royalist pamphlet of 1594 entitled *Satire Menipée de la vertu du Catholicon d'Espagne*, and Swift's "Tale of a Tub."

9. Northrop Frye, *Anatomy of Criticism*, Princeton: Princeton University Press, 1957, 309.

10. One exemplar Said never mentioned that comes close to his own Menippean performance in *Orientalism* is Fernand Braudel's *La Méditerranée et le Monde Méditerranéen à l'Époque de Philippe II*, Paris: Librarie Armand Colin, 1966. Considered by some to be the greatest history written during the twentieth century, the book's status as Menippean satire is a relatively late discovery, cf. J. H. Hexter, citing a "Rabelaisian picaresque" element in "Fernand Braudel and the *Monde Braudellien*," *Journal of Modern History*, 44, 1972, 529. Kellner, "Disorderly Conduct," 91, writes, "in sum, the commentary of three decades has not accepted *The Mediterranean and the Mediterranean World in the Age of Philip II* as a formal success"—even though it is "widely viewed as a classic"!

11. The creative treatment of exhaustive erudition is the organizing principle of the greatest Menippean satire in English before Swift, Burton's *Anatomy of Melancholy*.... We may as well adopt [the term anatomy] as a convenient name to replace the cumbersome and in modern times rather misleading "Menippean satire."

(Frye, *Anatomy*, 311–312)

12. Lecture notes from the class on Swift that Said taught at Columbia on April 5, 1999.
13. "A Tale of a Tub" (1704), *Gulliver's Travels and Other Writings by Jonathan Swift*, ed. Louis Landa, Boston: Houghton Mifflin, 1960, 277.
14. Swift, "Tale," 277.
15. Frye, *Anatomy*, 377.
16. Most distinguished of the core of postcolonial literature in which empathy appears as a weapon would be Homi Bhabha, "Of Mimicry and Man," *October: Anthology*, Boston: MIT Press, 1987; reprinted in Homi Bhabha, *The Location of Culture*, London and New York: Routledge, 1994, 85–92, and Stephen Greenblatt, "Improvisation and Power," in *Literature and Society: Selected Papers from the English Institute 1978*, ed. Edward W. Said, Baltimore and London: Johns Hopkins University Press, 1980, 57–99. Said gave me a copy of the latter in 1978, when it was still in manuscript. Further reading would have to include Clifford Geertz on thick description.
17. Lord William Bentinck and Warren Hastings exemplified a deep love of Indian culture, geography, smells, sights, and sounds.
18. François-René de Chateaubriand, *Oeuvres romanesques et voyages*, ed. Maurice Regard, Paris: Gallimard, 1969, 2, 702. Originally in *Itinéraire de Paris à Jérusalem, et de Jérusalem à Paris* (1810–11), a record of his trip taken in 1805–6.
19. Said's translation, O 182, from Gérard de Nerval, *Voyage en Orient*, in *Oeurves*, ed. Albert Béguin and Jean Richet, Paris: Gallimard, 1960, 2, 68.
20. John Buchan, cited in Alan Sandison, *The Wheel of Empire: A Study of the Imperial Idea in Some Late Nineteenth and Early Twentieth Century Fiction*, New York: St. Martin's Press, 1967, 158.
21. Sir J. Fitzjames Stephen, *History of the Criminal Law of England*, 3 vols., London 1883, vol. 111, 344–345.
22. Gil Anidjar, "Secularism," *Critical Inquiry*, 33, Autumn 2006, 52–77, argues correctly that secularism became a religion of the West.
23. Joseph Conrad, *Heart of Darkness*, ed. Ross C. Murfin, second edition, Boston and New York: Bedford/St. Martin's, 1996, 21:

> The conquest of the earth, which mostly means the taking it away from those who have a different complexion or slightly flatter noses than ourselves, is not a pretty thing when you look into it too much. What redeems it is the idea only. An idea at the back of it; not a sentimental pretence but an idea; and an unselfish belief in the idea—something you can set up, and bow down before, and offer a sacrifice to.

24. Commenting on "the personal dimension," Said remarked that he was educated entirely in the West, and that "in many ways my study of

Orientalism has been an attempt to inventory the traces upon me, the Oriental subject, of the culture whose domination has been so powerful a factor in the life of all Orientals" (O 25).

25. Gayatri Chakravorty Spivak, *The Post-Colonial Critic*, ed. Sarah Harasym, London and New York: Routledge, 1991, 154.

5. Secular Criticism

1. "I felt like a rather passive and isolated victim," "Interview with Edward Said," *Edward Said: A Critical Reader*, Oxford and Cambridge, MA: Blackwell, 1992, 228.
2. "His ill-informed and banal use of antireligious rhetoric, though endemic to the academy, lacks the knowledge and intellectual seriousness of critics such [sic] Hume and Nietzsche." William D. Hart, *Edward Said and the Religious Effects of Culture*, Cambridge: Cambridge University Press, 2000, 37.
3. "Donations Pour in at John Jay Awards: Prof. Eric Foner and Lt. Gov. David Paterson Honored," *Columbia Daily Spectator* CXXXI, 34, Friday March 2, 2007, 1.
4. Denis Donoghue, "An Organic Intellectual," *The New Republic*, April 18, 1983, 31. "Professor Said's analysis of contemporary literary theory in his *Beginnings: Intention and Method* (1975) was far more favorably inclined [towards literary theory and criticism] than any chapter in his new book." Said was a modernizer and innovator who had followed his father's trade as an importer. He was a proclaimed comparativist who brought the latest French literary theories into the United States. And like his dad, he had flourished. Thus, when he abruptly sold up and got out, literary journalists noticed his departure.
5. Alison Light, "The World, The Text and the Critic" (review essay), *Criticism*, 26, 2, Summer 1984, 282.
6. Jane Gallop, *Around 1981: Academic Feminist Literary Theory*, New York and London: Routledge, 1992.
7. Bruce Robbins, "*Re-Reading English*, Peter Widdowson, ed., London and New York: Methuen, 1982, and Edward W. Said, *The World, the Text, and the Critic*, Cambridge: Harvard University Press, 1983, review," *the minnesota review*, NS 21, Fall 1983, 147.
8. By making Said into a defender of professionalism in *Secular Vocations: Intellectuals, Professionalism, Culture*, London and New York: Verso Books, 1993, Robbins initiated a round of books and articles about professionalism. He accomplished a similar scholarly coup by investigating Said's cosmopolitanism. See *Cosmopolitics: Thinking and Feeling Beyond the Nation*, eds. Pheng Cheah and Bruce Robbins, Minneapolis and London: University of Minnesota Press, 1998. Said writes that Georg Lukács "shows how critics appropriate the function of starting to make values for the work they are judging. Wilde said it more flamboyantly: criticism 'treats the work of art as the starting point for a new creation'" (WTC 52); citing Lukács, *Die Seele und die Formen* (1911; rpt. Berlin: Luchterhand, 1971, 28; and Wilde, *The Artist as Critic: Critical Writings of Oscar Wilde*, ed. Richard Ellmann, New York: Vintage, 1970, 367.

9. Robbins's most recent book, *Upward Mobility and the Common Good: Toward a Literary History of the Welfare State*, Princeton and Oxfordshire: Princeton University Press, 2007, works an entirely new set of changes—the ties among the state, secularism, the general public, and careers.
10. Bruce Robbins, *Secular Vocations: Intellectuals, Professionalism, Culture*, London and New York: Verso, 1993.
11. Paul A. Bové, "Closing Up the Ranks: Xerxes' Hordes Are at the Gate," *In the Wake of Theory*, Hanover and London: University Press of New England, 1992, 81.
12. Bové, "Closing Up the Ranks," 81.
13. William D. Hart, *Edward Said and the Religious Effects of Culture*, Cambridge: Cambridge University Press, 2000.
14. "Interview with Edward Said," *Edward Said: A Critical Reader*, Oxford and Cambridge, MA: Blackwell, 1992, 232–233.
15. Said, "Religious Criticism," WTC, 291–292.
16. Gil Anidjar, "Secularism," *Critical Inquiry* 33, Autumn 2006, 52–77.
17. Joseph Conrad, *Heart of Darkness*, 21.
18. Anidjar, "Secularism," 68. Incidentally, Said took this point from Philip D. Curtin's pithy edited collection of primary documents, *Imperialism*, New York: Walker and Co., 1971. Curtin observes that some of these documents demonstrate that the shift from religious conversion to cultural conversion is the ideological justification of conquest. "If religious superiority carried an obligation to convert the heathen, cultural superiority might easily carry an obligation to convert the barbarian to civilization" (Curtin, xix). Cf., the selection by Charles Temple entitled, "The Relations Existing Between Dominant and Dependent Races. Quo Vadis?" in Curtin, 103. Said was assigning Curtin to seminars that I attended in 1977.
19. W.J.T. Mitchell, "Secular Divination: Edward Said's Humanism," *Critical Inquiry*, 31, 2, Winter 2005, 462.
20. Samuel Butler, *The Way of All Flesh*, Harmondsworth: Penguin, 1966 [first published 1903]. Cited by Said in a public lecture at the University of Colorado, Boulder, September 1991.
21. Biblical scholars are even more dazzling than literary critics in their use of the "find a problem and solve it" mode. Any standard biblical scholarly periodical, such as the *Journal of Biblical Literature*, will confirm their pre-eminence.
22. Stanley Fish, "Interpreting the *Variorum*," "Interpreting 'Interpreting the *Variorum*,'" and "What Makes an Interpretation Acceptable?" in *Is There a Text in This Class?* London and Cambridge, MA: Harvard University Press, 1980.
23. Derrida's relationship to Midrash has been studied most carefully by Susan Handelman, *The Slayers of Moses: The Emergence of Rabbinic Interpretation in Modern Literary Theory*, Albany: SUNY Press, 1982. Handelman feels Derrida exemplifies Midrashic tradition, whereas it is evident, to me at least, that he is devoted precisely to its undoing.
24. Jacques Derrida, "Like the Sound of the Sea Deep Within a Shell: Paul de Man's War," trans. Peggy Kamuf, *Critical Inquiry*, 14, Spring 1988;

reprinted in Derrida, *Memoires for Paul de Man*, revised edition, New York: Columbia University Press, 1986, 1989, 232.
25. Frank Kermode, *The Sense of an Ending*, Oxford: Oxford University Press, 1968 (first published in 1967).
26. So classified by Hayden White, "Criticism as Cultural Politics, Review of Edward W. Said, Beginnings: Intention and Method," *diacritics*, 6, 3, Fall 1976, 8–13.
27. Conversation with Harold Veeser after the Said memorial lecture 2006, Faculty House, Columbia University.
28. Frank Kermode, "Institutional Control of Interpretation," in Kermode, *Essays on Fiction 1971–82*, London: Routledge & Kegan Paul, 1983, 183.
29. According to Said, this power derives from the relationship between discourse and speaker, which is "governed by rules that antedate the speaker's appearance and postdate his disappearance" (B 299).
30. Gerald Bray, *Biblical Interpretation, Past and Present*, Downers Grove: InterVarsity Press, 1996, 57.
31. As an evangelical scholar, Bray is conservative theologically, but he belongs to that wing of evangelicalism that seeks to embrace critical biblical scholarship, so in the quoted passage he is reporting on the practice of earlier interpreters.
32. David Stern, "Midrash and the Language of Exegesis," in Geoffrey Hartman and Sanford Budick, eds., *Midrash and Literature*, New Haven: Yale University Press, 1986, 108.
33. Stern, "Midrash," 108.
34. James L. Kugel, "Two Introductions to Midrash," Geoffrey H. Hartman and Sanford Budick, eds., *Midrash and Literature*, New Haven: Yale University Press, 1986, 92.
35. Kugel, "Two Introductions," 91. When Bruce Grill tipped me off that I should write about Socrates' assessment of Agathon, he was pointing out just such a problem. In addition, it was hardly the most obvious topic of interest—it was not gay or straight love, it was not drunken parties, it was not the origin of philosophy or Socratic method. The out-of-the-wayness of Grill's suggested topic is intrinsic to Midrash. He unerringly felt out a snag in the text and deemed the mysterious Agathon a cavity just recherché enough to cause subliminal reader-discomfort and therefore to invite the attentions of a good cosmetic dentist.
36. Gerald Graff, *Clueless in Academe: How Schooling Obscures the Life of the Mind*, New Haven: Yale University Press, 2004, convincingly demonstrates that the impulse to conceal method remains widespread in the teaching of literature.
37. J. Hillis Miller, "Beginning with a Text," *diacritics*, 6, 3, Fall 1976, 2–7.
38. Miller, "Beginning," 7.
39. Derrida, "Like the Sound of the Sea Deep Within a Shell," 232. Ironically, Said's alliance with rhetoric aligned him—against his protests—with deconstruction, whose great discovery is the triumph of rhetoric over logic. As Paul De Man says in "The Resistance to Theory," in Robert Con Davis and Ronald Schleifer, eds., *Contemporary Literary Criticism: Literacy and Cultural Studies*, White Plains, New York: Longman, 1994, 105.

Rhetoric, by its actively negative relationship to grammar and to logic, certainly undoes the claims of the trivium (and by extension, of language) to be an epistemologically stable construct. The resistance to theory is a resistance to the rhetorical or tropological dimension of language.

Nevertheless, Said's historicism violated basic tenets of deconstruction and he championed a different rhetorical dimension: delivery.

40. Leila Ahmed, *A Border Passage: From Cairo to America—A Woman's Journey*, New York: Farrar, Strauss, Giroux, 1999, 123–125, describes the suffocatingly rote orthodoxy in Koranic interpretation that triumphed over Itjihad, which means scholars using the best judgment to issue a ruling on an affair that is not clear, and determining the meaning of an utterance from the context in which it was spoken or written.
41. "Tale of a Tub" was Said's closest model for secular criticism. In Swift's satiric postmodern allegory, three brothers (Protestant, Anglican, and Roman Catholic) twist and turn their father's simple words (in his Last Will and Testament) so as to evade his strictures and get their own desires. The narrative thread is frequently cut by prefaces, dedications, footnotes, missing sections, and digressions, which are the zaniest and most radically postmodern parts of the book. In Said's extensive scholarly writings on the Dean of St. Patrick's, Swift appears above all as unorthodox and thus a sympathetic model for experiments in secular criticism.
42. David Stern, "Midrash and the Language of Exegesis: A Study of Vayikra Rabbah, Chapter 1," in *Midrash and Literature*, ed. Geoffrey Hartman and Sanford Buddick, New Haven: Yale University Press, 1986, 105–124.
43. In a review of the expanded version of Foucault's *Madness and Civilization*, Andrew Scull wrote:

    The whole of Part One of *Madness* has a total of twenty-eight footnotes (out of 399) that cite twentieth-century scholars.... Foucault's bibliography for Part Two lists a single twentieth-century work.... Narrowness of this kind is not confined to footnotes. Foucault's isolation from the world of facts and scholarship is evident throughout *History of Madness*. It is as though nearly a century of scholarly work had produced nothing of interest or value to Foucault's project.
    ("Scholarship of Fools: The Frail Foundations of Foucault's Monument," *The Times Literary Supplement*, March 23, 2007, 3–4)

44. Said writes "Batinists" on one page and "Batinites" on the next, showing how unstable his own text is, and how careless he is of ordinary scholarly decencies.
45. Steven Mailloux, *Rhetorical Power*, Ithaca: Cornell University Press, 1989, 147–148.
46. Said's complete scholarly bibliography is available online: www.lib.uci.edu/libraries/pubs/scctr/Wellek/said/. An excellent archive of Said's occasional journalism is available online: http://themargins.net/said.html.

6. Rhetoric and Image

1. "The Palestinians have lost their greatest polemical champion." Alexander Cockburn, "Remembering Edward W. Said," Columbia University, March 3, 2004, 23.
2. Hardcover flyleaf, Edward W. Said, *The Question of Palestine*, New York: Times Books, 1979.
3. George Eliot, *Daniel Deronda*, London: Penguin Books, 1967, 594–595; in Said, *QP* 64.
4. Ranke's complete statement, in (old) German: *"Man hat der Historie das Amt, die Vergangenheit zu richten, die Mitwelt zum Nutzen zukünftiger Jahre zu belehren, beigemessen: so hoher Aemter unterwindet sich gegenwärtiger Versuch nicht: er will blos zeigen, wie es eigentlich gewesen."* Leopold von Ranke, "Vorrede zur ersten Ausgabe, Okt. 1824," *Geschichten der romanischen und germanischen Völker von 1494 bis 1514 zur kritik neuerer Geschichtsschreiber*, Leipzig: Verlag Duncker and Humblot, 3. Ausgabe, 1885, 5, vii. In Mary Fulbrook, "Jenseits der Totalitarismustheorie? Vorläufige Bemerkungen aus sozialgeschichtlicher Perspektive," in *The GDR and its History: Rückblick und Revision*, ed. Peter Barker, Amsterdam and Atlanta: Rodopi, 2000, 51.
5. Hayden White, *Metahistory*, Baltimore: Johns Hopkins University Press, 1973, 164–165.
6. John Berger and Jean Mohr, *A Seventh Man*, London: Penguin, 1976; Paris: Maspero, 1976. Susan Meiselas, *Nicaragua*, New York: Pantheon, 1981; rpt. Aperture/ICP, 2008.
7. Edward Said, "Homage to Joe Sacco," in Joe Sacco, *Palestine*, Seattle: Fantagraphics Books, 2001, i–v, and Edward W. Said, "The Art of Displacement: Mona Hatoum's Logic of Irreconcilables," in *The Entire World as a Foreign Land*, London: Tate Gallery, 2000, 7–17.
8. Page 271 in the edition Said assigned for the course, *Gulliver's Travels and Other Writings by Jonathan Swift*, ed. Louis A. Landa, Boston: Houghton Mifflin Co., 1960.
9. *Gulliver's Travels and Other Writings*, 333.

7. On Stage

1. Said, "Performance as an Extreme Occasion," *Musical Elaborations*, New York: Columbia University Press, 1991, 2; quoting Richard Poirier, *Performing Self*, xiv.
2. See Yves Lacoste, *Ibn Khaldun: The Birth of History and the Past of the Third World*, London: Verso, 1984, 136–137.
3. "Criticism, Culture, and Performance," Said interviewed by the editorial board of the magazine *Wedge*, in Gauri Viswanathan, ed., *Power, Politics, and Culture: Interviews with Edward Said*, New York: Pantheon Books, 2001, 96.
4. "Interview with Edward Said: Jennifer Wicke and Michael Sprinker," in Michael Sprinker, ed., *Edward Said: A Critical Reader*, Oxford and Cambridge, MA: Blackwell, 1992, 245–246.
5. Apparently, Said was a clumsy and defenseless public speaker—at first. He writes in his memoir that he used to remove his glasses so that he was unable to see his audience because the sight of them would have made

him too nervous to perform. Ibrahim Abu-Lughod recalled that Said almost stuttered as he read his early lectures and his performance as M.C. at a 1975 AAUG conference drew the comment "This is the first time in my life that I have seen the audience almost willing to lynch the M.C." from one of their friends. "But afterwards?" Abu-Lughod added, "you can't believe it's the same person" (personal communication with the author).

6. To say that Said liked to perform would be like saying Wimpy liked hamburgers. According to Alexander Cockburn's superlative epitaph, "Edward Said, Dead at 66, A Mighty and Passionate Heart," *Counterpunch*, September 25, 2003, 23–24 (www.zmag.org/content/showarticle.cfm?Section ID=22&ItemID_4251); reprinted in *Remembering Edward W. Said* (for the memorial service at Columbia University, St. Paul's Chapel, March 3, 2004), as a knockout artist and a professional hothead, Said "never lost his fire." This tribute from an accomplished rabble-rouser and wit like Cockburn is the highest praise Said could receive: Cockburn and he are fellow brawlers, professional nay-sayers and outsiders. Cockburn writes that "the Said prose that I most enjoyed, the fiery diatribes ... the searing sentences" poured forth to the end. He describes Said as a profoundly theatrical character, one who would call up and say, "with mock heroic English intonation, 'Alex-and-er, have you seen the latest *New Republic*? Have you read this filthy, this utterly disgusting diatribe? You haven't? Oh, I know, you don't care about the feelings of a mere black man such as myself.' I'd start laughing." Meanwhile, Said would "rehearse fiery rebuttals."

7. "Middle East: Boiling Again," *MacNeil/Lehrer News Hour* (October 1, 1985); in *Interviews with Edward Said*, eds. Amritjit Singh and Bruce G. Johnson, University Press of Mississippi, 2004, 39.

8. "Middle East: Boiling Again," 42.

9. "Middle East: Boiling Again," 43.

10. Edward Said, "Secular Interpretation, the Geographical Element and the Methodology of Imperialism," Davis Lecture, Princeton University, 1990, 9 (typescript).

11. *Yeats and Decolonization*, Field Day Pamphlets, Series, 5, *Nationalism, Colonialism and Literature. Field Day*, 1988, 17; excerpted but without this passage in Edward W. Said, "Yeats and Decolonization," in Seamus Deane, ed., *Nationalism, Colonialism, and Literature*, Minneapolis: University of Minnesota Press, 1990.

12. Jean Genet, *Le captif amoureaux*, Paris: Gallimard, 1986, 122; *The Prisoner of Love*, trans. Barbara Bray, Hanover: Wesleyan University Press, 1992, 88. Quoted in Said, "On Jean Genet," in *On Late Style: Music and Literature Against the Grain*, New York: Pantheon, 2006, 84. Genet, *Les Paravents*, Isère, France: Marc Barbezat, Décines, 1961; trans. Bernard Frechtman, *The Screens* (New York: Grove Press, 1962).

13. John Mowitt, "What Said Said," mss.

14. Published in "Forum," *PMLA* (*Publications of the Modern Language Association of America*) 114, 1, January 1999, 106–107.

8. Later Visions

1. Roland Barthes, *Camera Lucida*, Paris: Editions du Seuil, 1980; and Farrar, Straus and Giroux, 1981, 6.
2. Published in *CI* in 1993, the essay originally appeared as "The Imperial Spectacle," *Grand Street*, 6, 2, Winter 1987, 82–104. Even Said foe Aijaz Ahmad admits that this is his favorite among all Said's essays and praises "Said's highly convincing argument" (*In Theory: Classes, Nations, Literatures*, London and New York: Verso, 1992, 201).
3. Said, "The Imperial Spectacle," *Grand Street*, 6, 2, Winter 1987, 91.
4. Edward W. Said, "The Imperial Spectacle," *Grand Street*, 6, 2, Winter 1987, 103; this version is better than the revision in *Culture and Imperialism*.
5. A.R. Louch, "Critical Discussions: The World, the Text, and the Critic," *Philosophy and Literature*, 8, 2, October 1984, 276, provides one example of such complaints: "As Said does not appear to know what an argument is (judging by unexpected appearances of 'therefore' in his text), it is not surprising that he does not recognize a need for internal consistency."
6. Kaja Silverman, *The Threshold of the Visible World*, New York: Routledge, 1996, 18.
7. Some contemporary realities Said discussed include Anglo-Egyptian rivalry in East Africa, French and Italian ambitions in Somalia and Ethiopia, and how these would probably resonate in an opera that was about an Egyptian army that defeats an Ethiopian force (*CI* 125–126). This discussion occupies a small part of Said's article, which is in no sense a point-for-point allegorical reading of the opera, as it might have been in the hands of Marxist critics a generation earlier.
8. All references are to Quintin Hoare and Geoffrey Nowell Smith, eds., *Selections from the Prison Notebooks of Antonio Gramsci*, New York: International Publishers, 1971. Said read aloud the passages cited here during a graduate seminar. Cornel West was a student in the seminar and later had important insights into Gramsci.
9. A neighbor still appears to resent this injustice. Hoda Guindi, "Of the Place," *Alif*, 25, 2005, 10. Ms. Guindi writes that the Saids and the Guindis were friends and neighbors in Cairo's Zamalek district. Said was

    the subject of much envious mutterings as he was the first, ostensibly because he was the eldest, to be given a room of his own! I realize now with hindsight that this must have caused the first stirrings of feminism in the gaggle of girls who were, sometimes, vouchsafed, by Edward's lordly magnanimity, a glimpse of the room and even, on extremely rare occasions, the right to cross the threshold of the sacrosanct space and gasp at his books and, in pride of place, his piano.

10. "Interview with Edward Said (Jennifer Wicke and Michael Sprinker)," in Michael Sprinker, ed., *Edward Said: A Critical Reader*, Oxford and Cambridge, MA: Blackwell, 1992, 240.
11. Excerpts from *Remembering Edward W. Said*, November 1, 1935–September 25, 2003, memorial tributes given at Columbia University's St. Paul's Chapel, March 3, 2004.
12. Silverman, *Threshold*, 19.

13. Jonathan Crary, *Techniques of the Observer: On Vision and Modernity in the Nineteenth Century*, Cambridge, MA and London: MIT Press, 1990, 131. All references to Crary's work are from this edition.
14. Affectionate commentaries always remark on Said's impeccable dress. He stood out even within a preening group of colleagues among whom one found ebony cigarette holders, gold watch fobs, and suits by Ozwald Boateng. A colleague remarks that Said badgered him until he broke down and bought a black cashmere blazer, and adds that it was impossible to imagine Said "sitting around in his vest." See also Edward W. Said, "He Crinkled his Majestic Nose ..." *Columbia College Today*, 17, 1, Winter 1990, 26, for a comic description of how he led a colleague through the dark-paneled show rooms of London bootmakers and tailors. In interviews Said often described his weakness for fine fashions. The susceptibility went all the way back, for in *Out of Place*, he describes lovingly his Boy Scout uniform. In his youthful photographs, as in his late ones, he is a complete dandy.
15. Said begins his essay by recalling Kipling's birth in British India, where during the first six years of his life he spoke Hindustani. After school in England, he returned as an older teenager to work as a journalist in India, writing for *The Civil and Military Gazette* and then *The Pioneer*. His first stories were about this life in India, his first book of poems, *Departmental Ditties*, came out of the same experience (*CI* 133).
16. Peter Manning, author and professor of English, Q&A during Stony Brook University Graduate Conference, February 2006.
17. Said debated Stanley Fish and Jackson Bate on the topic of professionalism: "Response to Stanley Fish," *Critical Inquiry*, 10, 2, December 1983, 371–373. Fish responded in "Profession Despise Thyself: Fear and Self-Loathing in Literary Studies," *Critical Inquiry*, 10, 2, December 1983, 349–364. Said carried on the attack of what he called the cult of expertise in his Reith Lectures, later published as *Representations of the Intellectual*, New York: Pantheon, 1994, especially pages 77–83. His examples of non-expert intellectuals are most often fictional: Bazarov, Stephen Dedalus, and Moreau (creations of, respectively, Turgenev, James Joyce, and Flaubert). This might suggest that "the intellectual" is a convenient displacement of, or euphemism for, Literature Itself.
18. My opponent was Sa'eb Erekat, who was regularly promoted until, by 1997, he became the principle Arafat spokesperson and press secretary to the Western media. He continues in this role today, January 2009.
19. "In any case the idea that there is a kind of redemptive homeland doesn't answer to my view of things" (*PolD* 114).

9. Marquee Intellectual
1. Justus Reid Weiner, "'My Beautiful Old House,' and Other Fabrications by Edward Said," *Commentary Magazine*, September 1999.
2. He quoted often, with full approval, Hugo of St. Victor:

> he is perfect to whom the entire world is as a foreign land. The tender soul has fixed his love on one spot in the world; the strong man has extended his love to all places; the perfect man has extinguished his.
> (*RoE* 185)

3. See Immanuel Wallerstein, "The Brandt Report," *Towards One World? International Responses to the Brandt Report*, London: Temple Smith, 1981; reprinted in Wallerstein, *Geopolitics and Geoculture: Essays on the Changing World System*, Cambridge and New York: Cambridge University Press, 1991, 98–103.
4. Said, "A Changing World Order: The Arab Dimension," *Arab Studies Quarterly*, 3, 2, Spring 1981; quoted in *PolD* 231.
5. Edward W. Soja, *Postmodern Geographies: The Reassertion of Space in Critical Social Theory*, London and New York: Verso, 1989. Radical geographers moved from Said's university reading lists to his lectures and writings: Frantz Fanon's passages on the divided colonial city ceased to appear in Said's books (although Fanon received praise for recognizing "the primacy of geography in history") and Lacoste, Foucault on geography, and Henri Lefebvre began to crop up (*RoE* 446).
6. Timothy Mitchell, *Colonising Egypt*, Cambridge and New York: Cambridge University Press, 1988, 44–45. He adds that cutting up space so precisely coincides with the origins of private landownership: space becomes a commodity. Eric Stokes, *The English Utilitarians in India*, Oxford: Clarendon [Oxford University Press], 1959, 82–84, 99–100, 103–106, records the same process taking place in early nineteenth-century India.
7. Mitchell, *Colonising Egypt*, 50. My description of the upper and lower parts of the house comes from Pierre Bourdieu, *Outline of a Theory of Practice*, Cambridge: Cambridge University Press, 1977, 90.
8. Ahmed el-Nahas, General Manager, Ramses Hilton Hotel, Cairo, and member of the Old Victorians alumni association. "Those were the best days of our lives. Almost everyone believes so. The system of education has changed completely, and it is very hard to find documents about the Old Victorians" (Interview with Harold Veeser, Ramses Hilton Hotel, June 21, 1990).
9. Gloria Emerson, *Gaza*, New York: Atlantic Monthly Press, 1991, 107.
10. Frantz Fanon, *Les damnés de la terre* (1962), trans. Constance Farrington, *The Wretched of the Earth*, London: MacGibbon & Kee, 1965, 38–39. The antithetical structure of this passage mirrors the geographical antithesis that shapes much postcolonial writing on the topic of geography.
11. One postcolonial theorist, Abdul JanMohamed, in his accurately titled book, *Manichean Aesthetics: The Politics of Literature in Colonial Africa*, Amherst: University of Massachusetts Press, 1983, raises Fanon's Manichean thought to the eminence of a postcolonial universal. On apartheid geographies, see also Meena Alexander, *Fault Lines: A Memoir*, New York: The Feminist Press at the City University of New York, 1993, and Jacqueline Rose, *States of Fantasy*, Oxford and New York: Oxford University Press, 1996.
12. Michael Walzer, *Exodus and Revolution*, New York: Basic Books, 1985, 149.
13. Edward W. Said, "Michael Walzer's Exodus and Revolution: A Canaanite Reading," *Grand Street*, 5, 1985–1986, 86–106; "Michael Walzer's *Exodus and Revolution*: A Canaanite Reading," *Arab Studies Quarterly*,

8, 3, Summer 1986, 289–303; and see "An Exchange: Exodus and Revolution," *Grand Street*, Summer 1986 (Walzer 246–252; Said 252–259).

10. Political Roughhouse

1. Unsigned review of J.P. Mahaffy, *Greek Life and Thought: from the Age of Alexander to the Roman Conquest*, Pall Mall Gazette, XLVI, 7066, November 9, 1887, 3; in *The Artist as Critic*, ed. Richard Ellmann, Chicago: University of Chicago Press, 1982, 81.
2. Diana Jean Schemo, "America's Scholarly Palestinian Raises Volume Against Arafat," *New York Times*, March 4, 1994: "He plunged into the political arena after the Arab–Israeli war of 1967, rapidly becoming the most prominent Palestinian spokesman in the United States."
3. "to be a Palestinian in New York—in many ways *the* Palestinian—is not the easiest of fates." "On Palestinian Identity: A Conversation with Salman Rushdie," *New Left Review*, 160, November–December 1986, 67. Edward Alexander, "Professor of Terror," *Commentary*, August 1989.
4. Mustapha Marrouchi, *Edward Said at the Limits*, Albany: State University of New York Press, 2004.
5. Saïd K. Aburish, *Arafat: From Defender to Dictator*, New York: Bloomsbury, 1998, 202. All future citations are to this edition.
6. They were a mixed bag of people who included Faisal Husseini and Sari Nusseibeh as representatives of the Palestinian elite, and Hanan Ashrawi, Radwan Abu Ayyash, Ziyyad Abu Zayyad, Hanna Seniora, Sam'an Khoury and others who represented a new breed of leaders who did not fit the traditional mold. The activists of the UNL came from all factions comprising the PLO; the *intifadah* forced them to cooperate.

    (Aburish, *Arafat: From Defender to Dictator*, 208)

    The Unified National Leadership appears to be located physically in the Jerusalem/Ramallah area, if several seizures of freshly printed leaflets are any indication. All that is known is that each of the four major organizations is represented, probably by one delegate each who rotate frequently.

    (Joe Stork, "The Significance of Stones: Notes from the Seventh Month," *Intifada: The Palestinian Uprising Against Israeli Occupation*, Boston: South End Press, 1989, 72)

    The four major organizations are the Popular Front for the Liberation of Palestine, the Democratic Front for the Liberation of Palestine, Fatah, and the Communist Party.
7. Joe Stork, *Intifada*, 73.
8. Penny Johnson and Lee O'Brien with Joost Hiltermann, "The West Bank Rises Up," *Intifada: The Palestinian Uprising Against Israeli Occupation*, Boston: South End Press, 1989, 8.
9. Rashid Khalidi, "The Palestinian People: Twenty-two Years After 1967," *Intifada: The Palestinian Uprising Against Israeli Occupation*, Boston: South End Press, 1989, 124–125.

10. Glenn Frankel, *Beyond the Promised Land, Jews and Arabs on the Hard Road to a New Israel*, Beaverton: Touchstone, 1996, 57.
11. Nizar Qabbani, "Children Bearing Rocks," in *Intifada: The Palestinian Uprising Against Israeli Occupation*, Boston: South End Press, 1989, 100.
12. Unified National Leadership communiqué no. 6 (February 2, 1988), *Intifada: The Palestinian Uprising Against Israeli Occupation*, Boston: South End Press, 1989, 333–334.
13. All communiqués quoted from Appendix II, "Communiqués from the Unified National Leadership of the Uprising," in *Intifada: The Palestinian Uprising*, 328–394.
14. As, for example, Joan Peters, *From Time Immemorial*, New York: Harper and Row, 1984, and Alan Dershowitz, *The Case for Israel*, Hoboken: John Wiley and Sons, Inc., 2003. But this contradiction is grist for further interminable grinding, all of it in the astonishing high-Mannerist private language of contemporary postcolonial criticism. A more generous and accurate way to put it is that Said "insists on the need for a national narrative that does not reduce the Palestinian reality to a mere function of Zionism." Extremists held that Arabs entered the region only after Israel redeemed the land, and that these parasites batten on Israeli prosperity and confect their ersatz "Palestinian identity" as an alibi and excuse.
15. Mohammed Heikal, *Secret Channels*, New York: HarperCollins, 1996, 382, in Aburish, *Arafat: From Defender to Dictator*, 203.
16. This is a pattern of popular revolutions in the 1980s. The Nicaraguan Sandinista revolution was co-opted by the former Conservative Party, members of which occupied important positions a mere two years after the popular victory, and who succeeded within those same two years in disenfranchising the mass organizations—unions included. See H. Aram Veeser, "Addicted to Privilege," *The Nation*, September 30, 1996, 27–30 and H. Aram Veeser, "On the Genealogy of Murals," *The Nation*, May 27, 1996, 33–35.
17. Said, "Meeting with the Old Man," *Interview Magazine*, December 1988.
18. Rashid Khalidi, *The Iron Cage: The Story of the Palestinian Struggle for Statehood*, Boston: Beacon, 2006, 163.
19. "Interview with Edward Said," in *Edward Said: A Critical Reader*, ed. Michael Sprinker, Oxford and Cambridge, MA: Blackwell, 1992, 232.
20. "On Palestinian Identity: A Conversation with Edward Said," in Salman Rushdie, *Imaginary Homelands: Essays and Criticism, 1981–1991*, London: Granta Books/Viking Penguin, 1991, 182. See also Said's discussion of personal and mass displacement *Sky* 164: "We are migrants and perhaps hybrids in, but not of, any situation in which we find ourselves."
21. *Imaginary Homelands* 174.
22. This statement was published simultaneously in the weekend edition of the Kuwaiti daily *al-Qabas* and in the Lebanese daily *as-Safir*, and then reported with commentary in *Mideast Mirror*, October 9, 1989, 13–15.
23. Despite the astonishing flow of books, articles, journalism, media attention, and political debate, Israel/Palestine is just a detail within the larger U.S. strategy in the Arabian Gulf and the Middle East. Before World War II, Anglo-Persian Oil (later British Petroleum, BP) held half of the Ottoman Empire's old oil reserves. Royal Dutch/Shell and Deutsche Bank held

the rest. But the British were pulling out of the region, leaving a looming crisis over control of the world's oil reserves. A U.S. military base in Dhahran, the center of the Saudi oil fields, completed in 1946, was the biggest U.S. Air Force base outside of Europe and Japan. On the same day Harry Truman unfolded his Truman Doctrine, four U.S. oil companies signed a consortium agreement to share all Saudi oil among themselves. However, the U.S. withdrew from Dhahran in 1962 and abandoned its remaining regional military stronghold when Colonel Qaddafi led his junta to power seven years later. Other sites were drawing its attention away from the Middle East and direct involvement was becoming difficult. The Kennedy and then Johnson administrations were the first to use Israel as a surrogate; military credits from the U.S. increased from nothing (1948–58) to $90M in 1966, the year before Israel fought against Egypt, Syria, and Jordan. See Cheryl Rubenberg, *Israel and the American National Interest: A Critical Examination*, Chicago: University of Illinois Press, 1986, 91, on JFK's growing perception of the advantages of "an Israeli Sparta acting as a U.S. surrogate" and the initiation of the policy of providing it with sophisticated American weaponry. Israel's 1967 offensive exceeded every hope, not only sparing the U.S. any Vietnam-style political risk, but in the military yield of each dollar that had been invested. See Gilbert Achcar, *Eastern Cauldron: Islam, Afghanistan, Palestine, and Iraq in a Marxist Mirror*, trans. Peter Drucker, New York: Monthly Review Press, 2004.
24. Edward W. Said, "Thinking Ahead: After Survival, What Happens?" *Z Magazine*, April 2002 (http://listserv.linguistlist.org/cgi-bin/wa?A2=ind 0204&L=critics-l&P=792).
25. Said, "Thinking Ahead."

11. Dropping the PLO
1. "Orientalism Revisited: An Interview with Edward W. Said (interviewed by James Paul)," *Middle East Report*, January–February 1988; rpt. *Interviews with Edward W. Said*, eds. Amritjit Singh and Bruce G. Johnson, Jackson: University Press of Mississippi, 2004, 47–48.
2. Timothy Brennan, "The Illusion of a Future: *Orientalism* as Traveling Theory," *Critical Inquiry*, 20, Spring 2000, 558–583, contends that the need for a discursive shift accounted for the impact of *Orientalism*. He argues that Said intends a homology between nineteenth-century English and French philology and late-twentieth-century literary theory.
3. For Brennan, Said shares a hardcore communist emphasis on state power and in *Culture and Imperialism* ultimately became "more deliberately materialist" than Raymond Williams or even Antonio Gramsci ("The Illusion of a Future," 564). But actually Said refused to be associated with "labels like 'Marxism' or 'liberalism'" (*WTC* 28). Moreover, he had considerable antipathy to Marx based on the latter's prejudices against Asiatic societies and the Asiatic mode of production, and he found Williams fatally insular. He declares that he "can't identify with a Marxist party" or "a Marxist rhetoric," and that even the best Marxist theories are "perhaps historically important texts, but no more than that" ("Interview with Edward Said [interviewed by Jennifer Wicke and Michael Sprinker],"

Edward Said: A Critical Reader, ed. Michael Sprinker, Oxford and Cambridge, MA: Blackwell, 1992, 259, 261).
4. See Robert Young, *White Mythologies: Writing History and the West*, London and New York: Routledge, 1990. Young considers poststructuralism the basis of postcolonialism and traces its origins to French Algerian founders, such as Jacques Derrida and Hélène Cixous. Said's case was rather different from theirs because he was involved simultaneously with advanced theory and with militant struggle. Aside from the irony that a brilliant poststructuralist like Young could embrace so simplistic a myth of origin, the relationship between poststructuralism and postcolonialism is by no means direct or unmediated.
5. Said, *QP*, 167: "the conservative version of the Palestinian quest is both historically and morally intolerable: the idea that we can all go back to 1948, to our property, to an Arab country, presumably ruled by traditional Arab despots." The last phrase is a subtle punchline reminding us that the author also wrote Menippean satire. In *QP*, 119, he wrote:

> every thinking Palestinian, or those like myself whose trials have been cushioned by good fortune and privilege, knows somehow that all the real parallels between Israel and South Africa get badly shaken up in his consciousness when he reflects seriously on the difference between white settlers in Africa and Jews fleeing European anti-Semitism. But the victims in Africa and Palestine are wounded and scarred in much the same sort of ways.

6. Said, *PolD*, xxv. Said is paraphrasing his colleague Shafiq al-Hout, who actually said this to the assembled PNC in Algiers in 1983. It is also Said's position.
7. Bruce Robbins, "Homelessness and Worldliness," *diacritics*, 13, 3, Fall 1983, 71.
8. Said, *MidEast Mirror*, October 9, 1989.
9. "Yaser Abedrabbo Replies to Edward Said," *MidEast Mirror*, October 13, 1989, 13–15.
10. Michel Foucault, *Power/Knowledge*, ed. Colin Gordon, New York: Pantheon, 1980; Foucault, *Surveiller et punir*, Paris: Editions Gallimard, 1975; Foucault, *Discipline and Punish*, trans. Alan Sheridan, New York: Random House, 1979. In the context of the nation, see Foucault, "Governmentality," in *The Foucault Effect: Studies in Governmentality*, eds. Graham Burchell, Colin Gordon, and Peter Miller, Chicago: University of Chicago Press, 1991, 87–104. For a postcolonial reading, see Spivak, "More on Power/Knowledge," in *The Spivak Reader*, eds. Donna Landry and Gerald MacLean, New York and London: Routledge, 1996, 141–174.
11. Khalidi, *The Iron Cage*, 162.
12. Many of these critics faulted Said for his inconsistencies, assuming that these were unintended or somehow escaped his notice. See, for example, James Clifford, "On Orientalism," in *The Predicament of Culture: Twentieth Century Ethnography, Literature and Art*, Cambridge: Harvard University Press, 1988, 255–276; and Dennis Porter, "Orientalism and its Problems" (1983), reprinted in Patrick Williams and Laura Crisman, eds.,

Colonial Discourse and Postcolonial Theory: A Reader, Hemel Hempstead: Harvester Wheatsheaf, 1993, 150–161. Robert J. C. Young, *White Mythologies: Writing History and the West*, New York and London: Routledge, 1990, 134–135, describes Said's predicament as follows:

> positing a hegemonic Orientalism as a totality which has no reference—for there is no object to which it corresponds—nor inner conflict, but solely an intention to dominate, Said must then demand a counterintention from outside the system for any resistance. This double bind, instead of being recognized as such, is given a theoretical corollary through an awkward meshing of Foucault's discursive system with Gramsci's organic intellectual, embodied in a methodological distinction between "strategic location"—the author's position in a text with regard to the material he writes about—and "strategic formation"—the relationship between texts and the way in which groups of texts acquire referential power.

13. Said's *al-Qabas* exchanges with the PLO show that the PLO had a more sophisticated view of human agency as something that is possible only collectively. To a mass movement like the PLO, the single human person is more like Karl Marx's "divided and dislocated" subject, someone lost in the wilderness, or like Althusser's decentered subject held together by the illusion of free subjectivity—an illusion fostered by the interpellations of ideology.
14. Gilbert Achcar, "Where Is the PLO Going? The Long March ... Backwards," *Eastern Cauldron*, New York: Monthly Review Press, 2004, 151.
15. This was true at the time of the Veeser interview at 448 Riverside Drive in New York, August 1, 1989. In 1992, Said went to Gaza and the West Bank for the first time since 1947. See Said, "Palestine, Then and Now: An Exile's Journey Through Israel and the Occupied Territories," *Harper's Magazine*, December 1992, 47–55.
16. Said, "Palestine, Then and Now," 55.
17. Yet, in Said's essay on "Renan's Philological Laboratory," he demonstrated against his will that a great, impersonal "discourse," with its own immense institutional machinery and deep historical roots, governs Arab–European relations.
18. *The Edward Said Reader*, eds. Moustafa Bayoumi and Andrew Rubin, New York: Vintage, 2000, 17.
19. Said's "Orientalism Reconsidered," *Race & Class*, Autumn 1985, is an instance of his taking cues from his own contradictions.

12. Said in History

1. *Orientalism* was published in 1978; its third edition came out at the time of 9/11.
2. Bruce Robbins, "Homelessness and Worldliness," 76.
3. Richard E. Miller, session #202, and Lennard J. Davis, session #320, Program of the 124th Annual MLA Annual Convention (PMLA 123.6 [November 2008], 1917, 1934).
4. All published in 2008.

5. Daniel T. O'Hara, *Empire Burlesque: The Fate of Critical Culture in Global America*, Durham and London: Duke University Press, 2003, 33.
6. Aijaz Ahmad, *In Theory: Classes, Nations, Literatures*, London and New York: Verso, 1992, 210. All future citations are to this work.
7. Terry Eagleton, "The Death of Self-Criticism," [review of Stanley Fish, *Professional Correctness: Literary Studies and Political Change*, Oxford: Clarendon Press, 1995], *Times Literary Supplement*, November 24, 1995, 6.
8. Excerpts from *Remembering Edward W. Said*, November 1, 1935–September 25, 2003, memorial tributes given at Columbia University's St. Paul's Chapel, March 3, 2004.
9. Some of these were themselves path-breaking works, for instance, his former student Gauri Viswanathan's *Masks of Conquest*, a study of colonial education in India.
10. Escher's prints of impossible realities sometimes superpose a hyperbolic plane on a fixed two-dimensional plane or image irregular perspectives akin to the Möbius strip. A favorite practical joke in machine shops is to present a novice with a realistic-looking blueprint of one of Escher designs to be turned into a three-dimensional model.
11. Bruce Robbins, "Homelessness and Worldliness," 69–77.
12. Russell Jacoby, *The Last Intellectuals: American Culture in the Age of Academe*, New York: Noonday/Farrar, Straus and Giroux, 1987, laments the passing of the intellectual as an unfunded or at least non-academic amateur. For a more searching view of the intellectual's role, see also Jeffrey Williams, "The Romance of the Intellectual and the Question of Profession," in Henry A. Giroux with Patrick Shannon, eds., *Education and Cultural Studies: Toward a Performative Practice*, New York: Routledge, 1997, 49–64; Catherine R. Stimpson, "The Public Duties of Our Profession," *Profession 1996*, New York: MLA, 1996, 100–102; Pierre Bourdieu, "The Corporation of the Universal: The Role of Intellectuals in the Modern World," *Telos*, 81, 1989, 99–110; Lewis A. Coser, *Men of Ideas: A Sociologist's View*, 1965; rpt. New York: Free Press, 1997); and Alvin W. Gouldner, *The Future of Intellectuals and the Rise of the New Class: A Frame of Reference, Theses, Conjectures, Arguments, and an Historical Perspective on the Role of Intellectuals and Intelligentsia in the International Class Contest of the Modern Era*, New York: Seabury, 1979. For the least sanguine view of the figure of the powerful, freestanding intellectual, see Paul Bové, *Intellectuals in Power: A Genealogy of Critical Humanism*, New York: Columbia University Press, 1986, and the collected works of Noam Chomsky.
13. Bruce Robbins, *Secular Vocations: Intellectuals, Professionalism, Culture*, London and New York: Verso, 1993, 158.
14. D.D. Guttenplan, "An Obligation to Truth," *New Statesman*, June 14, 2004: www.newstatesman.com/200406140033.
15. Jonathan Culler, *Literary Theory: A Very Short Introduction*, Oxford: Oxford University Press, 1997; re-edition 1999, handily summarizes these central tenets of deconstruction.
16. According to Said, *WTC*, 16–20, the first step in any education is moving beyond filiation—the hand that was dealt to you at birth. This might be

understood as dropping your parents and your retarding companions, or in his terms, discarding your inherited and biological relationships. *Check*: Harold Veeser leaves Guilderland, NY, never to return. As a lumpish upstate New Yorker suddenly transplanted to the urbane settings of Ivy League New York and the nominal mentoring of well-to-do and very posh Edward Said, my situation obviously fit this model. My desires were primal and feudal: I wished to place myself under an individual's personal influence and protection. Step two in Said's description of the educational process is "pressure to produce new and different ways of conceiving human relationships." *Check*: Harold comes quickly to depend on Columbia for money, food, and emotional sustenance. He looks to his girlfriends for philosophical instruction and his teachers and friends for emotional support. In the third step, the new affiliative ties become "no less orthodox and dominant than culture itself." *Check*: Said, my girlfriend Bebe, Columbia, and my classmates all acquire the heavy burdensomeness of patriarchal families. Primitive hierarchies of authority, rules, obligations, and oppressions are put into place, and an "A" grade or a coveted Kellett fellowship substitute for parental approval.
17. Excerpts from *Remembering Edward W. Said*, November 1, 1935–September 25, 2003, memorial tributes given at Columbia University's St. Paul's Chapel, March 3, 2004.
18. "On Jean Genet," *Grand Street*. Reprinted in *On Late Style*, 75.
19. "On Jean Genet," *Grand Street*. Reprinted in *On Late Style*, 77.

Bibliography of Works Cited

Abdel-Malek, A., "L'orientalisme en crise," *Diogène*, 24, 1963, 109–142.
Abedrabbo, Y., "Yaser Abedrabbo replies to Edward Said," *MidEast Mirror*, October 13, 1989, 13–15.
Abu-Lughod, I., "Territorially-based Nationalism in the Politics of Negation," in Edward W. Said and Christopher Hitchens, eds., *Blaming the Victims: Spurious Scholarship and the Palestinian Question*, London and New York: Verso, 1988.
Aburish, S.K., *Arafat: From Defender to Dictator*, New York: Bloomsbury, 1998.
Achcar, G., *Eastern Cauldron: Islam, Afghanistan, Palestine, and Iraq in a Marxist Mirror*, trans. Peter Drucker, New York: Monthly Review Press, 2004.
—— "Where Is the PLO Going? The Long March ... Backwards," *Eastern Cauldron*, New York: Monthly Review Press, 2004.
Ahmad, A., *In Theory: Classes, Nations, Literatures*, London and New York: Verso, 1992.
Ahmad, E., *The Selected Writings of Eqbal Ahmad*, eds. Carollee Bengelsdorf, Margaret Cerullo, and Yogesh Chandrani, New York: Columbia University Press, 2006.
Ahmed, L., *A Border Passage: From Cairo to America—A Woman's Journey*, New York: Farrar, Strauss and Giroux, 1999.
Alexander, E., "Professor of Terror," *Commentary*, August 1989, 49–50.
Alexander, M., *Fault Lines: A Memoir*, New York: The Feminist Press at the City University of New York, 1993.
Anidjar, G., "Secularism," *Critical Inquiry*, 33, Autumn 2006, 52–77.
Anon., "Donations Pour in at John Jay Awards: Prof. Eric Foner and Lt. Gov. David Paterson Honored," *Columbia Daily Spectator*, CXXXI, 34, Friday March 2, 2007, 1.
—— *Remembering Edward W. Said*, November 1, 1935–September 25, 2003, memorial tributes given at Columbia University's St. Paul's Chapel, March 3, 2004.
Asad, T., *Anthropology and the Colonial Encounter*, London: Ithaca Press, 1973.
Ashcroft, B. and Ahluwalia, P., *Edward Said: The Paradox of Identity*, London and New York: Routledge, 1999.

Barthes, R., *Camera Lucida*, Paris: Éditions du Seuil, 1980; Farrar, Straus and Giroux, 1981.
Berger, J. and Mohr, J., *A Seventh Man*, London: Penguin, 1976; Paris: Maspero, 1976.
Bhabha, H., *The Location of Culture*, London and New York: Routledge, 1994.
Bourdieu, P., *Outline of a Theory of Practice*, Cambridge: Cambridge University Press, 1977.
—— "The Corporation of the Universal: The Role of Intellectuals in the Modern World," *Telos*, 81, 1989, 99–110.
—— "The Market for Symbolic Goods," *The Field of Cultural Production: Essays on Art and Literature*, ed. Randal Johnson, New York and Chichester: Columbia University Press, 1993, 112–144.
Bourdieu, P. and Passeron, J.-C., *Reproduction: In Education, Society and Culture*, trans. Richard Nice, London and Beverly Hills: Sage Publications, 1977.
Bové, P.A., *Intellectuals in Power: A Genealogy of Critical Humanism*, New York: Columbia University Press, 1986.
—— *In the Wake of Theory*, Hanover and London: University Press of New England, 1992.
Braudel, F., *La Méditerranée et le Monde Méditerranéen à l'Époque de Philippe II*, Paris: Librarie Armand Colin, 1966.
Bray, G.L., *Biblical Interpretation, Past and Present*, Downers Grove: InterVarsity Press, 1996.
Brennan, T., "Places of Mind, Occupied Lands: Edward Said and Philology," in Michael Sprinker, ed., *Edward Said: A Critical Reader*, Oxford: Blackwell, 1992, 74–95.
—— "The Illusion of a Future: *Orientalism* as Traveling Theory," *Critical Inquiry*, 20, Spring 2000, 558–583.
Butler, S., *The Way of All Flesh*, Harmondsworth: Penguin, 1966 [first published 1903].
Chateaubriand, F.-R. de, *Oeuvres romanesques et voyages*, ed. Maurice Regard, Paris: Gallimard, 1969.
Cheah, P. and Robbins, B., eds., *Cosmopolitics: Thinking and Feeling Beyond the Nation*, Minneapolis and London: University of Minnesota Press, 1998.
Clifford, J., *The Predicament of Culture: Twentieth Century Ethnography, Literature and Art*, Cambridge: Harvard University Press, 1988, 255–276.
Cockburn, A., "Edward Said, Dead at 66, A Mighty and Passionate Heart," *Counterpunch*, September 25, 2003, 23–24: www.zmag.org/content/showarticle.cfm?Section ID=22&ItemID_4251.
Conrad, J., *Joseph Conrad, Life & Letters*, 2 vols., Garden City: Doubleday, Page and Co., 1927.
—— *Heart of Darkness*, ed. Ross C. Murfin, second edition, Boston and New York: Bedford/St. Martin's, 1996.
Coser, L.A., *Men of Ideas: A Sociologist's View*, 1965; rpt. New York: Free Press, 1997.
Crary, J., *Techniques of the Observer: On Vision and Modernity in the Nineteenth Century*, Cambridge, MA and London: MIT Press, 1990.

Culler, J., *Literary Theory: A Very Short Introduction*, Oxford: Oxford University Press, 1997; re-edition 1999.
Curtin, P.D., ed., *Imperialism*, New York: Walker and Co., 1971.
De Man, P., "The Resistance to Theory," in Robert Con Davis and Ronald Schleifer, eds., *Contemporary Literary Criticism: Literary and Cultural Studies*, White Plains: Longman, 1994, 93–108.
Derrida, J., "Like the Sound of the Sea Deep Within a Shell: Paul de Man's War," trans. Peggy Kamuf, *Critical Inquiry* 14, Spring 1988; reprinted in Derrida, *Memoires for Paul de Man*, revised edition, New York: Columbia University Press, 1986, 1989.
Dershowitz, A., *The Case for Israel*, Hoboken: John Wiley and Sons, Inc., 2003.
Dickstein, M., *Lionel Trilling and the Critics: Opposing Selves*, ed. John Rodden, Lincoln and London: University of Nebraska Press, 1999.
Donoghue, D., "An Organic Intellectual," *The New Republic*, April 18, 1983, 30–33.
Eagleton, T., "The Death of Self-Criticism," *Times Literary Supplement*, November 24, 1995, 6.
Eliot, G., *Daniel Deronda*, London: Penguin Books, 1967.
Emerson, G., *Gaza*, New York: Atlantic Monthly Press, 1991.
Fanon, F., *Les damnés de la terre* (1962), trans. Constance Farrington, *The Wretched of the Earth*, London: MacGibbon & Kee, 1965.
Fish, S., *Is There a Text in This Class?* London and Cambridge, MA: Harvard University Press, 1980.
—— "Profession Despise Thyself: Fear and Self-Loathing in Literary Studies," *Critical Inquiry*, December 1983, 10, 2, 349–364.
Foucault, M., *Discipline and Punish*, trans. Alan Sheridan, New York: Random House, 1979.
—— *Power/Knowledge*, ed. Colin Gordon, New York: Pantheon, 1980.
—— "Governmentality," in Graham Burchell, Colin Gordon, and Peter Miller, eds., *The Foucault Effect: Studies in Governmentality*, Chicago: University of Chicago Press, 1991, 87–104.
Frankel, G., *Beyond the Promised Land, Jews and Arabs on the Hard Road to a New Israel*, New York: Simon and Schuster, 1994.
Frye, N., *Anatomy of Criticism*, Princeton: Princeton University Press, 1957.
Fulbrook, M., "Jenseits der Totalitarismustheorie? Vorläufige Bemerkungen aus sozialgeschichtlicher Perspektive," in Peter Barker, ed., *The GDR and Its History: Rückblick und Revision*, Amsterdam and Atlanta: Rodopi, 2000, 35–53.
Gallop, J., *Around 1981: Academic Feminist Literary Theory*, New York and London: Routledge, 1992.
Genet, J., *Le captif amoureaux*, Paris: Gallimard, 1986, 122; *The Prisoner of Love*, trans. Barbara Bray, Hanover: Wesleyan University Press, 1992.
—— *Les Paravents*, Isère, France: Marc Barbezat, Décines, 1961; trans. Bernard Frechtman, *The Screens*, New York: Grove Press, 1962.
Gillory, J., *Cultural Capital: The Problem of Literary Canon Formation*, Chicago and London: University of Chicago Press, 1993.
Gorman, D., "The Worldly Text: Writing as Social Action, Reading as Historical Reconstruction," in Joseph Natoli, ed., *Literary Theory's*

Future(s), Urbana and Chicago: University of Illinois Press, 1989, 181–220.
Gouldner, A.W., *The Future of Intellectuals and the Rise of the New Class: A Frame of Reference, Theses, Conjectures, Arguments, and an Historical Perspective on the Role of Intellectuals and Intelligentsia in the International Class Contest of the Modern Era*, New York: Seabury, 1979.
Graff, G., *Clueless in Academe: How Schooling Obscures the Life of the Mind*, New Haven: Yale University Press, 2004.
Gramsci, A., *Selections from the Prison Notebooks of Antonio Gramsci*, eds. Quintin Hoare and Geoffrey Nowell Smith, New York: International Publishers, 1971.
Greenblatt, S., "Improvisation and Power," in Edward W. Said, ed., *Literature and Society: Selected Papers from the English Institute 1978*, Baltimore and London: Johns Hopkins University Press, 1980, 57–99.
Guillory, J., *Cultural Capital: The Problem of Literary Canon Formation*, Chicago and London: University of Chicago Press, 1993.
Guindi, H., "Of the Place," *Alif*, 25, 2005, 9–11.
Guttenplan, D.D., "An Obligation to Truth," *New Statesman*, June 14, 2004: www.newstatesman.com/200406140033.
Handelman, S., *The Slayers of Moses: The Emergence of Rabbinic Interpretation in Modern Literary Theory*, Albany: SUNY Press, 1982.
Hart, W.D., *Edward Said and the Religious Effects of Culture*, Cambridge: Cambridge University Press, 2000.
Hartman, G., and Buddick, S., eds., *Midrash and Literature*, New Haven: Yale University Press, 1986.
Heikal, M., *Secret Channels*, New York: HarperCollins, 1996.
Hexter, J.H., "Fernand Braudel and the *Monde Braudellien*," *Journal of Modern History*, 44, 1972, 480–539.
Irwin, R., "Lured in the East: Tricky with Argument, Weak in Languages, Careless of Facts: But, Thirty Years On, Edward Said Still Dominates Debate," *Times Literary Supplement*, May 9, 2008, 3–5.
Jacoby, R., *The Last Intellectuals: American Culture in the Age of Academe*, New York: Noonday/Farrar, Straus and Giroux, 1987.
JanMohamed, A., *Manichean Aesthetics: The Politics of Literature in Colonial Africa*, Amherst: University of Massachusetts Press, 1983.
Johnson, B., *A World of Difference*, Baltimore: Johns Hopkins University Press, 1987.
Johnson, P. and O'Brien, L. with Hiltermann, J., "The West Bank Rises Up," in Zachary Lockman and Joel Beinin, eds., *Intifada: The Palestinian Uprising Against Israeli Occupation*, Boston: South End Press, 1989, 29–41.
Kellner, H., "Disorderly Conduct: Braudel's Mediterranean Satire," *History and Theory*, 18, 2, May 1979, 197–222.
Kermode, F., *The Sense of an Ending*, Oxford: Oxford University Press, 1968 [first published in 1967].
—— *Essays on Fiction 1971–82*, London: Routledge & Kegan Paul, 1983.
Khalidi, R., "The Palestinian People: Twenty-two Years After 1967," in Zachary Lockman and Joel Beinin, eds., *Intifada: The Palestinian Uprising Against Israeli Occupation*, Boston: South End Press, 1989, 113–126.

—— *The Iron Cage: The Story of the Palestinian Struggle for Statehood*, Boston: Beacon, 2006.
Klein, R., "That He Said That Said Said," *Enclitic*, 2, 1, Spring 1978, 81–96.
Kugel, J.L., "Two Introductions to Midrash," eds. Geoffrey H. Hartman and Sanford Budick, *Midrash and Literature*, New Haven: Yale University Press, 1986, 77–103.
Lacoste, Y., *Ibn Khaldun: The Birth of History and the Past of the Third World*, London: Verso, 1984.
Light, A., "The World, The Text and the Critic" (review essay), *Criticism*, 26, 2, Summer 1984, 282–284.
Louch, A.R., "Critical Discussions: The World, the Text, and the Critic," *Philosophy and Literature*, 8, 2, October 1984.
Lukács, G., *The Theory of the Novel*, trans. Anna Bostock, Cambridge, MA: MIT Press, 1971.
Mailloux, S., *Rhetorical Power*, Ithaca: Cornell University Press, 1989.
Marrouchi, M., *Edward Said at the Limits*, Albany: State University of New York Press, 2004.
Meiselas, S., *Nicaragua*, New York: Pantheon, 1981; rpt. Aperture/ICP, 2008.
Miller, J.H., "Beginning with a Text," *diacritics*, 6, 3, Fall 1976, 2–7.
Mitchell, T., *Colonising Egypt*, Cambridge and New York: Cambridge University Press, 1988.
Mitchell, W.J.T., "Secular Divination: Edward Said's Humanism," *Critical Inquiry*, 31, 2, Winter 2005, 462–471.
Neill, E., "Critical Condition," *Times Educational Supplement*, October 12, 1984, 32 (review of *The World, the Text, and the Critic*), 3563, 32.
Nerval, G. de, *Voyage en Orient*, eds. Albert Béguin and Jean Richet, *Oeuvres*, Paris: Gallimard, 1960.
O'Hara, D.T., *Empire Burlesque: The Fate of Critical Culture in Global America*, Durham and London: Duke University Press, 2003.
Peters, J., *From Time Immemorial*, New York: Harper and Row, 1984.
Poirier, R., *The Performing Self: Compositions and Decompositions in the Languages of Contemporary Life*, London and New York: Oxford University Press, 1971.
Porter, D., "Orientalism and its Problems" (1983), reprinted in Patrick Williams and Laura Crisman, eds., *Colonial Discourse and Postcolonial Theory: A Reader*, Hemel Hempstead: Harvester Wheatsheaf, 1993, 150–161.
Qabbani, N., "Children Bearing Rocks," in Zachary Lockman and Joel Beinin, eds., *Intifada: The Palestinian Uprising Against Israeli Occupation*, Boston: South End Press, 1989, 100.
Raad, W. and Toufic, J., "The Withdrawal of Tradition Past a Surpassing Disaster," United Nations Plaza Broadcast: Seminar 3, opening lecture, January 31, 2007: http://unp.kein.org/v2v?page=1.
Rabbo, I.A., "Land and the Intifada," *New York Times*, Op-Ed, May 16, 2001.
—— "Homelessness and Worldliness," *diacritics*, 13, 3, Fall 1983, 69–77.
Robbins, B., "Peter Widdowson, ed., *Rereading English* and Edward W. Said, *The World, the Text, and the Critic*" (review essay), *the minnesota review* NS 21, Fall 1983, 146–149.

—— *Secular Vocations: Intellectuals, Professionalism, Culture*, London and New York: Verso, 1993.
—— *Upward Mobility and the Common Good: Toward a Literary History of the Welfare State*, Princeton and Oxfordshire: Princeton University Press, 2007.
Rose, J., *States of Fantasy*, Oxford and New York: Oxford University Press, 1996.
Rubenberg, C., *Israel and the American National Interest: A Critical Examination*, Chicago: University of Illinois Press, 1986.
Rushdie, S., *Imaginary Homelands: Essays and Criticism, 1981–1991*, London: Granta Books/Viking Penguin, 1991.
Said, E.W., *Joseph Conrad and the Fiction of Autobiography*, Cambridge, MA: Harvard University Press; London: Oxford University Press, 1966.
—— *Beginnings: Intention and Method*, New York: Basic Books, 1975.
—— "Vico on the Discipline of Bodies and Texts," *Modern Language Notes*, 91, October 1976, 814–826; rpt. *RoE*, 85–86.
—— *Orientalism*, New York: Pantheon Books; London: Routledge & Kegan Paul; Toronto: Random House, 1978.
—— *The Question of Palestine*, New York: Times Books, 1979.
—— "A Changing World Order: The Arab Dimension," *Arab Studies Quarterly*, 3, 2, Spring 1981, 198–202.
—— *Covering Islam: How the Media and the Experts Determine How We See the Rest of the World*, New York: Pantheon; London: Routledge & Kegan Paul, 1981.
—— "Response to Stanley Fish," *Critical Inquiry*, 10, 2, December 1983, 371–373.
—— *The World, the Text, and the Critic*, Cambridge, MA: Harvard University Press, 1983.
—— "Michel Foucault, 1927–1984," *Raritan: A Quarterly Review*, 4, 2, Fall 1984, 1–11; rpt. *RoE, 187–197*.
—— "Orientalism Reconsidered," *Race & Class*, 27, 2, Autumn 1985, 1–15.
—— *After the Last Sky: Palestinian Lives*, photographs by Jean Mohr, New York: Pantheon; London: Faber, 1986.
—— "An Exchange: Exodus and Revolution," *Grand Street*, Summer 1986, 252–259.
—— "Michael Walzer's *Exodus and Revolution*: A Canaanite Reading," *Grand Street*, 5, 1985–6, 86–106.
—— "Michael Walzer's *Exodus and Revolution*: A Canaanite Reading," *Arab Studies Quarterly*, 8, 3, Summer 1986, 289–303.
—— "On Palestinian Identity: A Conversation with Salman Rushdie," *New Left Review*, 160, November–December 1986, 63–80.
—— "Cairo Recalled," *House and Garden*, 159, 4, April 1987, 20, 24, 28, 32.
—— "The Imperial Spectacle," *Grand Street*, 6, 2, Winter 1987, 82–104.
—— "Meeting with the Old Man," *Interview Magazine*, 18, 12, December 1988, 112–115, 194.
—— *MidEast Mirror*, October 9, 1989.
—— "He Crinkled His Majestic Nose …," *Columbia College Today*, 17, 1, Winter 1990.

―― *Yeats and Decolonization.* Field Day Pamphlets, Series, 5, *Nationalism, Colonialism and Literature.* Field Day, 1988, 17; excerpted but without this passage in Edward W. Said, "Yeats and Decolonization," in Seamus Deane, ed., *Nationalism, Colonialism, and Literature,* Minneapolis: University of Minnesota Press, 1990.

―― *Musical Elaborations,* New York: Columbia University Press, 1991.

―― "Palestine, Then and Now: An Exile's Journey Through Israel and the Occupied Territories," *Harper's Magazine,* 285, 1711, December 1992, 47–55.

―― *Culture and Imperialism,* New York: Knopf/Random House, 1993.

―― *The Politics of Dispossession: The Struggle for Palestinian Self-Determination, 1969–1994,* New York: Pantheon Books, 1994.

―― *Representations of the Intellectual,* New York: Pantheon, 1994.

―― *Peace and Its Discontents: Essays on Palestine in the Middle East Peace Process,* New York: Vintage, 1995. Published in Britain as *Peace and Its Discontents: Gaza-Jericho, 1993–1995,* London: Vintage, 1995.

―― *Out of Place: A Memoir,* New York: Knopf, 1999.

―― "The Art of Displacement: Mona Hatoum's Logic of Irreconcilables," in Mona Hatoum, *The Entire World as a Foreign Land,* London: Tate Gallery, 2000, 7–17.

―― *The Edward Said Reader,* eds. Moustafa Bayoumi and Andrew Rubin, New York: Random House, 2000.

―― *The End of the Peace Process: Oslo and After,* New York: Pantheon Books; London: Granta, 2000.

―― *Reflections on Exile and Other Essays,* Cambridge, MA: Harvard University Press, 2000.

―― *Parallels and Paradoxes: Explorations in Music and Society,* New York: Pantheon, 2002.

―― "Thinking ahead: After Survival, what Happens?" *Z Magazine,* April 2002: http://listserv.linguistlist.org/cgi-bin/wa?A2=ind0204&L=critics-l&P=792.

―― *Interviews with Edward W. Said,* eds. Amritjit Singh and Bruce G. Johnson, Jackson: University Press of Mississippi, 2004.

―― *Humanism and Democratic Criticism,* New York: Columbia University Press, 2004.

―― *From Oslo to Iraq and the Road Map,* New York: Pantheon, 2004.

―― *On Late Style: Music and Literature Against the Grain,* New York: Pantheon, 2006.

Sandison, A., *The Wheel of Empire: A Study of the Imperial Idea in Some Late Nineteenth and Early Twentieth Century Fiction,* New York: St. Martin's Press, 1967.

Schemo, D.J., "America's Scholarly Palestinian Raises Volume Against Arafat," *New York Times,* March 4, 1994.

Scull, A., "Scholarship of Fools: The Frail Foundations of Foucault's Monument," *Times Literary Supplement,* March 23, 2007, 3–4.

Silverman, K., *The Threshold of the Visible World,* New York: Routledge, 1996.

Soja, E.W., *Postmodern Geographies: The Reassertion of Space in Critical Social Theory,* London and New York: Verso, 1989.

Spivak, G.C., *The Post-Colonial Critic*, ed. Sarah Harasym, London and New York: Routledge, 1991.
—— "More on Power/Knowledge," eds. Donna Landry and Gerald MacLean, *The Spivak Reader*, New York and London: Routledge, 1996, 141–174.
Stephen, J.F., *History of the Criminal Law of England*, 3 vols., London 1883.
Stern, D., "Midrash and the Language of Exegesis," in Geoffrey Hartman and Sanford Budick, eds., *Midrash and Literature*, New Haven: Yale University Press, 1986.
—— "Midrash and the Language of Exegesis: A Study of Vayikra Rabbah, Chapter 1," in Geoffrey Hartman and Sanford Buddick, ed., *Midrash and Literature*, New Haven: Yale University Press, 1986, 105–124.
Stimpson, C.R., "The Public Duties of Our Profession," *Profession 1996*, New York: MLA, 1996, 100–102.
Stokes, E., *The English Utilitarians in India*, Oxford: Clarendon [Oxford University Press], 1959.
Stork, J., "The Significance of Stones: Notes from the Seventh Month," in Zachary Lockman and Joel Beinin, eds., *Intifada: The Palestinian Uprising Against Israeli Occupation*, Boston: South End Press, 1989, 67–79.
Swift, J., *Gulliver's Travels and Other Writings by Jonathan Swift*, ed. Louis Landa, Boston: Houghton Mifflin, 1960.
Temple, C., "The Relations Existing Between Dominant and Dependent Races: Quo Vadis?" ed. Philip D. Curtin, *Imperialism*, New York: Walker and Co., 1971, 93–105.
Tibawi, A.L., "English-Speaking Orientalists: A Critique of Their Approach to Islam and to Arab Nationalism," *Muslim World*, 53, 3–4, 185–204, 298–313.
Trilling, L., *Of This Time, Of That Place, and Other Stories*, New York: Harcourt Brace Jovanovich, 1979.
Varisco, D.M., *Reading Orientalism: Said and the Unsaid*, Seattle: University of Washington Press, 2008.
Veeser, H.A., "Addicted to Privilege," *The Nation*, September 30, 1996, 27–30.
—— "On the Genealogy of Murals," *The Nation*, May 27, 1996, 33–35.
Vico, G., *The New Science of Giambattista Vico*, eds. Thomas Goddard Bergin and Max Harold Fisch (Abridged Translation of the Third Edition, 1744), Ithaca and London: Cornell University Press, 1970.
Viswanathan, G., *Masks of Conquest: Literary Study and British Rule in India*, Delhi and New York: Oxford University Press, 1998.
—— ed., *Power, Politics, and Culture: Interviews with Edward Said*, New York: Pantheon Books, 2001.
Wallerstein, I., "The Brandt Report," *Towards One World? International Responses to the Brandt Report*, London: Temple Smith, 1981; reprinted in Wallerstein, *Geopolitics and Geoculture: Essays on the Changing World System*, Cambridge and New York: Cambridge University Press, 1991, 98–103.
Walzer, M., *Exodus and Revolution*, New York: Basic Books, 1985.
—— "An Exchange: Exodus and Revolution," *Grand Street*, Summer 1986, 246–252.

Warraq, I., *Defending the West: A Critique of Edward Said's* Orientalism, Amherst: Prometheus, 2008.
Weber, M., *On Charisma and Institution Building*, ed. S.N. Eisenstadt, Chicago: University of Chicago Press, 1968.
Weber, S., "The Intersection: Marxism and the Philosophy of Language," *diacritics*, 15, 4, 1985, 94–112.
Weiner, J.R., "'My Beautiful Old House,' and Other Fabrications by Edward Said," *Commentary Magazine*, September 1999, 23–31.
White, H., *Metahistory: The Historical Imagination in Nineteenth-Century Europe*, Baltimore and London: Johns Hopkins University Press, 1973.
—— "Criticism as Cultural Politics, review of Edward W. Said, Beginnings: Intention and Method," *diacritics*, 6, 3, Fall 1976, 8–13.
Wilde, O., "Review of J.P. Mahaffy, *Greek Life and Thought: from the Age of Alexander to the Roman Conquest*," *Pall Mall Gazette*, XLVI: 7066, November 9, 1887, 3; in *The Artist as Critic*, ed. Richard Ellmann, Chicago: University of Chicago Press, 1982.
Williams, J.J., "The Romance of the Intellectual and the Question of Profession," in Henry A. Giroux with Patrick Shannon, eds., *Education and Cultural Studies: Toward a Performative Practice*, New York: Routledge, 1997, 49–64.
—— "Name Recognition," *the minnesota review*, 52–54, 2001, 185–208.
Young, R.J.C., *White Mythologies: Writing History and the West*, London and New York: Routledge, 1990.
—— *Postcolonialism: An Historical Introduction*, Oxford and Malden, MA: Blackwell, 2001.

Index

Page numbers in **bold** denote figures.

Abdel-Malek, Anouar 63
Abedrabbo, Yasser 186, 198, 199, 201
Abu-Lughod, Ibrahim 51–4, 55–6, 144, 146, 177–8, 182–5, 200, 226–7 n.14
Aburish, S.K. 181, 185, 186
action figures 78–9
Adorno, Theodor 14
Aeschylus 92; *The Persians* 72
affective fallacy 28
After the Last Sky (*Sky*) 15, 32, 69, 106, 108, 110, 111–12, 113, 165, 171
Ahluwalia, Pal 25
Ahmad, Aijaz 136, 199, 207, 208, 209
Ahmad, Eqbal 68, 69, 125–7, 195–6
Ahmed, Leila 233 n.40
Aida (Verdi) 140–3, 144, 165, 167
Al-Ahram 15
al-'Azm, Sadiq Jalal 63
al-Bitar, Nadim 63
Al-Hayat 15
Al-Majalla 15
Al Qabas 125, 186
The Alchemist (Jonson) 76
Aleph (Borges) 66
Alexander, Edward 130
Alexander, Meena 238 n.11
Algiers Declaration 188
Althusser, Louis 214
American Medical Association 13
Anidjar, Gil 89–91, 93
Annales school 165
anthropology, interpretative 14
Arab-American Association of University Graduates (AAUG) 53, 54, 55, 56–7, 144
Arab–Israeli conflict 36, 107, 169, 170, 176–91
The Arab Israeli Confrontation 53
"The Arab Portrayed" 51
Arab Studies Quarterly 53
Arafat, Yasir 7, 178, 179, 180, 185, 186, 198, 199–200, 201

The Archeology of Knowledge (Foucault) 196
Aristotle, *The Rhetoric* 120
Arnold, Matthew 90, 100
Ashcroft, Bill 25
Ashrawi, Hanan Michail 125–6
Auerbach, Berthold 208
Auerbach, Erich 62; *Mimesis* 100

Bachelard, Gaston 165
Balfour, Arthur 51, 68–70, 71
Barenboim, Daniel 154
Baring, Evelyn (Lord Cromer) 76–7
Barsamian, David 124
Barthes, Roland 41, 140, 142, 167
Barzun, Jacques 17
Batinists 99–100
The Battle of Algiers (Pontecorvo) 167
Bayley, John 85
Beginnings: Intention and Method (B) 18, 24, 27, 31, 40, 41, 42, 43, 45, 46, 57, 66, 95, 207, 208
Belloc, Hilaire 90
Berger, John 110
Bergson, Allen 218
Bhabha, Homi K. 166, 194
biblical criticism 95, 97
Blair, Hugh 28
Blake, William 95
Bloom, Harold 4
Boateng, Oswald 137 n.14
Borges, Jorge Luis, *Aleph* 66
Bourdieu, Pierre 4, 5, 6, 7, 8, 9, 153, 204, 221 n.4
Bouvard et Pecuchet (Flaubert) 65
Bové, Paul 86–7
Boyarin, Daniel and Jonathan 130
Brandt, Willy 165
Braudel, Fernand, *The Mediterranean* 68, 228 n.10
Bray, Gerald 232 n.31

Brennan, Timothy 23–4, 25, 211, 213
Brombert, Victor 63
brotherhood 79
Buchan, John 79
bullying 122–3
Burton, Richard 79, 80
Butler, Samuel 94; *Erewhon* 65; *The Way of All Flesh* 65
Byron, George Gordon, Lord 15

Cabral, Amilcar 151
"Cairo Recalled" 20
Camp David (2000) 199
Canguilem, 41
"The Capitive" (Michelangelo) 47, **48**, 49–50, 99, 107
captivity 49–50
Castiglione, Baldessar 50
Chareaubriand, François-René 92
charisma 1–22; Bourdieu on 5, 6, 8; religious 3, 8; Weber on 3, 8, 10, 12
Charismatic Activism 17
charismatic heroes 26, 28, 30
Charlie Rose (TV show) 146
"Children Bearing Rocks" (Qabbami) 180
Chinese, "quick brains" of 73
Christianity 90
Cicero 223 n.16
class 146
Clifford, James 199
Clinton, Bill **148**, 199
Cole, Jonathan 6, 11–12
colonialism 63–4
Colonizing Egypt (Mitchell) 166
Columbia University 6, 159
Comédie Français 146
Commager, Henry Steele 17
Commentary magazine 158
Conrad, Joseph 23, 25–8, 33–4, 36, 41, 57, 90; *The Heart of Darkness* 229 n.23; *The Nigger of the Narcissus* 26; *Nostromo* 26, 41–2; *The Secret Agent* 224n. 8; "The Secret Sharer" 26
Covering Islam 9, 15
Crary, Jonathan 143, 150–1, 167
Critical Inquiry 130, 135, 175–6
criticism: as activism 144; as *article de luxe* 155; as box of utensils 154; as branch of rhetoric 153; as eternal coitus 140; as extreme occasion 116; as heterotopia 168; as local knowledge 14–15, 153; Lucianic 61; as Menippean satire 64–8, 71, 72, 114, 186; as parasite 9; as performance 166; as personal example 151, 154; religious 86–9, 94–101; repetition in 139; secular 23–5, 83–105, 122, 144–5, 165–6
Cromer, Lord (Evelyn Baring) 76–7
cultural capital 208

Cultural Studies 206
culture 9
Culture and Imperialism (*CI*) 32, 101–2, 152, 154

Daniel Deronda (Eliot) 108–9
de Man, Paul 3, 10, 214
deconstruction 10, 13, 14, 41, 98, 214
dérapage 45–7, 57, 68, 166
Derrida, Jacques 4, 10, 15, 41, 66, 95, 96–7, 99, 110
determinism 42, 222 n.12
Diacritics 24
Dictionnaire des idées reçues (Flaubert) 65, 66
Dirks, Nicholas B. 149
Discipline and Punish (Foucault) 165
disenchantment 42
displacement, Palestinian 159, 165
Donoghue, Denis 85
Donohue, Phil 8
Dopico, Ann 21
Duchamp, Marcel 4–5
Duke, Josie Biddle 59
Dunsimore, Barrie 132–3

Eagleton, Terry 28, 209
The Edward Said Reader 28
Egypt 35–6
el-Nahas, Ahmad 166
Eliot, George: *Daniel Deronda* 108–9; *Middlemarch* 109
Emerson, Gloria 167
The End of the Peace Process 15, 33, 194
Engel, Monroe 28
English Institute 223 n.18
Enlightenment 12
Erekat, Sa'eb 130
Erewhon (Butler) 65
Escher, M.C. 213, 244 n.10
Essa, Zeyad 156
ethnocentrism 87
Eurocentrism 13
Exodus & Revolution (Walzer) 158, 168–9

Fanon, Frantz 167–8
Fatah 177, 178, 179, 181, 185, 196
fatalism 35
feminism 85
Fish, Stanley 5
Flaubert, Gustave 75, 92; *Bouvard et Pecuchet* 65; *Dictionnaire des idées reçues* 65, 66
Foucault, Michel 10, 15, 41, 61, 73, 96, 100, 105, 195–6, 201, 212; *The Archeology of Knowledge* 196; *Discipline and Punish* 165; heterotopias 167, 168; power/knowledge 152; Said's Memorial to 11

"The Fountain" (Duchamp) 4–5
Freedberg, David 149
Freud, Sigmund 41
From Oslo to Iraq and the Road Map 15
Frye, Northrop 40–1, 114, 229 n.11

Gallagher, Catherine 199
Gallop, Jane 85
Gellner, Ernest 63
Genet, Jean 1, 129, 130, 212, 219; *Les Paravents* 129
Geneva School 28
geography 158, 165–6
Gibb, Sir Hamilton A.R. 62
Gorman, D. 47, 226 n.11
Gould, Glenn 117, 124
Gourgouris, Stathis 211
Graff, Gerald 232 n.36
Gramsci, Antonio 144–5, 158, 165, 191, 194, 208, 214; on the intellectual 144, 145, 146; *Prison Notebooks* 139, 144–5
Grand Street 130, 169
Greenblatt, Stephen 223 n.18
Greenmantle (Buchan) 79
Griffin, Robert 130
Guillory, John 3
Gulliver's Travels (Swift) 81
"Gunga Din" (Kipling) 79, 152

Habbash, George 177
Harper's Magazine 170–1, 176
Hart, W.D. 87, 89
Hatoum, Mona 110
The Heart of Darkness (Conrad) 229 n.23
heterotopias 167, 168
historical criticism 28
historicism 14, 36; *see also* New Historicism
House & Garden 20, 176
humanism 62
Humanism and Democratic Criticism 16
Husserl, Edmund 28
Huyssen, Andreas 206–7

Ibn-Khaldun 117
identity 187, 200
"Impediments" (Trilling) 19
imperialism 9, 152–3
Institute of Arab Studies 53–4, 55–6
intellectuals 144, 145, 146, 188
intentional fallacy 28
interpretative anthropology 14
Interventions 175
intifadah 176, 178–81, 185–6, 198
irrationalism 10–11, 13
Irwin, Robert 61
Islam 99–100
Israeli–Arab conflict 36, 107, 169, 170, 176–91

James, C.L.R. 194
JanMohammed, Abdul 167, 238 n.11
Jesus Christ 3
Jewish Defense League 202
Johnson, Barbara 221 n.3
Jones, William 72
Jonson, Ben: *The Alchemist* 76; *Volpone* 68
Joseph Conrad and the Fiction of Autobiography (JC) 25–8, 33–4
Joyce, James 11

Kafka, Franz 29
Kermode, Frank 96
Kerr, Malcolm 63
Khadder, George 161–5, 166
Khalidi, Rashid 179, 218
Kim (Kipling) 78, 79, 152
Kipling, Rudyard 152; "Gunga Din" 79, 152; *Kim* 78, 79, 152; "Rikki Tikki Tavi" 152; "The White Man's Burden" 152
Kirkpatrick, Jeane 130, 131–5, 136
Klein, R. 46–7, 68
knowledge/power 152, 199
Kojève, Alexandre 212
Koppel, Ted 8, 126
Koran 99–100
Kugel, J.L. 97–8
Kurick, Maire 36, 208

Lane, Edward, *Modern Egyptians* 92
language proficiency 208–9
late style 29, 210
Lawrence, T.E. 1, 3, 71, 79, 92; *The Seven Pillars of Wisdom* 78, 92, 175, 201
"Leda and the Swan" (Yeats) 153
Lehrer, Jim 8
Levin, Harry 28
Lewis, Bernard 63
"liberating" of classrooms 58
Light, Alison 85
literary critics, as superstars 3–4, 5
local knowledge 10, 14–15, 152, 153
London Review of Books 4, 7
Lukács, Georg 31, 34, 212, 214

Machiavelli, Niccolo 199
Mackenzie, John 63
McNeil, Robert 8
Mailloux, Steven 101
Malik, Charles 63–4
Mandela, Nelson 194
Manning, Peter 154
Mariette, Auguste 141–2, 144
Marx, Karl 150, 241 n.3
Marxism 14, 153, 214, 241 n.3
Masser, Kamal 187
Massignon, Louis 62, 71

258 • Index

The Mediterranean (Braudel) 68, 228 n.10
Meiselas, Susan 110
Menand, Louis 210
Menippean satire 64–8, 71, 72, 114, 186
Menorah Journal 19
Merleau-Ponty, Maurice 28
Michelangelo, "The Capitive" 47, 48, 49–50, 99, 107
Michelet, Jules 34–5, 40
Middlemarch (Eliot) 109
Mideast Mirror 186
Midrash 97–8
Mikhail, Hanna 219–20
Miller, J. Hillis 28, 98–9
Milton, John 95
Mimesis (Auerbach) 100
Mitchell, Timothy, *Colonizing Egypt* 166
Mitchell, W.J.T. 89, 93–4
Modern Language Association (MLA) 135, 213–14
Modernists 41, 93
"Modest Proposal" (Swift) 81
Mohr, Jean 110
molestation, theory of 41
Moore-Gilbert, Bart 199
Mowitt, John 130
Mozart, Wolfgang Amadeus 72
Murphy, Geraldine 18
music/musical performance 116, 124; *see also Aida* (Verdi); West-Eastern Divan Workshop and Orchestra
Musical Elaborations (ME) 116

Napoleon Bonaparte 72, 77, 142, 199
narrative 106–13
Nasser, Sylvia 172–4
national identity 187
nationalism 87
The Nation 176
Nerval, Gérard de 75, 92
New Criticism 28–9, 36, 89
New Historicism 14, 153, 223 n.18
The New Science (Vico) 34, 222 n.12
New Social Movements 14
Nietzsche, Friedrich 41
The Nigger of the Narcissus (Conrad) 26
Nightline (TV show) 130, 131–5, 146
Nostromo (Conrad) 26, 41–2

On Late Style 16
Orientalism 9, 10, 13, 34, 35, 51, 61–81, 89–91, 93, 151
Orientalism 9, 61–6, 68–81, 83, 100–1, 151, 195–6, 227 n.1; as anti-Western polemic 176; the case against 62–3; as celebration of Orientalist achievements 91–3; as elegy 9; theme of passivity in 31, 33
Out of Place 33, 151, 165

Palestine Liberation Organization (PLO) 7–8, 130, 176, 177–8, 184, 187, 188, 196–201; and *intifadah* 179, 181, 185, 186; Said's criticism of 125, 186, 196–8
Palestine National Council 177, 179, 188
Palestine/Palestinians 35, 51, 106–8, 109–10, 167, 169, 170, 171, 176–91; displacement 159, 165; *intifadah* 176, 178–81, 185–6, 198
Palestinian Declaration of Principles (1988) 131–5
"The Palestinian Perspective" (Speech, 1989) 118–19
Les Paravents (Genet) 129
Passeron, J.-C. 204
passivity 25–6, 29–34, 35, 41, 153, 225 n.13
performance 116–38, 210
Perlmutter, Amos 123–4
The Persians (Aeschylus) 72
phenomenology 165
photo-essays 110–12
photographs, image and referent 140, 142, 143–4
place 158, 159
Poirier, Richard 7, 40, 47, 49–51, 54, 226 n.12
politics 35, 51–6, 175–202
The Politics of Dispossession (PolD) 15, 32, 35, 107, 158, 165, 188, 207
Pollock, Jackson 7
Pontecorvo, Gilles, *The Battle of Algiers* 167
Popular Front for the Liberation of Palestine 177
Poradowska, Marguerite 27
Porter, Dennis 199
postcolonialism 66, 167, 196, 199, 200, 227 n.1, 242 n.4
poststructuralism 85, 196, 242 n.4
Poulet, Georges 28
power 152
power/knowledge 152, 199
press 6–7
Prison Notebooks (Gramsci) 139, 144–5
professionalism 84, 154, 155, 213, 237 n.17
The Progressive 176

Qabbami, Nizar, "Children Bearing Rocks" 180
question-and-answer sessions 118–22
The Question of Palestine 9, 15, 69, 107, 109, 113, 196

Raad, Walid 204
Race & Class 136
racism 13
Rahman, Hasan 198
Ranke, Leopold von 110

Raritan 175
Read, Herbert 66
Reagan, Ronald 147
reason 222–3 n.15; as cause of civilization's fall 12–13
Reflections on Exile (*RoE*) 212, 213, 214–15
religious charisma 3, 8
religious criticism 86–9, 94–101
Renan, Ernest 73, 75
Representations of the Intellectual (*RI*) 188, 207
rhetoric 14, 153, 223 n.16
The Rhetoric (Aristotle) 120
"Rikki Tikki Tavi" (Kipling) 152
Robbins, Bruce 85–6, 196, 213, 214
romanticism 34, 35
Rose, Charlie 8
Rousset, Jean 28
Rushdie, Salman 187

Sacco, Joe 110
Sacy, Silvestre de 151
Said, Boulos 161
Said, Edward: anchoring the self 158; and anger 169; as Anglican 94; as athlete 149; as bastard 20–2; and class 146; as connoisseur 149; as cultural critic 169; and *dérapage* 45–7, 57, 68, 166; and discipline of detail 29, 110, 112; and exile 151, 179; hair 138; as intellectual de luxe 146; italics usage 109; as *khawaga* bourgeois 35; and Koran 99–100; and local knowledge 10, 14–15, 152, 153; and passivity 25–6, 29–34, 35, 41, 153, 225 n.13; as Princeton man 57–8; and professionalism 84, 154, 155, 213, 237 n.17; question-and-answer sessions 118–22; as self-contradictory 13, 24–5, 39; style 45–7, 57; television apearances 126–7, 130, 131–5, 146, 147; as Tory 64, 65; and Tory anarchy 154; as undergraduate advisor 36–9; as vampire 214
Said, Wadir 161, 162, 163
Saint-Mandé, Wilfred de 78
Salina, Kansas 227 n.15
Sardar, Ziauddin 63
satire, Menippean 64–8, 71, 72, 114, 186
Schapiro, Meyer 17
Schopenhauer, Arthur 29, 34, 41
Scull, Andrew 233 n.43
The Secret Agent (Conrad) 224n. 8
"The Secret Sharer" (Conrad) 26
secular criticism 23–5, 83–105, 122, 144–5, 165–6
secularism 89–91
The Seven Pillars of Wisdom (Lawrence) 78, 92, 175

Shultz, George 180–1, 182–4, 199
Siegel, Robert 190
Silverman, Kaja 143, 147
slippage (dérapage) 45–7, 57, 68, 166
sociology 14
Soja, Edward 165, 166
Sonnenberg, Ben 204
Soueif, Ahdaf 149
spatial analysis 165–6
Spitzer, Leo 93
Spivak, Gayatri 29, 166, 194
Spotts, Eric 207
Sprinker, Michael 146–7, 214
Starobinski, Jean 28
Stephen, J. Fitzjames 83
stereoscope 150
Stern, David 211, 218, 233 n.42
Stokes, Eric 104
stone-throwing episode 1, **2**, 6, **7**, 141, 143–4, 201
Strouse, Jean 149
structuralism 41
Students for a Democratic Society 58–9
style 43–7, 57, 149; late 29, 210
Sweetman, John 63
Swift, Jonathan 16–17, 24, 66–8, 70, 77, 81, 83, 99, 100, 110, 113–15, 214, 234 n.8; *Gulliver's Travels* 81; "Modest Proposal" 81; *Tale of a Tub* 65, 66, 67–8, 71, 81, 113, 158, 233 n.41
symbolic capital 4

Taine, Hippolyte-Adolphe 18
Tale of a Tub (Swift) 65, 66, 67–8, 71, 81, 113, 158, 233 n.41
Tang, Chenxi 207
television appearances 126–7, 130, 131–5, 146, 147
theater 77
theory 210–11
third space 166
Third Space 166, 175
The Thirty Nine Steps (Buchan) 79
Times Literary Supplement (TLS) 4, 61
The Times 107
Tooke, Horne 28
Torah 95
Tory anarchy 154
Toscanini, Arturo 124
translation 208
"Traveling Theory" 130, 210, 212
Trilling, Lionel 17, 18–19
Turner, Bryan 63
Turner, Victor 153

UNESCO 165
Unified National Leadership (UNL) 180–1, 186

Valéry, Paul 76
Vance, Cyrus 8
vapors, Swiftean attributes of 72
Verdi, Giuseppe, *Verdi* 140–3, 144, 165, 167
Verso Books 136
Vico, Gian'Battista 10–13, 42–3, 47, 50, 54, 57, 93, 107, 117; and the body 12; on reason 222–3 n.15; *The New Science* 34, 222 n.12; style 43, 44, 45
Viswanathan, Gauri 213
Volpone (Jonson) 68

Wallerstein, Immanuel 238 n.3
Walzer, Michael 130, 168–9; *Exodus & Revolution* 158, 168–9
Warner, Marina 218
The Way of All Flesh (Butler) 65
Weber, Max 3, 8, 10, 12, 152, 153
Weber, Samuel 23
Wedge 124, 175
weight lifting 49
West, Cornel 209
West-Eastern Divan Workshop and Orchestra 16, 154–6, 223 n.19
White, Edmund 116
"The White Man's Burden" (Kipling) 152
Whitman, Jon 135
Wicke, Jennifer 213
Wilde, Oscar 175
Wilentz, Sean 57–8
will 41
Williams, Jeffrey 61
Williams, Raymond 194, 241 n.3
Winkiel, Laura 207
Wise, Mary 21–2
Wordsworth, William 33
The World, the Text, and the Critic (*WTC*) 31, 62, 83, 85, 99–100, 206, 224 n.8
worldliness 9

"Yeats and Decolonization" 129
Yeats, W.B. 129, 152–3; "Leda and the Swan" 153
Young, Robert 199, 227 n.1, 242 n.4